First World War
and Army of Occupation
War Diary
France, Belgium and Germany

14 DIVISION
Headquarters, Branches and Services
General Staff
1 November 1918 - 24 March 1919

WO95/1877B

The Naval & Military Press Ltd
www.nmarchive.com
Published in association with The National Archives

Published by

The Naval & Military Press Ltd

Unit 10 Ridgewood Industrial Park,

Uckfield, East Sussex,

TN22 5QE England

Tel: +44 (0) 1825 749494

www.naval-military-press.com

www.nmarchive.com

This diary has been reprinted in facsimile from the original. Any imperfections are inevitably reproduced and the quality may fall short of modern type and cartographic standards.

Contents

Miscellaneous	C Form. Messages And Signals.		
Miscellaneous	A Form Messages And Signals.		
Miscellaneous	C Form. Messages And Signals.		
Miscellaneous	A Form Messages And Signals.		
Operation(al) Order(s)	41st Infantry Brigade Order No. 35	04/11/1918	04/11/1918
Miscellaneous	J.B.1. Adjt. Mezi. Ref. Map Sheet 29 S.W.	05/11/1918	05/11/1918
Miscellaneous	Operation Report. Carried Out by 13 Platoon & 2 L.G. Sections Of 16 Platoon And By O.C. Coy.	04/11/1918	04/11/1918
Miscellaneous	Report On Operations On Right Coy. Front (Mezi) Night 3rd/4th.	04/10/1918	04/10/1918
Operation(al) Order(s)	14th Divisional Order No. 238.	05/11/1918	05/11/1918
Miscellaneous	14th Division-General Staff War Diary-Nov. 1918 Vol. XLV Operations-6 Nov. 1918 Appendix A (6)		
Miscellaneous	C Form. Messages And Signals.		
Miscellaneous	A Form. Messages And Signals.		
Miscellaneous	C Form. Messages And Signals.		
Miscellaneous	C.R.A. Q. G.O. 65		
Miscellaneous	C Form. Messages And Signals.		
Miscellaneous	Telephone Messages	06/11/1918	06/11/1918
Miscellaneous	C Form. Messages And Signals.		
Miscellaneous	A Form. Messages And Signals.		
Miscellaneous	14th Division-General Staff War Diary-Nov. 1918 Vol. XLV Operations 7 Nov. 1918 Appendix A (7)		
Miscellaneous	C Form. Messages And Signals.		
Miscellaneous	A Form. Messages And Signals.		
Miscellaneous	C Form. Messages And Signals.		
Miscellaneous	A Form. Messages And Signals.		
Miscellaneous	14th Division. 40th Division. XV Corps No. I.G. 116/8.	08/11/1918	08/11/1918
Miscellaneous	Messages And Signals.		
Miscellaneous	A Form Messages And Signals.		
Miscellaneous	C Form. Messages And Signals.		
Miscellaneous	XV Corps H.A. C.B.S.O. XV Corps R.A.F. 16/121	08/11/1918	08/11/1918
Miscellaneous	XV Corps Heavy Artillery. Counter Battery Staff Officer.	08/11/1918	08/11/1918
Miscellaneous	C.R.E. G.O. 92 8		
Miscellaneous	C Form. Messages And Signals.		
Miscellaneous	Telephone Messages	08/11/1918	08/11/1918
Miscellaneous	A Form. Messages And Signals.		
Miscellaneous	C Form. Messages And Signals.		
Miscellaneous	A Form Messages And Signals.		
Miscellaneous	C Form. Messages And Signals.		
Miscellaneous	Messages And Signals.		
Miscellaneous	C Form. Messages And Signals.		
Miscellaneous	Messages And Signals.		
Miscellaneous	C Form. Messages And Signals		
Miscellaneous	14th Division-General Staff War Diary-Nov. 1918 Vol. XLV Operations-8 Nov. 1918 Appendix A (8)		
Operation(al) Order(s)	14th Division Order No. 240.	07/11/1918	07/11/1918
Miscellaneous	14th Division-General Staff War Diary-Nov 1918 Vol. XLV Adjustment Of Div Areas Nov. 1918 Appendix B		
Operation(al) Order(s)	XV Corps Order No. 258.	02/11/1918	02/11/1918
Miscellaneous	14th Division. XV Corps No. G.S. 2/156 G.	02/11/1918	02/11/1918
Map	Issued With XV Corps Order No 258 Dated		
Miscellaneous	Reference XV Corps Order No. 256	02/11/1918	02/11/1918
Miscellaneous	March Table Issued With XV Corps No. G.S. 2/157.		
Operation(al) Order(s)	14th Division Order No. 237	02/11/1918	02/11/1918

Miscellaneous	March Table To Accompany 14th Division Order No. 237.		
Miscellaneous	41 Inf. Bde. 14 M.G. Bn. 14 Div. Gas Officer		
Miscellaneous	A Form Messages And Signals.		
Miscellaneous	14th Division-General Staff War Diary-November 1918 Volume Extension of Front On L'Escaut 6/7 November 1918 Appendix C		
Miscellaneous	Messages And Signals.		
Operation(al) Order(s)	XV Corps Order No. 259.	06/11/1918	06/11/1918
Miscellaneous	C Form. Messages And Signals.		
Operation(al) Order(s)	14th Division Order No. 239	06/11/1918	06/11/1918
Miscellaneous	A Form. Messages And Signals.		
Miscellaneous	C Form. Messages And Signals.		
Miscellaneous	14th Division-General Staff War Diary-Nov 1918 Vol. XLV Extension Of Front-7/8 Nov. 1918 Appendix D		
Operation(al) Order(s)	14th Division Order 238/1	06/11/1918	06/11/1918
Miscellaneous	Messages And Signals.		
Operation(al) Order(s)	14th Divisional Order No. 238.	05/11/1918	05/11/1918
Miscellaneous	41st Infantry Bde.	06/11/1918	06/11/1918
Map	Edition 3A (Local) Provisional Issue. Sheet		
Miscellaneous	D.A.G. G.H.Q. 3rd Echelon		
Miscellaneous	14th Division-General Staff War Diary-November 1918 Volume Appendix Orders And Instructions For Forcing Passage Of River Escaut		
Miscellaneous	Proceedings Of Conference Held by Corps Commander At Second Army Headquarters At 1000 On 7th November, 1918.	07/11/1918	07/11/1918
Operation(al) Order(s)	XV Corps Order No. 261.	07/11/1918	07/11/1918
Map	Issued With XV Corps O/261 Dated 7-11-18		
Miscellaneous	Addendum No. 1 To XV Corps Order No. 261.	07/11/1918	07/11/1918
Miscellaneous	14th Division Instructions No. 1.	07/11/1918	07/11/1918
Miscellaneous	14th Division S.G. 1497 Amendment To 14th Division Instructions No 1 (S.G. 1486) Para 90 Line 5 Should Read:-	08/11/1918	08/11/1918
Miscellaneous	Signal Communications. (Issued In Conjunction With 14th Div. Instructions No. 1)		
Diagram etc	Identification Trace For Use With Artillery Maps.		
Miscellaneous	Addendum No. 8 To XV Corps Order No. 261.	07/11/1918	07/11/1918
Miscellaneous	Addendum No. 3 To XV Corps Order No. 261 Dated 7th November, 1918	08/11/1918	08/11/1918
Miscellaneous	Addendum No. 4 To XV Corps Order No. 261 Dated 7th November, 1918	08/11/1918	08/11/1918
Miscellaneous	XV Corps No. 57/173 G, Dated 1/11/1918.	01/11/1918	01/11/1918
Miscellaneous	Signal Communication.	01/11/1918	01/11/1918
Miscellaneous	XV Corps No. 819/33 G, Dated 8/11/1918.	08/11/1918	08/11/1918
Miscellaneous	Reference 14th Division S.G. 1486 of 7/11/1918		
Miscellaneous	Addendum No. 5 To XV Corps Order No. 261, Dated 7th November, 1918	08/11/1918	08/11/1918
Miscellaneous	C Form. Messages And Signals.		
Miscellaneous	14th Division-General Staff War Diary-November 1918 Volume Pursuit Of Enemy From L'Escaut River 9 Nov. 1918		
Miscellaneous	Reference 14th Division S.G. 1486 of 7/11/1918	08/11/1918	08/11/1918
Miscellaneous	C Form. Messages And Signals.		
Miscellaneous	A Form. Messages And Signals.		
Miscellaneous	C Form. Messages And Signals.		

Miscellaneous	A Form. Messages And Signals.		
Miscellaneous	Telephone Messages	09/11/1918	09/11/1918
Miscellaneous	A Form. Messages And Signals.		
Miscellaneous	Messages And Signals.		
Miscellaneous	Telephone Messages	09/11/1918	09/11/1918
Miscellaneous	C Form. Messages And Signals.		
Miscellaneous	GOC Urgent Opens Priority		
Miscellaneous	Telephone Messages	09/11/1918	09/11/1918
Miscellaneous	C Form. Messages And Signals.		
Miscellaneous	G 57 Urgent Opens Priority		
Miscellaneous	C Form. Messages And Signals.		
Miscellaneous	C Form. Messages And Signals		
Miscellaneous	A Form Messages And Signals.		
Miscellaneous	C Form. Messages And Signals.		
Miscellaneous	B Form. Messages And Signals.		
Miscellaneous	Messages And Signals		
Miscellaneous	B Form. Messages And Signals.		
Miscellaneous	A Form Messages And Signals.		
Miscellaneous	C Form. Messages And Signals.		
Miscellaneous	Messages		
Miscellaneous	C Form. Messages And Signals.		
Miscellaneous	A Form Messages And Signals.		
Operation(al) Order(s)	Operation Order No. 21 by Colonel J. Hay Campbell, D.S.O., A.M.S., Commanding R.A.M. Corps, 14th Division	09/11/1918	09/11/1918
Operation(al) Order(s)	14th Division Order No. 241	09/11/1918	09/11/1918
Miscellaneous	43rd Infantry Bde.	09/11/1918	09/11/1918
Operation(al) Order(s)	43rd Infantry Brigade Order No. 56	09/11/1918	09/11/1918
Operation(al) Order(s)	40th Division Order No. 230	09/11/1918	09/11/1918
Miscellaneous	14th Division Instructions No. 1.	07/11/1918	07/11/1918
Miscellaneous	14th Division S.G. 1497	08/11/1918	08/11/1918
Miscellaneous	Signal Communications. (Issued In Conjunction With 14th Div. Instructions No. 1).	08/11/1918	08/11/1918
Miscellaneous	14th Division-General Staff War Diary-Nov. 1918 Vol. XLV Move Orders-November 1918 Appendix G.		
Operation(al) Order(s)	14th Division Order No. 242.	13/11/1918	13/11/1918
Miscellaneous	To All Recipients of 14th Divisional Order No. 242	13/11/1918	13/11/1918
Miscellaneous	A Form Messages And Signals.		
Operation(al) Order(s)	14th Division Order No. 243	14/11/1918	14/11/1918
Operation(al) Order(s)	14th Divisional Order No. 244	15/11/1918	15/11/1918
Miscellaneous	March Table-To Accompany 14th D.O. No 244		
Miscellaneous	14th Division-General Staff War Diary-Nov. 1918 Vol. XLV Thanks Giving Service Roubaix 17 Nov. 1918 Appendix H.		
Miscellaneous	14th Division G.S. 1552	15/11/1918	15/11/1918
Map	A Parade Ground "B" Cinema Hall-For Church Service "C" Army Comd & "D" Band		
Miscellaneous	To All Recipients of 14th Division, G.S. 1552	15/11/1918	15/11/1918
Miscellaneous	14th Division No. G.S. 1560	16/11/1918	16/11/1918
Miscellaneous	14th Division-General Staff War Diary-Volume Intelligence Summaries 1-8 Nov. 1918		
Miscellaneous	Not To Be Taken Beyond Battalion Headquarters.	01/11/1918	01/11/1918
Miscellaneous	Not To Be Taken Beyond Battalion Headquarters.	02/11/1918	02/11/1918
Miscellaneous	The News.	02/11/1918	02/11/1918
Miscellaneous	Not To Be Taken Beyond Battalion Headquarters.	03/11/1918	03/11/1918
Miscellaneous	Not To Be Taken Beyond Battalion Headquarters.	04/11/1918	04/11/1918

Miscellaneous	Not To Be Taken Beyond Battalion Headquarters.	06/11/1918	06/11/1918
Miscellaneous	Preliminary Examination	06/11/1918	06/11/1918
Miscellaneous	Not To Be Taken Beyond Battalion Headquarters.	07/11/1918	07/11/1918
Miscellaneous	Not To Be Taken Beyond Battalion Headquarters.	08/11/1918	08/11/1918
Miscellaneous	14th Division-General Staff War Diary-Nov. 1918 Vol. XLV Locations Nov. 1918 Appendix J		
Miscellaneous	14th Division Location Table Forecast To 06.00 2nd November 1918	01/11/1918	01/11/1918
Miscellaneous	Location Table (Forecast To 06.00 5th November, 1918.)	03/11/1918	03/11/1918
Miscellaneous	Location Table (Forecast To 06.00 9th November, 1918.)	08/11/1918	08/11/1918
Miscellaneous	Location Table (Forecast To 06.00 11th November, 1918.)	10/11/1918	10/11/1918
Miscellaneous	Location Table Forecast To 06-00 18/11/18		
Miscellaneous	14th Division-General Staff War Diary-Vol. XLV-Nov. 1918 Corps Commanders Inspections Appendix K		
Miscellaneous	14th Division. 40th Division.	12/11/1918	12/11/1918
Heading	14th Division-General Staff War Diary-December (1-31) 1918 Volume XLVI Appendices A-Army Commanders Inspection B-Recreation		
War Diary	Tourcoing	01/12/1918	31/12/1918
Miscellaneous	14th Division G.S. 1570 XV Corps.	18/11/1918	18/11/1918
Miscellaneous	14th Division No. G.S. 1565	17/11/1918	17/11/1918
Miscellaneous	14th Division G.S. 1578 XV Corps.	20/11/1918	20/11/1918
Miscellaneous	14th Division No. G.S. 1575	19/11/1918	19/11/1918
Miscellaneous	14th Division G.S. 1583	21/11/1918	21/11/1918
Miscellaneous	14th Division G.S. 1578	20/11/1918	20/11/1918
Miscellaneous	14th Division No. G.S. 1595	23/11/1918	23/11/1918
Miscellaneous	A Form Messages And Signals.		
Miscellaneous	14th Division-General Staff War Diary-December 1918 Vol. XLVI Army Commanders Inspection 10 Dec 1918 App. A		
Miscellaneous	XV Corps No. A.C. 75/8	27/11/1918	27/11/1918
Miscellaneous	14th Division S.G. 1607	26/11/1918	26/11/1918
Miscellaneous	14th Division G.S. 1684	08/12/1918	08/12/1918
Miscellaneous	March Table To Accompany G.S. 1684. Reference Sheet No 9799		
Miscellaneous	14th Division-General Staff War Diary-December 1918 Volume XLVI Torchlight Tattoo Cross-Country Racing Baxing		
Miscellaneous	A. 321/1.	13/11/1918	13/11/1918
Miscellaneous	14th Divisional Boxing Competition		
Miscellaneous	14th Divisional Cross Country Race.	18/11/1918	18/11/1918
Miscellaneous	14th Division. G.S. 1678.		
Miscellaneous	14th Division No. G.S. 1703	11/12/1918	11/12/1918
Map	Belgium And Part of France		
Miscellaneous	28 SE 1/20000		
Heading	14th Division-General Staff War Diary Volume XLVII-1st-31st January 1919		
War Diary	Tourcoing	01/01/1919	31/01/1919
Miscellaneous	Presentation of Colours To Units of 14th Division.	20/01/1918	20/01/1918
Diagram etc	Sketch Map To Accompany 14th Division G.S. 2067		
Diagram etc	Sketch Map To Accompany		
Miscellaneous	Presentation of Colours.		

Heading	14th Division-General Staff War Diary 1st-28th February, 1919-Volume XLVIII		
War Diary	Turcoing	01/02/1919	16/02/1919
War Diary	Turcoing Franes	17/02/1919	28/02/1919
War Diary	Tourcoing	01/03/1919	24/03/1919
Miscellaneous	A.D. 316.	19/03/1919	19/03/1919

19

HQ GS 14 D

SL 43

November 1918

23 JAN 19

Confidential

14th Division - General Staff

War Diary - November (1-30) 1918

VOLUME XLV

Appendices

A - Operations 1-8 Nov.
B - Adjustment of Areas
C - Extension of front
D - " ditto "
E - Orders for forcing L'ESCAUT River
F - Pursuit of enemy over L'ESCAUT
G - Moves
H - Thanksgiving Service, ROUBAIX
I - Intelligence Summaries - Nov.
J - Locations - Nov.
K - Corps Commander's Inspections

19

Instructions regarding War Diaries and Intelligence Summaries are contained in F. S. Regs., Part II, and the Staff Manual respectively. Title pages will be prepared in manuscript.

WAR DIARY
or
INTELLIGENCE SUMMARY.
(Erase heading not required.)

Army Form C. 2118.

Place	Date	Hour	Summary of Events and Information	Remarks and references to Appendices
	Nov.			
MOUSCRON	1		41st Inf Bde relieved 42nd Inf Bde in line. On relief 42nd Inf Bde went into reserve with H.Q. at HERSEAUX. Hostile patrol approached post of 41st Bde at C.9.d.55.50 from south but were driven off by rifle & M.G. fire. Situation generally quiet. Fine day.	App A(1)
	2		41st Bde front heavily shelled during night 1st/2nd a large percentage of gas shells being used. Situation quiet during the day. G.O.C. visited Brigade in line. We extended our line as far as [illegible] central, during night 1st/2nd. Weather unsettled some rain.	App A(2)
	3		Situation unusually quiet. G.O.C. visited 41st Inf Bde in the line. The following moves took place. M.G. Battn from LUINGNE to HERSEAUX. 6th [illegible] from LUINGNE to WATTRELOS, 20th Middlesex from LUINGNE to ESTAIMPUIS. II Corps took over area evacuated by above. Weather unsettled, some rain.	App A(3) App B
	4		A successful minor operation was carried out by the 41st Bde posts being established at C.4.b.6.4, C.5.a.2.4, C.5.a.20.05, C.5.b.40.45 [illegible]. Div H.Q. closed at MOUSCRON at 11.00 & opened at 12 Rue [illegible] TOURCOING (F.10.b.6.8) at the same hour. Fine day.	App A(4)

[signature] Capt.

D. D. & L., London, E.C.
(A7883) Wt W809/M1672 350,000 4/17 Sch. 52a Forms/C/2118/14

Instructions regarding War Diaries and Intelligence Summaries are contained in F. S. Regs., Part II. and the Staff Manual respectively. Title pages will be prepared in manuscript.

WAR DIARY
or
INTELLIGENCE SUMMARY.
(Erase heading not required.)

Army Form C. 2118.

Place	Date	Hour	Summary of Events and Information	Remarks and references to Appendices
TOURCOING	5		Another very successful minor enterprise was carried out by 33rd London Regt 41st Inf Bde on night 4th/5th posts being established from U 30 c 40.00 to U 24 b 6 5 on the E bank of the ESCAUT. Three footbridges were thrown across the river at U 30 c 40.50, U 30 c 80.95 and U 24 b 60.60. 15 of the enemy were killed, 20 were taken prisoners & 3 M Gs captured. Situation quiet during the day. Conference at Corps HQ at 15.30 which was attended by G.O.C. & G.S.O.1. Prisoners belonged to 95th and 96th I.R. 38th Division (normal). Wet day.	App A.5
	6		On night 5th/6th 29th DLI relieved 33rd London Regt in line: both 41st Bde. The enemy attempted to rush our post at C.5.b.4.5 but without success. Wet day	App A.6
	7		On night 6th/7th 41st Inf Bde took over from 40th Div that part of the front from present right Divisional boundary to C 15 c 7.3. 96th Brigade Army Field Art. moved from BOSSUYT arriving at HERSEAUX about midday at which hour they came under the command of G.O.C. 14th Div. Warning from Corps that if an enemy officer bearing a flag of truce	App C

[illegible] Capt.

Army Form C. 2118.

Instructions regarding War Diaries and Intelligence Summaries are contained in F. S. Regs., Part II. and the Staff Manual respectively. Title pages will be prepared in manuscript.

WAR DIARY
or
INTELLIGENCE SUMMARY.
(Erase heading not required.)

Place	Date	Hour	Summary of Events and Information	Remarks and references to Appendices
TOURCOING ~~MOUSCRON~~	7		appeared on our front he was to be detained + conducted to D.H.Q. pending orders from Corps H.Q. Owing to rain of 2 preceding days, level of river Lys rose 10 to 18 inches. Fine day.	App. A (7)
	8		On night 7/8th 41st Inf Bde handed over to 29th Div that part of the Divisional front from U.24 b. central to U.30 c central. Situation unchanged. A further slight rise in river ESCAUT reported by the Division on our right	App. D. App. A. 8
	9		On night 8th/9th 43rd Inf Bde relieved 41st Inf Bde in line. During the night the enemy opposite the Army front started to withdraw. By 9 30 the 43rd Bde were on the line CHEMIN VERT – D 20 d with the 40th Div (XV Corps) on their right + 29th Div (X Corps) on their left. The XV Corps was ordered to stand fast + our front was eventually covered by 29th Div from the north who joined hands with 59th Division (XI Corps). The XV Corps was withdrawn into Army reserve the 14th Division billeting in depth as follows: 43rd Inf Bde RESET DE SEBLE – HELCHIN area, 42nd Inf Bde EVREGNIES-DOTTIGNIES	App. E App. F

D. D. & L., London, E.C.
(A7883) Wt. W809/M1672 350,000 4/17 Sch. 52a Forms/C/2118/14

Instructions regarding War Diaries and Intelligence Summaries are contained in F. S. Regs., Part II. and the Staff Manual respectively. Title pages will be prepared in manuscript.

WAR DIARY
or
INTELLIGENCE SUMMARY.
(*Erase heading not required.*)

Army Form C. 2118.

Place	Date	Hour	Summary of Events and Information	Remarks and references to Appendices
TOURCOING	9		COYGHEM area, 41st Bde HERSEAUX area. During the advance no enemy were seen. Fine day. Pontoon bridge at HELCHIN completed by 1700	App. F.
	10		In accordance with orders received on night of 9th from XV Corps, all troops of 14th Div north of the GRAND ESPIERRES river were moved to the south side to clear aforesaid area for X Corps & the pontoon bridge at HELCHIN was handed over to them: at the same time 14th Div was given prior right of bridge at WARCOING.	
	11		Wire from Corps to say hostilities cease at 1100 today. Division to stand fast on its present line & await further orders.	
	12		Division stood fast. 43 Inf Bde employed filling in mine craters & generally repairing roads East of ESCAUT. Remainder of Division training & drilling. Fine day	[illegible] Capt
	13		GOC proceeded on leave his place being taken by Brig General G. E. Pereira CB. CMG DSO (43 Inf Bde). Work same as previous day. Fine day.	
	14		41st Inf Bde moved to BONDUES area. 42nd Inf Bde moved to HERSEAUX area	App. G.

Instructions regarding War Diaries and Intelligence Summaries are contained in F. S. Regs., Part II. and the Staff Manual respectively. Title pages will be prepared in manuscript.

WAR DIARY
or
INTELLIGENCE SUMMARY.
(Erase heading not required.)

Army Form C. 2118.

Place	Date	Hour	Summary of Events and Information	Remarks and references to Appendices
TOURCOING	15		43rd Inf Bde group including 44th Field Ambulance moved from WARCOING area to TOURCOING area. Training & education programmes carried out. 62nd Field Coy RE moved to LA MADELEINE for work under C E XV Corps	App. G
	16		61st & 89th Field Coys RE, 15th Bn L N Lan Regt (Pioneers) & 14th M G Battn moved from DOTTIGNIES area to TOURCOING area. Fine day.	App. G
	17		Thanksgiving service held at CINEMA HALL, ROUBAIX. Detachments from all troops of the Division attended, & afterwards marched past the Army Commander (acting) after the service. Voluntary service held in afternoon at the CIRQUE CINEMA HALL TOURCOING. Fine day.	App. H
	18.		Normal routine	
	19		ditto.	
	20		61st Field Coy moved to ESPIERRES & 89th Field Coy RE to HELCHIN to reconstruct these villages. Lecture in CINEMA HALL ROUBAIX by Commander Spicer Simpson DSO RN on the Work of the Navy during the war. Weather foggy.	App. G

[signature] Capt

1577 Wt. W10791/1773 500,000 1/15 D. D. & L. A.D.S.S./Forms/C. 2118.

Instructions regarding War Diaries and Intelligence Summaries are contained in F. S. Regs., Part II. and the Staff Manual respectively. Title pages will be prepared in manuscript.

WAR DIARY
or
INTELLIGENCE SUMMARY.
(Erase heading not required.)

Army Form C. 2118.

Place	Date	Hour	Summary of Events and Information	Remarks and references to Appendices
TOURCOING	21		Normal routine. Weather fine.	
	22		" " " "	
	23		42nd Inf Bde inspected by Divisional Commander in the absence of the Corps Commander. Weather fine	
	24		Usual church parades. Sacred concert held at TOURCOING. Recreational training. Weather fine	
	25		Corps Commander inspected 43rd Inf. Bde. Weather fine.	App. K
	26		Normal routine. Weather fine	
	27		Corps Commander inspected 41st Inf Bde. Weather fine	K
	28		Normal Routine	
	29		do.	
	30th		Corps Commander inspected the Divisional Artillery, 15th L.N. Lancs and 14th M.G. Battn at MOUVEAUX.	
			Intelligence Summaries Nov 1918 – See App I Locations do – See App J	App I App J

[signature]
Capt
for General Staff
14th Division
1/12/18

1577 Wt. W10791/1773 500,000 1/15 D. D. & L. A.D.S.S./Forms/C. 2118.

Army Form C. 2123.
(In books of 100.)

"C" FORM.
MESSAGES AND SIGNALS.

No. of Message ....

Prefix SM Code 0915 Words 22 Received from Pcs By [illegible] Service Instructions	Sent, or sent out. At .... m. To .... By	Office Stamp. G.S.O. G.S.O.1 G.S.O.2 G.S.O.3

Handed in at Pcs Office 0918 m. Received 0917 m.

TO 14 Divn

*Sender's Number.	Day of Month.	In reply to Number.	AAA
G189	5	M	
Corps	commander	congratulates	
you	and	all	concerned
on	successful		operations
carried	out	last	night

Repeat
4th R.B.
CRA
CRE
NGP

G.C.R.

FROM
PLACE & TIME 15 Corps. 0855

* This line, except AAA, should be erased, if not required.

(3287) Wt. W54/P738 691,000 Pads 3/18. A.P.Ltd. (E3013)

G.O.C.	
G.S.O.1	
G.S.O.2	
G.S.O.3	

14th Division.
G.S.1470.

M/26

41st Infantry Brigade. 5
42nd Infantry Brigade. 5
43rd Infantry Brigade. 5
C.R.A. 16
C.R.E. 4
14th Machine Gun Battn. 5
15th L.N. Lancs. Regt. 1
14th Div. Sig. Coy. 1
14th Div. Train, A.S.C. 1
A.D.M.S. 4
"Q". 1

It is with the utmost pride and pleasure that I congratulate the troops of the 14th Division on the highly successful operation carried out last night.

Once more this success was due to the close and cordial co-operation of every arm of the Service and I offer my most sincere thanks to the 41st Infantry Brigade and all the troops associated with them.

P. C. B. Skinner
Major-General
Commanding 14th Division.

5th Novr. 1918.

M/26

14th Division G.S.1511

43rd Infy. Bde.

Please convey my thanks to the Officer Commanding the left front Company of the 10th H.L.I. and the other Officers of the Company concerned, for their energy in securing their objective during todays' operations.

(sd) P.C.B.SKINNER

Major-General
Commanding
14th Division.

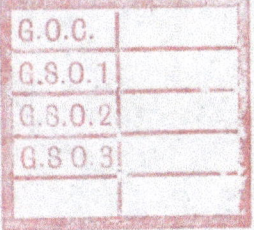

9/11/18.

G.O.C.	
G.S.O.1	
G.S.O.2	
G.S.O.3	

A. 320.

With all my heart I congratulate my splendid Division on the conclusion of an Armistice which means the end of a victorious war, an end which they have borne so full a share in bringing about.

I wish All Ranks to realize the admiration I feel for them and the esteem and affection with which I regard them.

Especially am I delighted at the spirit of comradeship and of co-operation which has been displayed by each and every Arm of the Service and which has contributed so much to the successes of the Division.

It is my earnest hope that the sense of comradeship engendered as the result of the sufferings, the trials, and the triumphs of this war, shared in common, may continue in civil life ; that the spirit of endurance and of self-sacrifice acquired may serve to strengthen the British People, and that, in after life, as a consequence of the experiences of this war, the Military Virtues may not be forgotten.

P.C.B. Skinner

Major-General,

Commanding 14th DIVISION.

11th November, 1918.
H.M.

Appendix A (1)

14th Division – General Staff

War Diary – Nov 1918

Vol. XLV

Operations – 1st Nov. 1918

Appendix A(2)

14th Division - General Staff

War Diary - Nov. 1918

Vol. XLV

Operations - 2 Nov. 1918

"C" FORM.

Army Form C. 2123.
(In books of 100.)

MESSAGES AND SIGNALS. No. of Message..........

Prefix Om Code 0015 Words 9

Received from .... By ....

Service Instructions

Handed in at OAKJ Office 0015 m. Received 0017 m.

Sent, or sent out. At .... m. To .... By ....

Office Stamp.

TO GSA.

*Sender's Number.	Day of Month.	In reply to Number.	AAA
Om 265	2	G025	

Complied with 2335

G.O.O.
G.S.O.1
G.S.O.2
G.S.O.3

0045

FROM OAKJ

PLACE & TIME

* This line, except A A A, should be erased, if not required.

[illegible]

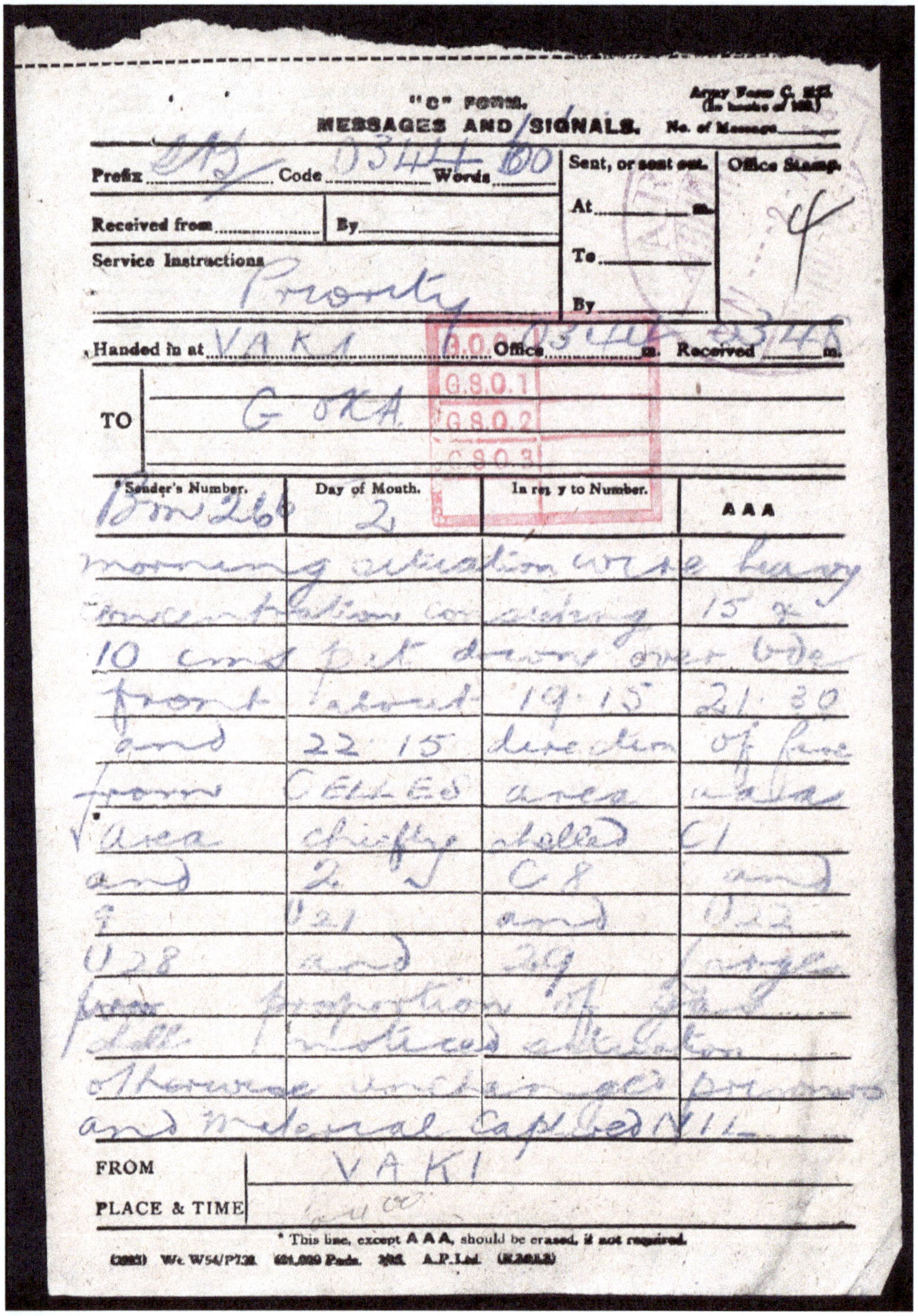

"C" FORM.
MESSAGES AND SIGNALS.

Army Form C. 2121 (In books of 100.)
No. of Message

Prefix OA/ Code 0344 Words 60

Received from | By

Service Instructions: Priority

Sent, or sent out. At m. To By

Office Stamp. 4

Handed in at VAKI Office 0344 m. Received 0348 m.

G.O.C.
G.S.O.1
G.S.O.2
G.S.O.3

TO G OKA

*Sender's Number.	Day of Month.	In reply to Number.	AAA
BM 266	2		

morning situation were heavy concentration consisting 15 & 10 cms put down over bde front about 19.15 21.30 and 22.15 direction of fire from CELLES area [illegible] area chiefly [illegible] C1 and 2 S C8 and 9 U21 and U22 U28 and 29 larger proportion of [illegible] [illegible] [illegible] [illegible] otherwise unchanged prisoners and material captured NIL

FROM VAKI
PLACE & TIME [illegible]

* This line, except AAA, should be erased, if not required.

(2023) Wt. W54/P738. 621,000 Pads. 2/15. A.P.Ltd. (E.2612.)

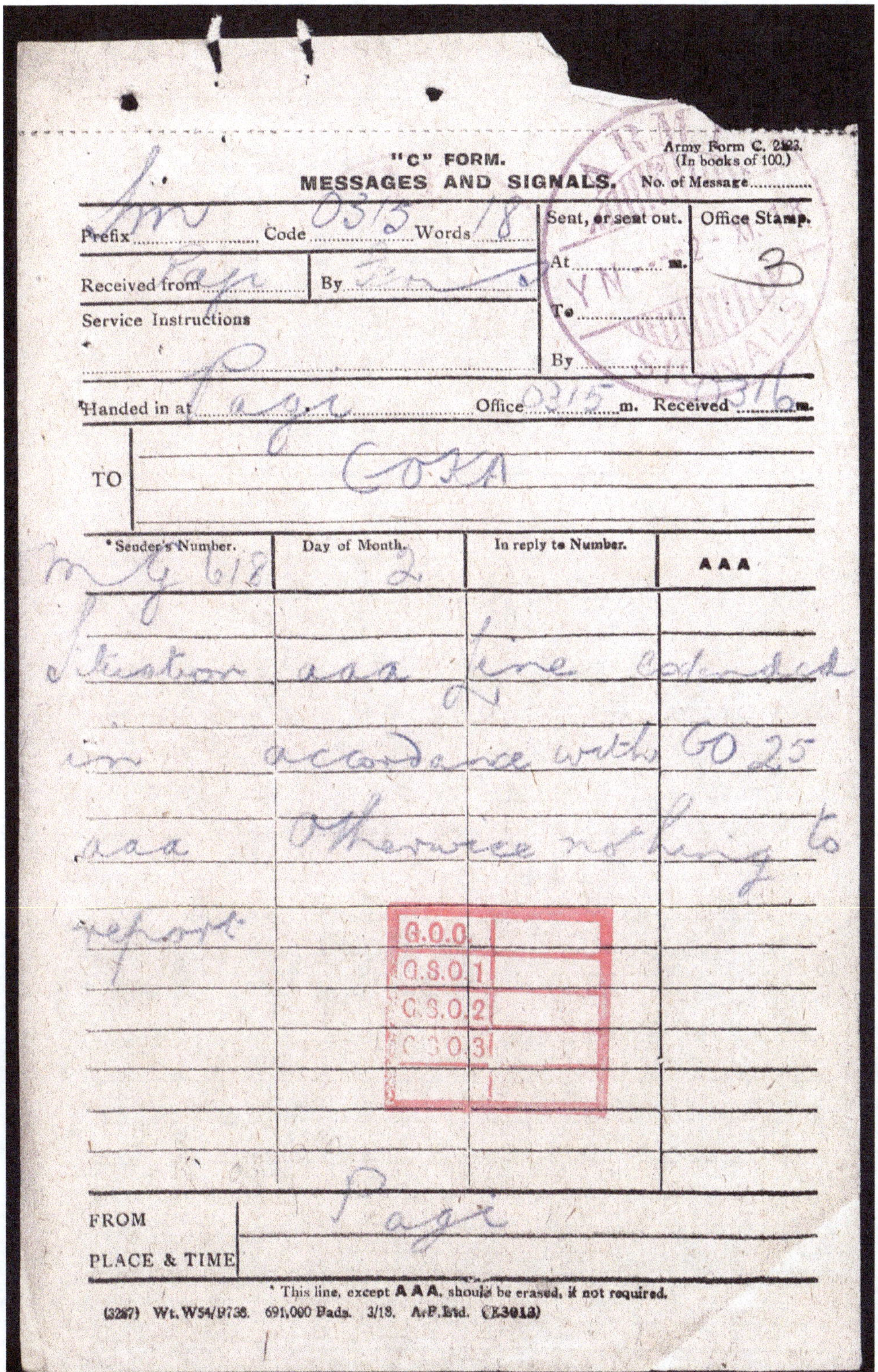

"C" FORM.
MESSAGES AND SIGNALS.

Army Form C. 2123.
(In books of 100.)
No. of Message............

Prefix SM Code 0315 Words 18	Sent, or sent out.	Office Stamp.
Received from Page By	At .... m.	3
Service Instructions	To	
	By	

Handed in at Page Office 0315 m. Received 0316 m.

TO COKA

* Sender's Number.	Day of Month.	In reply to Number.	AAA
MG 618	2		

Situation aaa line extended in accordance with GO 25 aaa Otherwise nothing to report

G.O.O.
G.S.O.1
G.S.O.2
G.S.O.3

FROM Page
PLACE & TIME

* This line, except AAA, should be erased, if not required.

(3287) Wt. W54/9738. 691,000 Pads. 3/18. A.F.Ltd. (E3013)

"A" Form

Army Form C. 2121
(In pads of 100.)

MESSAGES AND SIGNALS.

No. of Message..............

Prefix........ Code..........m	Words. Charge.	This message is on a/c of:	Recd. at..........m.
Office of Origin and Service Instructions	Sent	G.S.O.1 ✓ Service.	Date............
	At..............m.	G.S.O.2	From ....
	To..................	G.S.O.3	By ....
	By..................	(Signature of "Franking Officer.")	

TO: 15 Corps | 30 Div | 40 Div

Sender's Number.	Day of Month.	In reply to Number.	AAA
* G.O.30	2		

morning report AAA. Heavy concentration of 15 and 10 cm put down on brigade front about 19.15 21.30 and 22.15 direction of fire CELLES area AAA area chiefly shelled C1 2 and 8 U 21 22 28 and 29 large proportion gas shell AAA situation otherwise unchanged AAA captures Nil AAA line extended as ordered

From	[illegible] DIV
Place	
Time	04.20

The above may be forwarded as now corrected.

.... *Censor.*

(Z) [illegible signature] Capt

Signature of Addressor or person authorised to telegraph in his name.

* This line should be erased if not required.

(4715) Wt. W[illegible] [illegible] 2/18 C. & Co. (.024)

…AND SIGNALS.

Army Form C. 2121.
(In pads of 100.)

No. of Message............

Prefix......... Code............m. | Words. | Charge.

Office of Origin and Service Instructions.

Sent
At............m.
To
By

This message is on a/c of:
..................Service.
(Signature of "Franking Officer.")

Recd. at.......m.
Date
From
By

G.S.O.
G.S.O 1
G.S.O 2
G.S.O 3

TO XV Corps "I"

* Sender's Number.	Day of Month.	In reply to Number.	AAA
* G.O 33	2nd		

Intelligence	Summary	aaa	Hostile
Artillery	unusually	active	aaa
Several	heavy	concentrations	
Gas	and	HE	between
1800	and		20.00
aaa	Again	unusually	active
this	morning	aaa	Enemy
MGs	active	during	night
firing	into	HELCHIN	area
and	against	our	low
flying	planes	by	day
aaa	Suspected	MG	posts
CHAPEL	V26a11		CHATEAU
and	HOUSES	V26c14	C6a3075
aaa	Enemy light	TMs	fired
into	HELCHIN	and	vicinity
by	day	large	percentage

From
Place
Time

The above may be forwarded as now corrected. (Z)
Censor. Signature of Addressor or person authorised to telegraph in his name.

* This line, except AAA, should be erased if not required.

Wt. W 3253/P511. 500,000 Pads. 1/18. H. & S. Ltd. (E2389.)

...rm. Army Form C. 2121.
(In pads of 100.)

...GES AND SIGNALS.

No. of Message............

Prefix......... Code............m.	Words.	Charge.	This message is on a/c of:	Recd. at........m.
Office of Origin and Service Instructions.	Sent		........................Service.	Date............
	At...........m.			From
	To			
	By		(Signature of "Franking Officer.")	By

TO Q

Sender's Number.	Day of Month.	In reply to Number.	AAA
	2w		

phosgene aaa EA inactive aaa New Camouflage erected between C10d 60 45 and C10d 40 20 aaa Summary follows

From 14 Div
Place
Time

The above may be forwarded as now corrected. (Z)

Censor. Signature of Addressor or person authorised to telegraph in his name.

* This line, except A A A, should be erased if not required.

Wt. W 3253/P511. 500,000 Pads. 1/18. H. & S. Ltd. (E2389.)

37

"C" FORM.
Army Form C. 2121.
(In books of 100.)

MESSAGES AND SIGNALS.

No. of Message ______

G.O.C.
G.S.O.1
G.S.O.2
G.S.O.3

Prefix ______ Code ______ Words ______	Sent, or sent out. At ______ m. To ______ By ______
Received from ______ By ______	Office Stamp. YN 2 - XI. 1
Service Instructions: Rly	

Handed in at Vaki Office 1605 m. Received 1615 m

TO: Evoka

Sender's Number.	Day of Month.	In reply to Number.	AAA
IV 2/11/18	2/11/18		

Evening wire aaa Situation Quiet aaa Intermittent Shelling by enemy artillery in neighbourhood of HELCHIN and back areas aaa Our own artillery inactive our planes fairly active during morning aaa slight enemy mg fire at our planes aaa wind Slight SE observation fair aaa Captures NIL aaa

FROM: Vaki

PLACE & TIME

* This line, except AAA, should be erased, if not required.

(1023) Wt. W54/P728. 601,000 Pads. 1/16. A.P.Ltd. (E.2612)

"A" Form
Army Form C. 2121
(In pads of 100.)

MESSAGES AND SIGNALS.

No. of Message..............

G.O.C.
G.S.O.1
G.S.O.2
G.S.O.3

Prefix.............. Code..............m. Words. Charge.

Office of Origin and Service Instructions

Priority 15 Corps S.

XV Corp

Sent
At..............m.
To..............
By..............

This message is on a/c of:
.... *Service.*
....
(Signature of "Franking Officer.")

Recd. at..........m.
Date..................
From..................
By..................

TO: 15 Corps | 30 Div | HQ RFC

Sender's Number.	Day of Month.	In reply to Number.	AAA
* GO 32	2		

Morning	report	AAA	Situation
quiet	AAA	Intermittent	shelling
vicinity	of	HELCHIN	~~and~~
AAA	Some	M.G.	fire
against	our	planes	AAA
Captures	nil	AAA	Good
Corps	left	flank	Done.

From 14 KR			
Place			
Time			

The above may be forwarded as now corrected. (Z) [illegible] Capt

.... *Censor.*

Signature of Addressor or person authorised to telegraph in his name.

* This line should be erased if not required.

(4715) Wt. W3253/P312 1,123,336 Sbts. 2/18 C. & Co. (C34)

Army Form C. 2123.
(In books of 100)

"C" FORM.
MESSAGES AND SIGNALS.

No. of Message

Prefix Code Words

Received from By

Service Instructions

Sent, or sent out. At m. To By

Office Stamp

Handed in at TDZ Office 2322 m. Received 2346 m.

G.O.C.
G.S.O.1
G.S.O.2
G.S.O.3

TO 14 Divn

*Sender's Number.	Day of Month.	In reply to Number.	AAA
GB 171	2		
Hostile	Art	fire	prevented
Post	being	established	on
Causeway	C 20 D	aaa	5
posts	established	N	of
Inundated	area	in	C 21
of	which	left	is
in	touch	with	14
Divn	aaa	Addsd	15
Corps	Repted	Flank	Divns
CRA	CRE		
			2350

FROM 40 Divn

PLACE & TIME

* This line, except AAA, should be erased, if not required.

(5287) Wt. W54/P738. 691,000 Pads. 3/18. A.P.Ltd. (E3613)

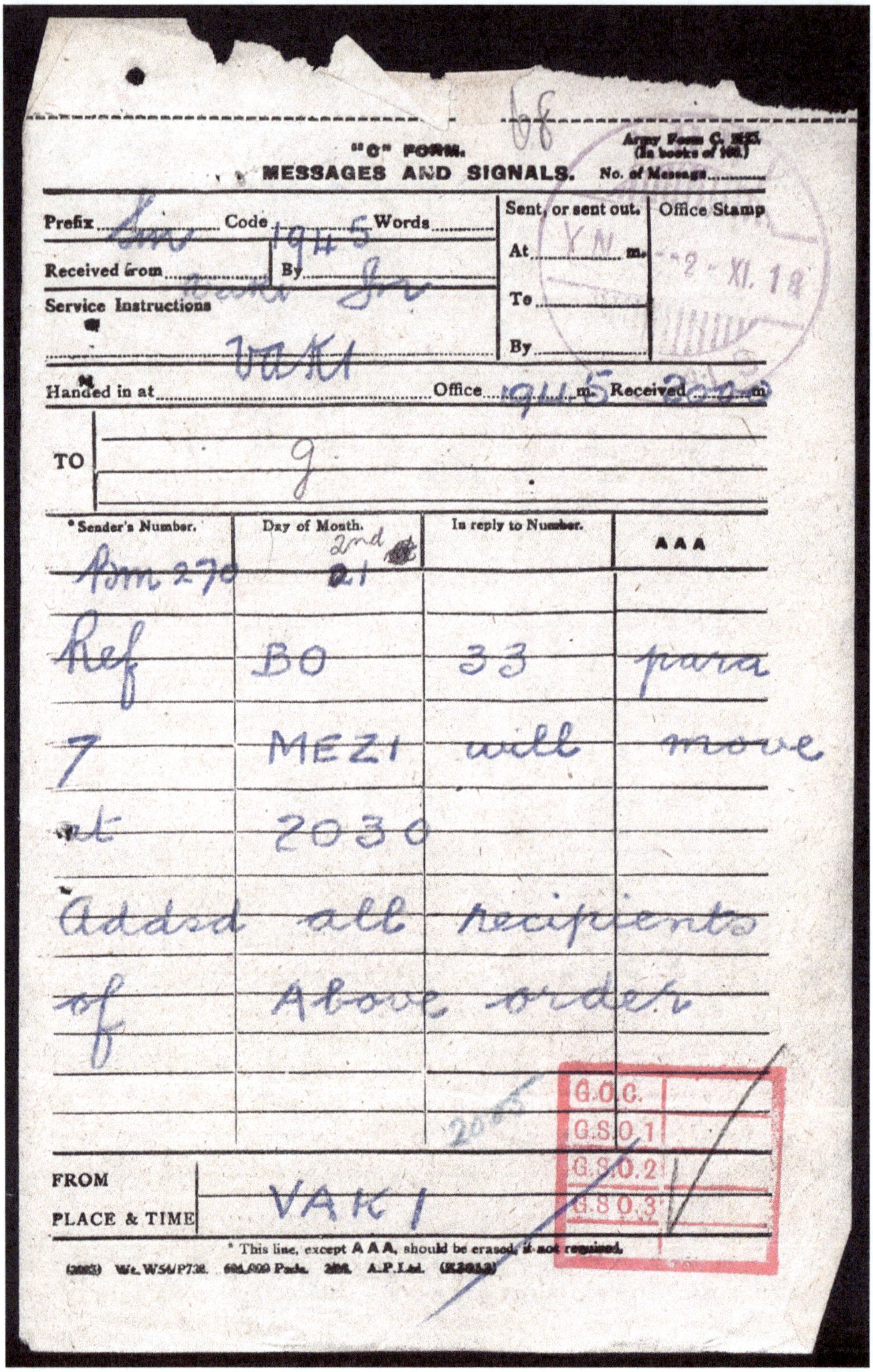

68

"C" FORM.
MESSAGES AND SIGNALS.

Army Form C. 2121.
(In books of 100.)
No. of Message............

Prefix Sm Code 1945 Words

Received from By

Service Instructions sent Sr

VAKI

Sent, or sent out.
At YN m.
To
By

Office Stamp
2 - XI. 18

Handed in at .... Office 1945 m. Received 2000 m.

TO g

*Sender's Number.	Day of Month.	In reply to Number.	AAA
Bm 270	2nd		
Ref	BO	33	para
7	MEZI	will	move
at	2030		
Addsd	all	recipients	
of	Above	order	

2005

G.O.C.
G.S.O.1
G.S.O.2
G.S.O.3

FROM
PLACE & TIME VAKI

* This line, except A A A, should be erased, if not required.

(2003) Wt. W56/P738. 600,000 Pads. 2/18. A.P.Ltd. (E2012)

Army Form C. 2128.
(In books of 100.)

"C" FORM.

MESSAGES AND SIGNALS. 8 No. of Message

Prefix SB Code 0348 Words 72

Received from 7DA By WW

Service Instructions Pty

Sent, or sent out. At m. To By

Office Stamp

Handed in at VAKI Office 0348 m. Received 0355 m.

TO GOKA

G.S.O. 1
G.S.O. 2
G.S.O. 3

*Sender's Number.	Day of Month.	In reply to Number.	AAA
BM 254	1		

Situation	report	aaa	Strong
enemy	patrol	approached	our
posts at	C9D55.50	at	2045
driven	off	AAA Patrol	of WIBI
proceeded	to	C5A2.4	and
was	fired on	from	house
at	C5B30.40	by	MG and
snipers	AAA	Intermittent	shelling
of	HELCHIN	between	2245
and	0130	and	right Coy
of	MERA	AAA Area	round
DOTTIGNIES	shelled	by	HV from
2330	to	2345	AAA MG's
less	active on	left batt	front

FROM

PLACE & TIME VAKI 0040

* This line, except A A A, should be erased, if not required.

(2082) Wt. W54/P72 [illegible] Pads. 2/38. A.P.Ltd. [illegible]

"A" Form

MESSAGES AND SIGNALS.

Army Form C. 2121
(In pads of 100.)

No. of Message 1

Prefix .... Code .... m	Words. Charge.	This message is on a/c of:	Recd. at .... m.
Office of Origin and Service Instructions	Sent	Service.	Date
	At .... m.	G.O.C.	From
	To	G.S.O. 1	
	By	(Signature of "Franking Officer.") G.S.O. 2	By
		G.S.O. 3	

TO: XV Corps

Sender's Number.	Day of Month.	In reply to Number.	AAA
* G022	1		

Inter Brigade relief complete.

From: 14th Div

Place

Time

The above may be forwarded as now corrected. (Z) W Beaumont Capt

Censor. Signature of Addressor or person authorised to telegraph in his name.

* This line should be erased if not required.

Wt. W3253/F311 1,250,396 Shts. 2/18 C. & Co. (E634)

"A" Form
MESSAGES AND SIGNALS.

Army Form C. 2121
(In pads of 100.)

No. of Message..............

Prefix.............. Code..............m | Words. | Charge. | This message is on a/c of: | Recd. at..........m.

Office of Origin and Service Instructions
Priority
to XV Corps

Sent
At..............m.
To..............
By..............

.... Service.
(Signature of "Franking Officer.")

Date..........
From..........
By..........

G.O.C.
G.S.O.1
G.S.O.3

TO: XV Corps, 30th Division, 40th Division

Sender's Number.	Day of Month.	In reply to Number.	AAA
* GO 21	1st		

Morning report AAA Strong enemy patrol approached post C9d5550 ~~[illegible]~~ off at 2045 hrs driven off AAA Patrol proceeding C5a24 fired on by M.Gs and snipers from C5b34 AAA Intermittent shelling HELCHIN 2245 to 0130 hrs AAA Area round DOTTIGNIES shelled with H.V. gun 2330 AAA addsd XV Corps repeated flank Divns

From: 14th Division
Place
Time

The above may be forwarded as now corrected. (Z)

Censor.

J. Beaumont Capt
Signature of Addressor or person authorised to telegraph in his name.

* This line should be erased if not required.

(4715) Wt. W3253/P122 2,125,125 Shts. 2/28 C. & Co. (574)

"A" Form

Army Form C. 2121
(In pads of 100.)

MESSAGES AND SIGNALS.

No. of Message..............

Prefix.............. Code..............m

Office of Origin and Service Instructions

Words. Charge.

Sent

At..................m.

To......................

By......................

This message is on a/c of:

.... *Service.*

(Signature of "Franking Officer.")

Recd. at............m.

Date......................

From ....

By ....

G.O.C.
G.S.O.1
G.S.O.2
G.S.O.3

TO 41st Inf. Bde.

Sender's Number.	Day of Month.	In reply to Number.	AAA
* G.O. 23	1		

Contact Patrol report 07.45 begins aaa Flew over squares D.1 - C.12 - 18- 23- 27 - I.3 at 100 - 200 ft. aaa 1 enemy soldier seen on road C.11.b.7.3 aaa Rifle fire whilst over C.12 and 18 apparently coming from Railway embankment at D.13 and 28 aaa Rifle fire whilst over C.27.d and I.6.cent apparently from Wood on hill at I.3.b.8.3 aaa No further hostile movement seen aaa No M.G. fire encountered aaa Civilians in HERINNES walking about streets aaa No flags and did not wave to us aaa Trenc es and Rifle pits have been dug along E bank of river about 100 - 200 yds from road at intervals between C.16.a and C.27.a aaa Apparently unoccupied aaa Our troops are in trenches on East bank of ESCAUT between C.4.b.6.2 and C.4.c.3.5 aaa Map Reference sheet 37 1/40000 aaa ends

From 14th Divn.

Place

Time 09.15

The above may be forwarded as now corrected.

.... *Censor.*

(Z)

Signature of Addressor or person authorised to telegraph in his name.

[signature] Capt

* This line should be erased if not required.

(4715) Wt. W3sss/P5n 1,183,336 Shts. 2/18 C. & Co (C34)

Army Form C. 2123.
(In books of 100.)

"C" FORM.

MESSAGES AND SIGNALS. No. of Message..........

Prefix OFN Code 0901 Words 140

Received from PCo By Cmo

Service Instructions

Handed in at RP Office 0907 m. Received 0925 m.

Sent, or sent out.	Office Stamp.
At .... m.	1-XI-18
To	
By	

G.O.C.
G.S.O 1
G.S.O 2
G.S.O 3

TO 14 Divn

*Sender's Number.	Day of Month.	In reply to Number.	AAA
E21G	1		
following	message	dropped	by
aeroplane	begins	Pledne	over
Squares	D16	C12	18
23	27	13	at
100	to	200	feet
one	enemy	soldier	seen
on	road	C11b43	rifle
fire	whilst	over	C12
at	18	apparently	coming
from	railway	embankment	in 18c
D13a28	rifle	fire	also
whilst	over	C27d	and
16	Cmll	apparently	from
wood	on	hill	at

FROM

PLACE & TIME

* This line, except A A A, should be erased, if not required.

Army Form C. 2123.
(In books of 100.)

"C" FORM.

MESSAGES AND SIGNALS.

No. of Message ....

Prefix .... Code .... Words	Sent, or sent out.	Office Stamp.
Received from .... By	At .... m.	
Service Instructions	To	
	By	

Handed in at .... Office .... m. Received 9.25 m.

TO 14 Div

*Sender's Number.	Day of Month.	In reply to Number.	AAA

I 26 B 3 [illegible] [illegible] [illegible] [illegible]
[illegible] [illegible] [illegible] [illegible]
[illegible] [illegible] HERINNES walking
about [illegible] [illegible] [illegible]
[illegible] [illegible] trenches [illegible]
[illegible] [illegible] [illegible] E [illegible]
[illegible] [illegible] 1600 yards
[illegible] [illegible] [illegible]
between C 16 [illegible] & C 27 a apparently
occupied [illegible] troops [illegible]
trenches [illegible] E [illegible] of ESCAUT
between C 4 b 6 2 and C 2 c 3 6
[illegible] sheet 37 1/40000
pilot R. H. Schroeder [illegible] Observer

FROM W. [illegible]

PLACE & TIME HQ 15 Corps

* This line, except A A A, should be erased if not required.

W15831—9201 45,000 3/17 HWV(M1609)
15831—9201 225,000 3/17

Army Form W. 3750.

No. of Message	Date	Aeroplane No.	Time	Place:—
1	1/11/18	2725	0745	

G.O.O.
G.S.O.1
G.S.O.2
G.S.O.3
I.3

To:— XV Corps. 14 & 40th Div

Flew over squares D.1. C.12, 17, 23, 29, I 3 at 100-200 ft. 1 Enemy soldier seen on road C11 D43. Rifle fire whilst over C12 & 17 apparently coming from Rly. Embankment at C 17 & 28. Rifle fire also whilst over C 27 d & I 6 C & d. apparently from wood on hill at I 3 b 8 3.

No further hostile movement seen.

No M.G. fire encountered.

Civilians in Hemmes walking about streets. No flags & did not wave to us.

Trenches & rifle pits have been dug along E bank of River (about 100-200 yds from road) at intervals between C 16 a and C 24 a.

Apparently unoccupied.

P.T.O.

Copies to:—

Signature R.H. Schroder. Pilot
MacCharles. Obs

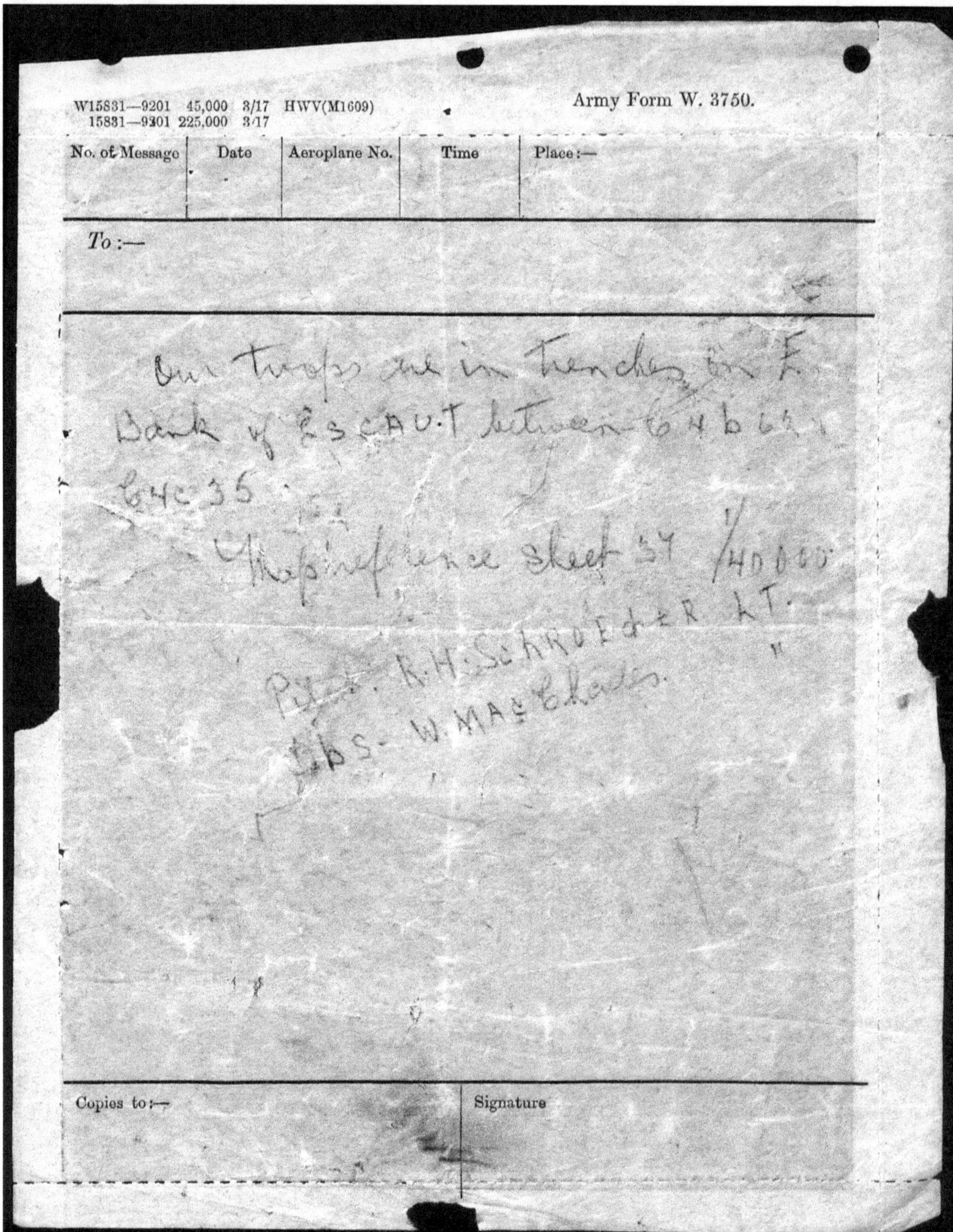

W15831—9201 45,000 3/17 HWV(M1609)
15831—9201 225,000 3/17

Army Form W. 3750.

No. of Message	Date	Aeroplane No.	Time	Place:—

To:—

Our troops are in trenches on E. Bank of ESCAUT between 64 b 6? & 64 c 35.

Map reference sheet 57 1/40000

Pilot. R.H. SCHROEDER LT.
Obs. W. MacClaren "

Copies to:—

Signature

"C" FORM.
MESSAGES AND SIGNALS.

Army Form C. 2123.
(In books of 100.)
No. of Message 64

Prefix OW Code 1302 Words 39	Sent, or sent out.	Office Stamp.
Received from .... By [illegible]	At .... m.	
Service Instructions	To	
	By	

Handed in at P Co Office 1302 m. Received 1314 m.

TO 14 Divn

*Sender's Number.	Day of Month.	In reply to Number.	AAA
5134	1		
Alert	your	left	[illegible]
to	stand	[illegible]	[illegible]
aaa	acknowledge	aaa	
addsd	14 Divn	Divn	repeated
15	Corps	GOC	RA
"Q"	15	Corps	
	Ack G.R.112		13.28

FROM 15 Corps
PLACE & TIME 1300

* This line, except A A A, should be erased, if not required.

(3287) Wt.W34/P778. 691,000 Pads. 2/18. A.P.Ltd. (E.2055)

"A" Form
MESSAGES AND SIGNALS.

Army Form C. 2121
(In pads of 100.)

No. of Message..............

Prefix.......... Code..........m	Words. Charge.	This message is on a/c of:	Recd. at..........m.
Office of Origin and Service Instructions	Sent	G.O.C.	Date.....
	At..........m.	G.S.O.1	
	To..........	G.S.O.2 .... Service.	From .....
	By..........	G.S.O.3 (Signature of "Franking Officer.")	By.....

TO 41 Bde - CRA - CRE - 14 MG Bn - 30 Divn

Sender's Number.	Day of Month.	In reply to Number.	AAA
* G.O. 25	1		

41 Inf Bde will take over line tonight up to U.24.b.55 from 21st Inf Bde under arrangements made by BGsC. concerned AAA CRA and O.C. 14 M.G. Bn will make necessary arrangements for covering new front AAA ACKNOWLEDGE AAA Added 41 Bde - CRA - CRE - 14 M.G. Bn reptd 30th Division

From
Place 14 Divn.
Time

The above may be forwarded as now corrected. (Z) [illegible] Capt. GS

Censor. Signature of Addressor or person authorised to telegraph in his name.

* This line should be erased if not required.

(4715) Wt. W3253/P321 1,125,336 Sbts. 2/18 C. & Co. (634)

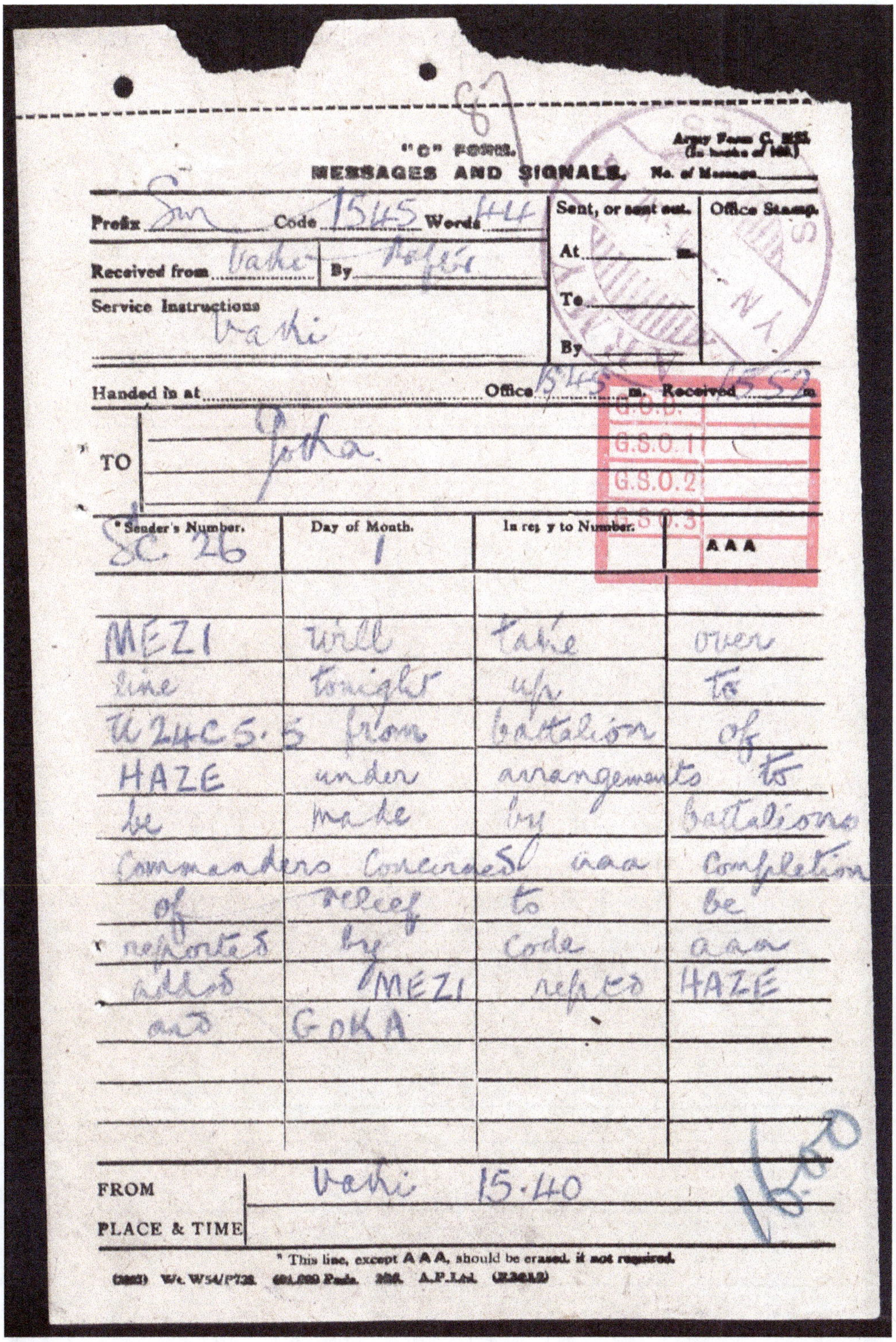

Army Form C. 2121. (In books of 100.)

"C" FORM.

MESSAGES AND SIGNALS. No. of Message ______

67

Prefix Sm Code 1545 Words 44	Sent, or sent out. At ______ m. To ______ By ______
Received from Vaki By Roger	Office Stamp.
Service Instructions Vaki	

Handed in at ______ Office 1545 m. Received 1552 m.

G.S.O.
G.S.O. 1
G.S.O. 2
G.S.O. 3

TO Goka

*Sender's Number.	Day of Month.	In reply to Number.	AAA
SC. 26	1		

MEZI	will	take	over
line	tonight	up	to
U24C5.5	from	battalion	of
HAZE	under	arrangements	to
be	made	by	battalions
Commanders	Concerned	aaa	Completion
of	relief	to	be
reported	by	code	aaa
addsd	MEZI	repted	HAZE
and	GOKA		

FROM PLACE & TIME Vaki 15.40

1600

* This line, except A A A, should be erased if not required.

(2823) Wt. W54/P728. 600,000 Pads. 3/16. A.F.Ltd. (E.2612)

"A" Form

Army Form C. 2121
(in pads of 100.)

MESSAGES AND SIGNALS.

No. of Message.................

Prefix .... Code ....m. | Words. | Charge.

Office of Origin and Service Instructions.

Sent

At.....................m.

To ....

By ....

DRLS

This message is on a/c of:

G.S.O.
G.S.O.1
G.S.O.2
G.S.O.3

Service.

(Signature of "Franking Officer.")

Recd. at ....m.

Date ....

From ....

By ....

TO 121st I.Bde. C.R.A.
C.R.E. 14th Division.

Sender's Number.	Day of Month.	In reply to Number.	AAA
* Gc 738	1		

121st Brigade will establish posts night 2nd/3rd November East of the river in C.15. and 21 to prevent the enemy approaching our positions through the gap of dry ground between the inundated areas in C.21 and C.15 aaa The C.R.E. will arrange in conjunction with 121st Brigade for a footbridge to be constructed about C.15.central and placed in position as soon as patrols are East of River and can cover its erection aaa Arrangements for use of footbridge in C.9.d. if required will be made between 121st Bde and 41st Brigade aaa Acknowledge aaa Addressed 121st Brigade C.R.E. repeated C.R.A. and 14th Division.

From
Place 40th Division.
Time

The above may be forwarded as now corrected. (Z)

Censor. Signature of Addressor or person authorised to telegraph in his name.

Lt. Col.
G.S.

* This line should be erased if not required.

(1539). Wt. W3253/P511. 200,000 Pads. 2/18. H. C. & L., Ltd.

"A" Form.

MESSAGES AND SIGNALS.

Army Form C. 2121. (In pads of 100.)

No. of Message..........

Prefix......... Code.......... m.	Words.	Charge.	This message is on a/c of:	Recd. at....... m.
Office of Origin and Service Instructions.	Sent		Service.	Date
	At .... m.			From
	To			
	By		(Signature of "Franking Officer.")	By

G.S.O. 1 / G.S.O. 2 / G.S.O. 3

TO XV Corps I

Sender's Number.	Day of Month.	In reply to Number.	AAA
* G O 28	1st		

Intelligence	Summary	aaa	Enemy
Arty	05.30	15	0645
light	barrage	SW	to
NE	through	C 3 a	U 27 d
few	guns	used	but
rapid	~~fire~~	sweeping	fire
aaa	Chateau	C 4 a	shelled
from	direction	REJET	MOULEUX
aaa	Slight	~~slight~~	activity
ESPIERRES	shelled	with	long
range	gas	and	HE
aaa	Chateau	C 4 a	also
shelled	again	long	range
aaa	Enemy	MGs	slightly
active	on	left	Bn
front. MG	suspected	firing	from
house	C 5 b 35	aaa	Party

From			
Place			
Time			

The above may be forwarded as now corrected. .... *Censor.* | (Z) .... Signature of Addressor or person authorised to telegraph in his name.

* This line, except A A A, should be erased if not required.

Wt. W 3253/P511. 500,000 Pads. 1/18. B. & S. Ltd. (E2389.)

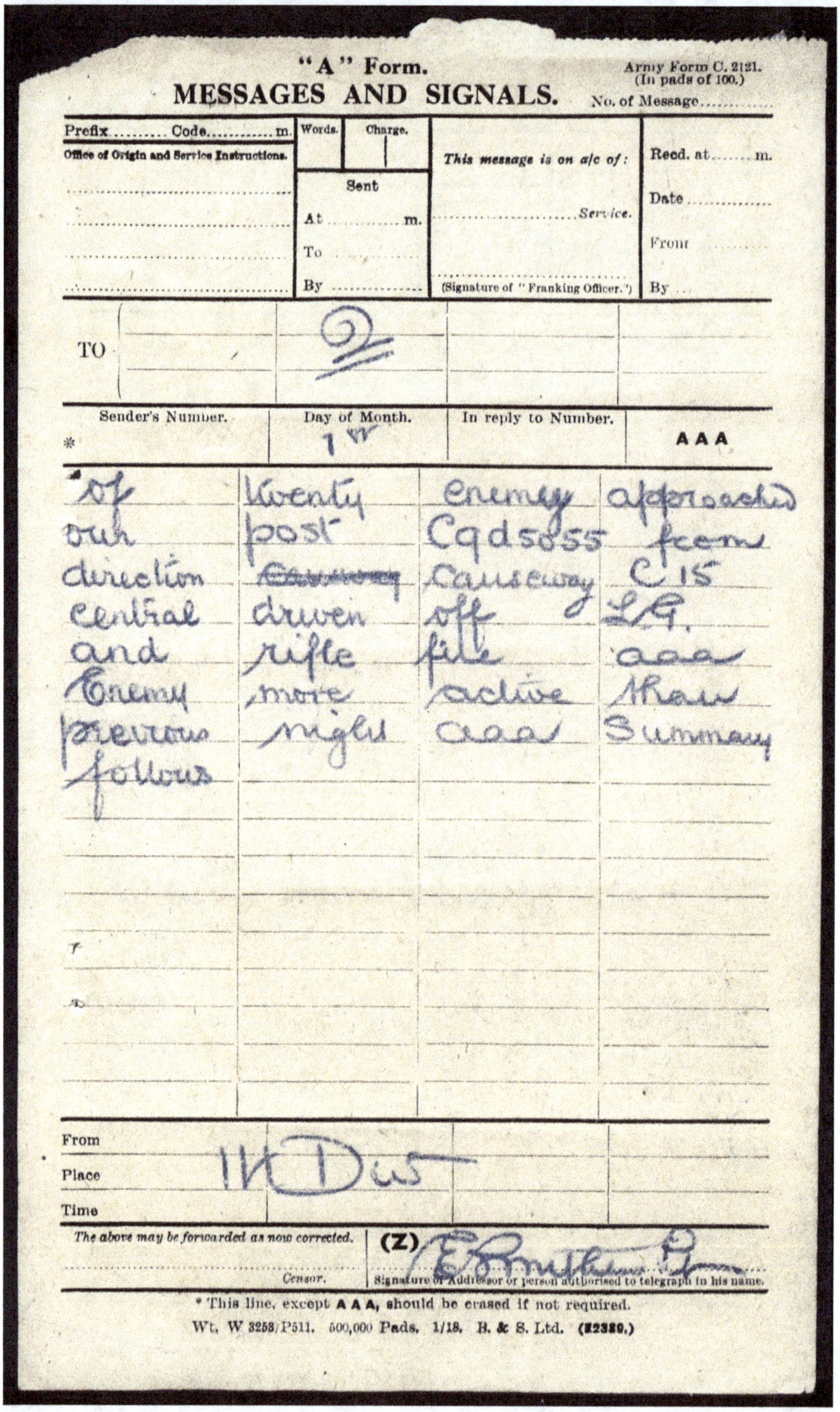

"A" Form.
Army Form C. 2121.
(In pads of 100.)
MESSAGES AND SIGNALS.
No. of Message..........

Prefix........ Code........... m.
Office of Origin and Service Instructions.

Words.	Charge.

Sent
At .... m.
To
By

This message is on a/c of:
.... *Service.*
(Signature of "Franking Officer.")

Recd. at .... m.
Date
From
By

TO: "Q"

Sender's Number.	Day of Month.	In reply to Number.	AAA
*	1st		

of	twenty	enemy	approached
our	post	C9d5055	from
direction	~~Causeway~~	Causeway	C15
central	driven	off	L.G.
and	rifle	fire	aaa
Enemy	more	active	than
previous	night	aaa	Summary
follows			

From
Place
Time
11th Div

The above may be forwarded as now corrected.
(Z) E Smithers [illegible]
.... *Censor.*
Signature of Addressor or person authorised to telegraph in his name.

* This line, except AAA, should be erased if not required.
Wt. W 3253/P511. 500,000 Pads. 1/18. B. & S. Ltd. (E2380.)

Army Form C. 2121.
(In books of 100.)

"C" FORM.

MESSAGES AND SIGNALS. No. of Message.

Prefix Sm Code 1545 Words 27

Received from Vathi By Sager

Service Instructions

Vathi 2 adds

Sent, or sent out. At m. To By

Office Stamp.

Handed in at Office 1525 m. Received 1553 m.

TO Jotha

G.O.O. G.S.O.1 G.S.O.2 G.S.O.3

*Sender's Number.	Day of Month.	In reply to Number.	AAA
J3	1/11/18		
Evening	wire	situation	quiet
weather	clear	wind	slight
SE	artillery	activity	slight
enemy	aircraft	nil	our
own	active	occasionally	
engaged	by	aa	aaa

FROM Vathi

PLACE & TIME 16 D

* This line, except A A A, should be erased, if not required.

(2803) Wt. W54/P728. 400,000 Pads. 285. A.P.Ltd. (E.3045)

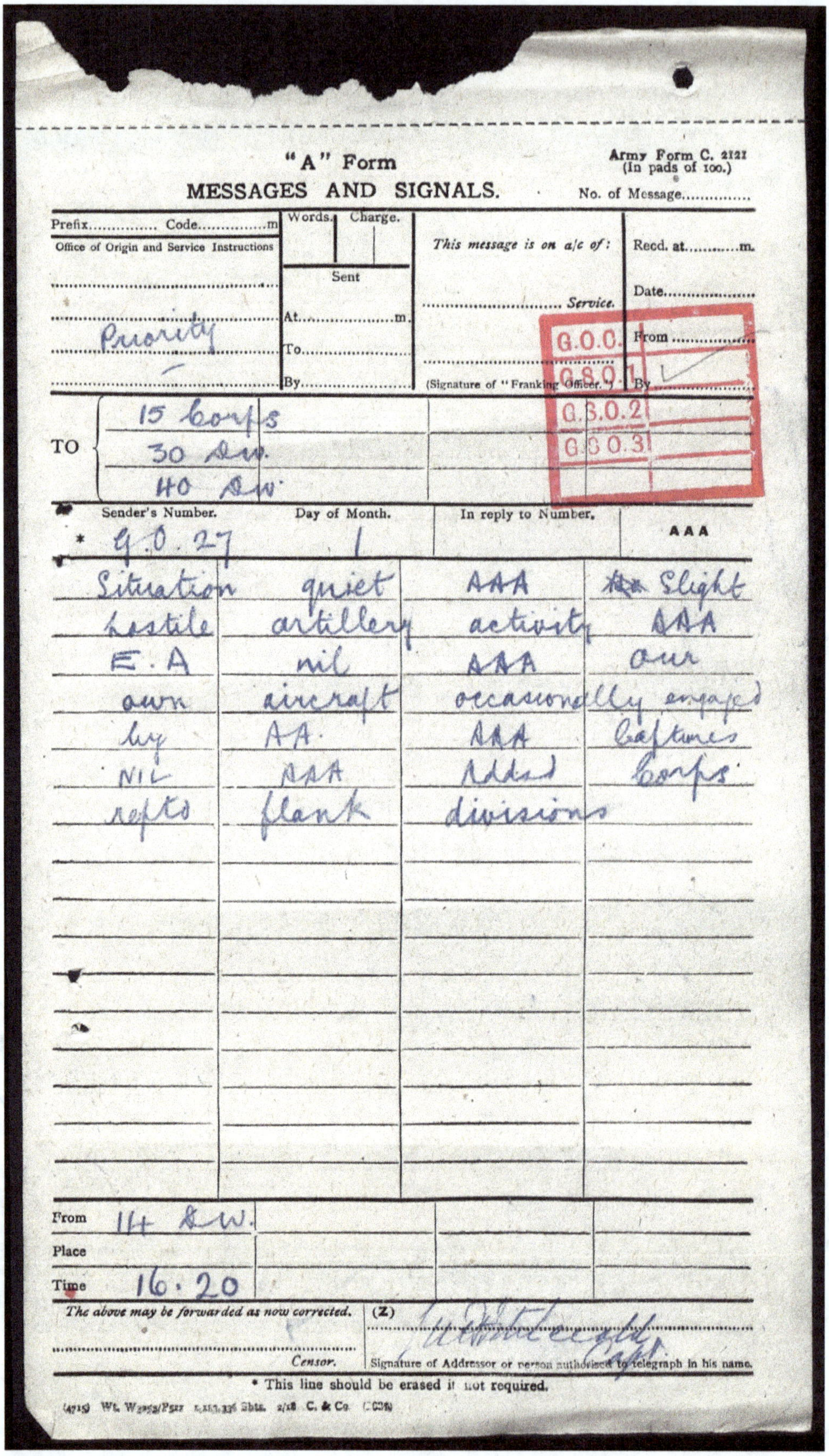

"A" Form

MESSAGES AND SIGNALS.

Army Form C. 2121 (In pads of 100.)

No. of Message..............

Prefix.......... Code..........m	Words. Charge.	This message is on a/c of:	Recd. at..........m.
Office of Origin and Service Instructions	Sent	.... Service.	Date..............
Priority	At..........m.		From ....
	To........		
	By........	(Signature of "Franking Officer.")	By........

Stamp: G.O.C. / G.S.O.1 / G.S.O.2 / G.S.O.3

TO: 15 Corps / 30 Div. / 40 Div.

Sender's Number.	Day of Month.	In reply to Number.	AAA
* G.O. 27	1		

Situation quiet AAA Slight hostile artillery activity AAA E.A nil AAA our own aircraft occasionally engaged by AA. AAA Captures NIL AAA Added Corps repto flank divisions

From: 14 Div.

Place

Time: 16.20

The above may be forwarded as now corrected. (Z)

Censor. Signature of Addressor or person authorised to telegraph in his name. [signature] Capt.

* This line should be erased if not required.

(4715) Wt. W2953/P522 5,125,336 Stbs. 2/18 C. & Co. (C0B)

SECRET & URGENT. Copy No 8

41st INFANTRY BRIGADE ORDER No. 35.

2nd November, 1918.

Refce. Map Sheet 29 S.W. 1/20,000.
37 N.W. 1/20,000.

1. The following operation will be carried out to-day, 2nd November, and during night 2nd/3rd November, by 121st Inf. Bde. on the right of 41st Inf. Bde. front.

   (a) Posts to be established on causeway about C 21 c 0.5.
   (b) Posts to be established on E side of L'ESCAUT to connect with pos[t] of 18th Y. & L. Regt.

2. In order to assist the operation referred to in para 1(b) the bridge at C 9 d is placed at the disposal of 121st Inf. Bde.
   In the event of the operation being successful a bridge is to be constructed about C 15 central by 121st Inf. Bde.

3. All details as to times of crossing and position of combined Liaison Post to be established on E side of L'ESCAUT will be arranged between 18th Y. & L. & 23rd Cheshire Regt. direct.

4. While the operation referred to in para 1(b) is in progress, 33rd London Regt. R.B. will endeavour to establish the following posts having first dislodged hostile M.Gs. from suspected emplacements in houses at C 5 b 40.45 and C 5 a 85.45 :-

   (a) Liaison Post with 18th Y. & L. at approximately C 4 a 90.25.
   (b) Post at SLUICE at C 5 a 2.4.
   (c) Post at house at C 5 a 85.45 with a listening post in vicinity of house at C 5 b 40.45.
   (d) Post at C 5 b 2.6.

5. 33rd L.R.B. will arrange direct with D.T.M.O. and O.C. Left M.G.Coy. for any assistance required.

6. If the above operation referred to in para 4 is successful O.C. 61st Field Coy., R.E. will arrange for light bridge to be thrown across the L'ESCAUT at approximately C 4 b 85.45.

7. Time at which operation referred to in para 1(b) is to be carried out will be notified later.

8. All concerned to acknowledge.

Issued at: 14.30

A.W. Watson
Captain,
Brigade Major,
41st Infantry Brigade.

Copies to:
1. 18th Y. & L.
2. 29th D.L.I.
3. 33rd L.R.B.
4. 41st T.M.B.
5. 61st Field Coy.R.E.
6. O.C. Left M.G.Coy.
7. D.T.M.O.
8. 14th Div. "G".
9. 14th D.A.
10. 46th Bde. R.F.A.
11. 47th Bde. R.F.A.
12. 36th Bde. R.G.A.
13. 14th M.G.Battn.
14. 121st Inf. Bde.
15. 90th Inf. Bde.
16. A.D.S. 44th Field Amb.
17. B.G.C.
18. S.C.
19. B.I.O.
20. B.S.O.
21. File.
22. W.D.

"A" Form

MESSAGES AND SIGNALS.

Army Form C. 2121
(In pads of 100.)

No. of Message..............

Prefix.............. Code..............m | Words. | Charge. | This message is on a/c of: | G.O.C. / G.S.O.1 / G.S.O.2 / G.S.O.3 | Recd. at..........m.

Office of Origin and Service Instructions

Priority

Sent
At.................m.
To..................
By..................

Service.

(Signature of "Franking Officer.")

Date..............
From..............
By................

TO		
	15	Corps
	30	Division
	40	Division

Sender's Number.	Day of Month.	In reply to Number.	AAA
* G.O. 50	4		

Evening	report	AAA	Slight
enemy	artillery	activity	which
caused	fire	at	ESPIERRES
Church	1215	AAA	
Captures	nil	AAA	Added
Corps	repts	flank	divisions

From 14. Division

Place

Time

The above may be forwarded as now corrected.

(Z) J. F. Beaumont Capt.

..............................Censor.

Signature of Addressor or person authorised to telegraph in his name.

* This line should be erased if not required.

(4715) Wt. W3255/P322 1,125,35d Shts. 2/18 C. & Co. (E34)

Army Form C. 2123.
(In books of 100.)

"C" FORM.

MESSAGES AND SIGNALS.

No. of Message 61

Prefix AM Code 1600 Words 45

Received from Vaki By Gbr. T

Service Instructions Vaki

Sent, or sent out. At ... m. To ... By ...

Office Stamp.

Handed in at ... Office 1600 m. Received 4.10 m.

0.8.0.1

0.8.0.1

0.8.0.1

0.8.0.1

TO GOKA

* Sender's Number.	Day of Month.	In reply to Number.	AAA
8/4	11/18		

Evening were aaa situation quiet slight enemy artillery activity aaa Some activity by our artillery and aeroplanes reported aaa Church at ESPIERRES caught fire owing to enemy shelling at 12.15 considerable damage fire now extinguished aaa

16.12 RD

FROM Vaki

PLACE & TIME

* This line, except AAA, should be erased, if not required.

(3287) Wt. W54/P738. 691,000 Pads. 3/18. A.P.Ltd. (E3013)

Army Form C. 2123.
(In books of 100.)

"C" FORM.
MESSAGES AND SIGNALS. No. of Message..........

Prefix SM Code 0835 Words 15

Sent, or sent out. At ....m. To .... By ....

Office Stamp. -4. XI. 18

*Received from ZAA By Jem

Service Instructions

Handed in at VAKI Office 0835 m. Received 0836 m.

TO GOKA

*Sender's Number.	Day of Month	In reply to Number	AAA
BM 279	4		

Bridge completed at C5a

0545

FROM VAKI

PLACE & TIME

* This line, except AAA, should be erased, if not required.

(3287) Wt. W54/P738 691,000 Pads 1/18 A.P.Ltd (E3613)

"A" Form

Army Form C. 2121 (In pads of 100.)

MESSAGES AND SIGNALS.

No. of Message..............

Prefix........ Code..............m | Words. Charge.

Office of Origin and Service Instructions

Priority 15 Corps

Sent

At..............m.

To..............

By..............

This message is on a/c of: G.O.C. / G.S.O.1 / G.S.O.2 / G.S.O.3 .... Service.

(Signature of "Franking Officer.")

Recd. at..........m.

Date..............

From..............

By..............

TO 15 Corps 30 + 40 Divs

Sender's Number.	Day of Month.	In reply to Number.	AAA
* G.O. 47	4		

Morning Report aaa Situation
quiet aaa Posts established
on left on front
C 6 b 6 4 C 5 a 2 4 C 5 a 20 05
C 6 b 40 45 aaa Slight
long range shelling and
shelling U 26 cent

From 14 Div.

Place

Time 04 17

The above may be forwarded as now corrected. (Z) [signature] Capt

Censor. Signature of Addressor or person authorised to telegraph in his name.

* This line should be erased if not required.

(4715) Wt. W3013/P522 5,113,336 Sbks. 2/18 C. & Co. (534)

6

Army Form C. 2123.
(In books of 100.)

"C" FORM.
MESSAGES AND SIGNALS. No. of Message..........

Prefix .... Code .... Words	Sent, or sent out.	Office Stamp.
Received from .... By	At .... m.	4 XI. 18 SIGNALS
Service Instructions	To	
	By	

Handed in at Vaki Bty Office 0342 m. Received 0352 m.

TO	Goka

G.O.C.
G.S.O.1
G.S.O.2
G.S.O.3

*Sender's Number.	Day of Month	In reply to Number	AAA
SC43	4		
Situation	quiet	aaa	Posts
established	on	left	bn
front	at	C4B6.4	C5A2.4
C5A2.0.05	and	C5B4.0.45	aaa
Slight	long	range	shelling
and	some	mg	fire
on	left	and	some
shelling	on	Central	aaa
Added	Goka	repeat	flanks

FROM: Vaki
PLACE & TIME: 0325

* This line, except **AAA**, should be erased, if not required.

(3287) Wt W54/P738 691,000 Pads 1/18 A P Ltd (E3013)

"C" FORM.
MESSAGES AND SIGNALS.

Army Form C. 2123.
(In books of 100.)
No. of Message 4

Prefix Sm Code 0200 Words 17

Received from ZDA By Cowin

Service Instructions

Sent, or sent out.
At .... m.
To ....
By ....

Office Stamp.
SIGNALS 4 VI 18

Handed in at VAKI Office 0200 m. Received 0209 m.

G.O.C.
G.S.O.1
G.S.O.2
G.S.O.3

TO GOKA

*Sender's Number.	Day of Month.	In reply to Number.	AAA
SC 41	4		

Posts established at C4 B6·4 C5A24 C5 A20 0.5 and C5 B4 0·45 aaa Situation quiet

FROM
PLACE & TIME VAKI 01·50

* This line, except A A A, should be erased if not required.

(2807) Wt. W5867CK. 625,000 Pads. 2/18. A.P.Ltd. (E2012)

Appendix A(4)

14th Division - General Staff

War Diary - Nov 1918

Vol XLV

Operations 4. Nov. 1918

Appendix A(3)

14th Division – General Staff

War Diary – Nov 1918

VOL XLV

Operations. 3 Nov. 1918

"C" FORM.

MESSAGES AND SIGNALS. No. of Message

Prefix .... Code .... Words ....

Received from .... By ....

Service Instructions

Sent, or sent out. At YN m. To .... By ....

Office Stamp. YN 3 - XI. 18 SIGNALS

Handed in at VAKI Pty Office 0330 m. Received 0534 m.

G.S.O. / G.S.O. 1 / G.S.O. 2 / G.S.O. 3

TO GOKA

*Sender's Number.	Day of Month.	In reply to Number.	AAA
J5	3/11/18		
morning	wire	aaa	Situation
unusually	quiet	aaa	Some
Slight	Enemy	Shelling	on
left	BATT	Front	our
artillery	inactive	aaa	Our
Patrols	are	out	aaa
DOTTIGNIES	was	lightly	Shelled
2230	Some	Casualties	reported
aaa	added	GOKA	and
Reptd	MAQE	JIIGI	
			0400

FROM VAKI

PLACE & TIME

* This line, except AAA, should be erased, if not required.

(3287) Wt.W54/P736. 691,000 Pads. 3/18. A.P.Ltd. (E3013)

"A" Form

Army Form C. 2121
(In pads of 100.)

MESSAGES AND SIGNALS.

No. of Message..............

Prefix............ Code..............m | Words. | Charge.

Office of Origin and Service Instructions

Priority.

[illegible signature]

Sent

At..................m.

To..................

By..................

This message is on a/c of:

.... *Service.*

(Signature of "Franking Officer.")

Recd. at..........m.

Date..................

From..................

By..................

TO		
	15	Corps
	30	Division
	40	Division

Sender's Number.	Day of Month.	In reply to Number.	AAA
* G.O.40	3		

Morning	Report	aaa	Enemy
Artillery	slightly	active	aaa
DOTTIGNIES	lightly	shelled	aaa
Otherwise	nothing	to	report

G.O.C.
G.S.O.1
G.S.O.2
G.S.O.3

0410

From 14 Division

Place

Time

The above may be forwarded as now corrected. (Z)

Censor.

Signature of Addressor or person authorised to telegraph in his name.

[illegible signature]

* This line should be erased if not required.

(4715) Wt. W3253/P522 1,333,336 Shts. 2/18 C. & Co. (634)

26

"C" FORM.

MESSAGES AND SIGNALS.

Army Form C. 2121.
(In books of 100.)

No. of Message..........

Prefix SB Code 10 35 Words 38	Sent, or sent out.	Office Stamp
Received from PCo By Comm	At .... m.	
Service Instructions Priority	To	
	By	

Handed in at YDZ Office 10 35 m. Received 10 52 m.

TO 14th Divn

G.O.C.
G.S.O 1
G.S.O 2
G.S.O 3

*Sender's Number.	Day of Month.	In reply to Number.	AAA
GC 745	3rd		

Posts established on East bank of canal as follows aaa C9D2.3 (Liaison) C9D2.1 C15B1.9 C15B4.1 C15 Central C15D1.6 aaa Footbridge erected at C15 Central aaa Addsd Corps repts Flank Divns CRA CRE RIZ

Put on G.O.C.

Disposition map. 1055

FROM 40 Divn Completed

PLACE & TIME

* This line, except A A A, should be erased, if not required.

(2082) Wt. W54/P738. 600,000 Pads. 2/18. A.P.Ltd. (R2012)

"A" Form

Army Form C. 2121
(In pads of 100.)

MESSAGES AND SIGNALS.

No. of Message..........

Prefix..........Code..........m | Words | Charge.

Office of Origin and Service Instructions

Sent
At..........m.
To..........
By..........

This message is on a/c of:

.... *Service.*

(Signature of "Franking Officer.")

Recd. at..........m.
Date..........
From..........
By..........

G.O.C.
G.S.O.1
G.S.O.2
G.S.O.3

TO 15 CORPS

Sender's Number.	Day of Month.	In reply to Number.	AAA
* G. 342	3		

Intelligence summary aaa Our patrols active reports follows aaa Enemy Arty very active largely with 77 mm and 10.5 cm but gas shelling much less than ~~yesterday~~ preceding 24 hours aaa Enemy TMs active firing on HELCHIN from GUERMIGIES aaa Emplacements located at C.10.d 75.80 and C.16.a aaa Considerable enemy transport heard aaa Enemy MG reported firing from house C.6.a 2.8 aaa Suspected OP in Chapel Tower POTTES

From 14 DIV
Place
Time 16.35

The above may be forwarded as now corrected. (Z) [illegible] Capt

.... *Censor.* Signature of Addressee or person authorised to telegraph in his name.

* This line should be erased if not required.

(1806.) Wt. W12952/M1294. 187,500 Pads. 1/17 H.P.Ltd.,S. (E. 818).

64

Army Form C. 2123.
(In books of 100.)

"C" FORM.
MESSAGES AND SIGNALS. No. of Message........

Prefix AD Code 1530 Words 23	Sent, or sent out. At ..... m. To ..... By .....
Received from Da By	Office Stamp. YN — 3 - XI. 18
Service Instructions Priority	
Handed in at DASA Office 1530 m. Received 1535 m.	

TO COKA

*Sender's Number.	Day of Month.	In reply to Number.	AAA
G 7	3		
Evening	wire	aaa	Situation
quiet	aaa	Slight	aerial
activity	by	our	planes
aaa	Some	slight	shelling
on	left	Daa	front
aaa			

G.O.C.	
G.S.O.1	
G.S.O.2	
G.S.O.3	

FROM VAKI
PLACE & TIME

* This line, except AAA, should be erased if not required.

(2367) Wt. W3689/P.28. 400,000 Pads. 3/18. A.P.Ltd. (E.2013)

"A" Form
Army Form
(In pads of ...)

MESSAGES AND SIGNALS.

No. of Message..............

Prefix............ Code..............m | Words. | Charge.

Office of Origin and Service Instructions

Sent

At..................m.

To......................

By......................

This message is on a/c of:

.... *Service.*

....

(Signature of "Franking Officer.")

Recd. at...........m.

Date..................

From ....

By ....

TO 15 Corps – 40 Div – 30 Div

Sender's Number.	Day of Month.	In reply to Number.	AAA
* G.O.42	3		

Evening	report	AAA	Quiet
AAA	Slight	shelling	on
left	Bn	front	AAA
Captures	nil	AAA	
addsd	Corps	repts	flank
divisions			

G.O.C.	
G.S.O.1	
G.S.O.2	
G.S.O.3	

From 14 Division

Place

Time

The above may be forwarded as now corrected. (Z) [illegible]

.... *Censor.*

Signature of Addressor or person authorised to telegraph in his name.

* This line should be erased if not required.

(4715) Wt. W3253/P331 2,253,336 Sbts. 2/18 C. & Co. (E034)

SECRET. Copy No 25

14th DIVISION ORDER No. 237

Ref. Sheets. 29 and 37 1/40,000
and TOURNAI. 1/100,000.

2nd November 1918

1. The Divisional Boundary has been extended Northwards to U.24.b.6.3.

2. The Northern Boundary runs as follows :-

U.24.b.5.5 - U.4.a.0.0 - A.3.d.0.0.

Southern Boundary. ESPIERRES Canal (inclusive) to B.23.a.6.6 thence along North bank of Canal to Railway A.27.a.2.6.

3. Troops of 14th Division at present outside these boundaries will move in accordance with attached March Table.

4. Refilling Point for Nos. 2 and 4 Coys. Divisional Train will be in the Square WATTRELOS at 13.00 hours Nov. 3rd.

5. Divisional H.Q. will close at MOUSCRON at 11.00 on 4th. inst. and re-open at TOURCOING at the same hour.

6. ACKNOWLEDGE.

T.E.Hamilton Johnston
Lieut-Colonel.
General Staff.
14th Division.

Issued at 20.00.

Copies to - No. 1 - 41st Inf. Bde.
2 - 42nd Inf. Bde.
3 - 43rd Inf. Bde.
4 - C.R.A.
5 - C.R.E.
6 - 15th L.N.Lancs.Rogt. Pioneers.
7 - 14th Machine Gun Bn.
8 - 14th Signal Coy.
9 - 14th Div. Train.
10 - S.S.O.
11 - 14th Div. M. T. Coy.
12) 13) - AQ Branch.
14 - A.D.M.S.
15 - D.A.D.V.S.
16 - D.A.D.O.S.
17 - D.A.P.M.
18 - D.G.O.
19 - O.C. 14th Div.Reception Camp.
20 - XV Corps G.
21 - XV Corps Q.
22 - XV Corps R.A.
23 - 30th British Division
24 - 40th British Division.
25 - War Diary.
26 - File.

SECRET

MARCH TABLE TO ACCOMPANY 14th DIVISION ORDER NO. 237.

Serial No.	Date.	Unit.	From	To	Route	Remarks
1.	Nov. 3	Battn. 42 Inf.Bde.	LUINGNE	WATTRELOS	HERSEAUX - PETIT AUDENARDE	To be clear of LUINGNE by 10.00. Billets from Area Cmdnt. WATTRELOS.
2	Nov. 3	Battn. 42 Inf.Bde.	LUINGNE	PETIT AUDENARDE - ESTAMPUIS area	HERSEAUX PETIT AUDENARDE	Available accommodation in Sqs A 12 c & d, A 18, B 7, B 12. Not to move before 10.00 and to be clear of LUINGNE by 11.00.
3	Nov. 3	14th M.G.Bn. H.Q.	LUINGNE	HERSEAUX		Billets from Area Cmdnt HERSEAUX
4	Nov. 3	No. 4 Coy. Div. Train.	28/ X 17 c 87.	WATTRELOS	No. restrictions	Billets from Area Cmdnt. WATTRELOS.
5	Nov. 3	No. 2 Coy. Div. Train	29/ S 22 d 8540	PETIT AUDENARDE - ESTAMPUIS area		Billets to be arranged by O.C. Div. Train in conjunction with 43 Infantry Bde.
6	Nov. 4	Divisional H.Q.	MOUSCRON	TOURCOING		To be clear of MOUSCRON by 11 00.

Appendix A(5)

14th Division - General Staff

War Diary - Nov. 1918

Vol XLV

Operations - 5 Nov. 1918

Army Form C. 2123.
(In books of 100.)

"C" Form.

MESSAGES AND SIGNALS. No. of Message ....

Prefix ...... Code ...... Words	Received.	Sent, or sent out.	Office Stamp.
£ s. d.	From	At .... m.	
Charges to Collect	By	To	
Service Instructions. Priority		By	

Handed in at VAKI Office 0331 m. Received 0328 m.

TO GOKA

*Sender's Number.	Day of Month.	In reply to Number.	AAA
BM 284	5	—	

Operations referred to in Bde orders 55 successfully carried out posts being established on E bank of LESCAUT our casualties slight details follow aaa Enemy artillery active especially on U22 and U228 aaa Our artillery active in support of operation referred to aaa Prisoners captured details of identification follow

3.40

G.O.C.
G.S.O. 1
G.S.O. 2
G.S.O. 3

FROM VAKI
TIME & PLACE

*This line should be erased if not required.

300,000.—John Bissen, Ltd.—5/17.—3280. Forms C2123.

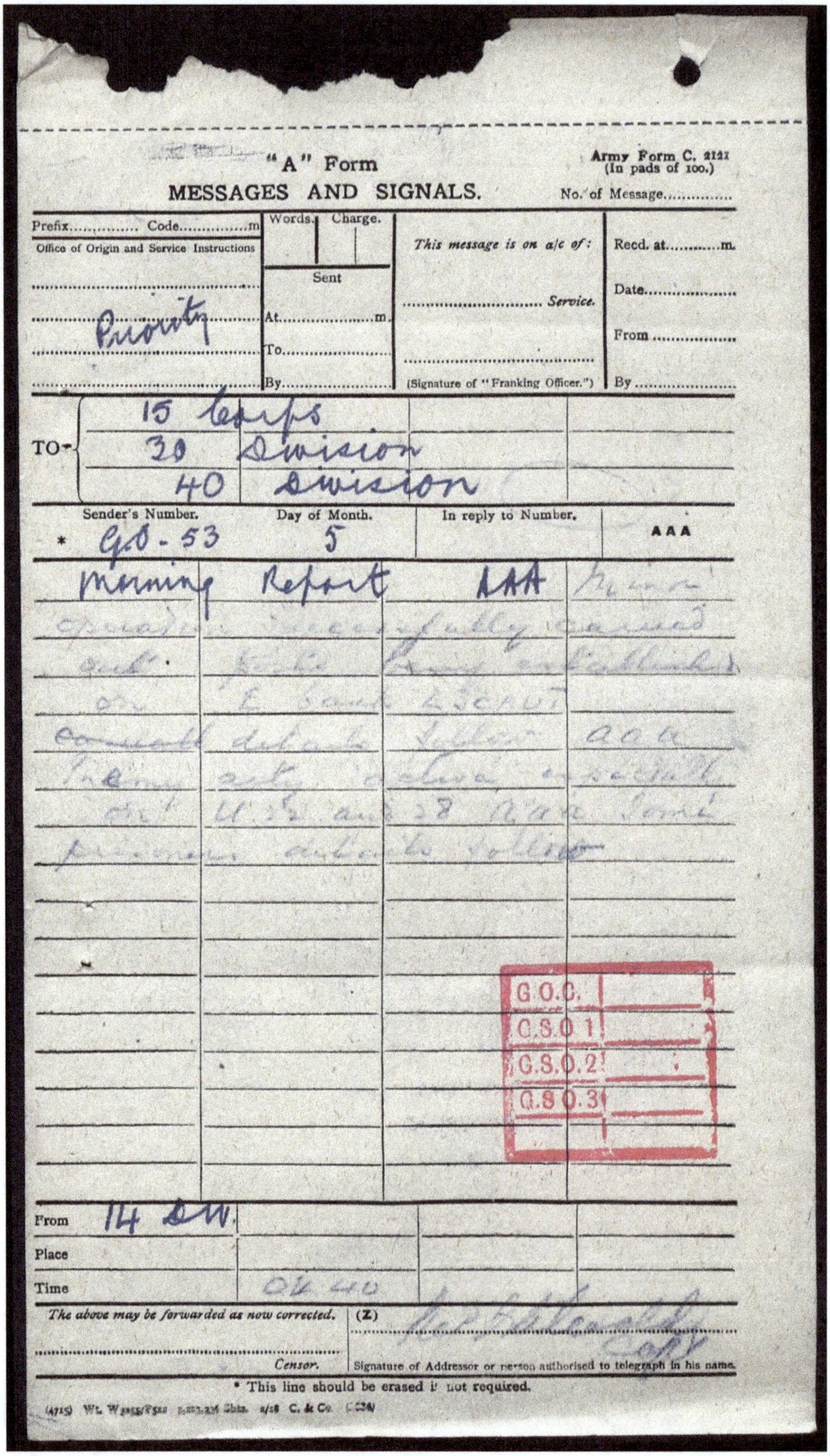

"A" Form

MESSAGES AND SIGNALS.

Army Form C. 2121
(In pads of 100.)

No. of Message..............

Prefix.......... Code..........m	Words. Charge.	This message is on a/c of:	Recd. at..........m.
Office of Origin and Service Instructions	Sent	.... Service.	Date..............
Priority	At..........m.		From..............
	To..............		
	By..............	(Signature of "Franking Officer.")	By..............

TO– 15 Corps
30 Division
40 Division

Sender's Number.	Day of Month.	In reply to Number.	AAA
* G.O-53	5		

Morning Report AAA Minor operation successfully carried out. Posts being established on E bank L'Escaut consolidated details follow AAA Enemy arty active especially on U 32 and 28 AAA Some prisoners details follow

G.O.C.
G.S.O 1
G.S.O 2
G.S.O 3

From 14 Div.
Place
Time 04 40

The above may be forwarded as now corrected. (Z) [illegible] Capt
Censor. Signature of Addressor or person authorised to telegraph in his name.

* This line should be erased if not required.

(4715) Wt. W[illegible] [illegible] C. & Co. ([illegible])

"C" Form.

Army Form C. 2123.
(In books of 100.)

MESSAGES AND SIGNALS. No. of Message

Prefix SM Code 0419 Words	Received. From ZDA By AW	Sent, or sent out. At ... m. To ... By ...	Office Stamp.
£ s. d. Charges to Collect			
Service Instructions.			

Handed in at VAKI Office 0419 m Received 0421 m.

TO GOKA

*Sender's Number.	Day of Month.	In reply to Number.	AAA
BM 285	5		

30 prisoners captured belonging to 95TH IR 38TH Div

G.O.C.
G.S.O. 1
G.S.O. 2
G.S.O. 3

FROM VAKI
TIME & PLACE

*This line should be erased if not required.

300,000.—John Bissen, Ltd —5/17.—3280. Forms C2123.

"A" Form
Army Form C. 2121
(In pads of 100.)

MESSAGES AND SIGNALS.

No. of Message..............

Prefix........ Code........m	Words. Charge.	This message is on a/c of:	Recd. at........m.
Office of Origin and Service Instructions	Sent	.... Service.	Date........
Priority	At........m.		From........
	To........		
	By........	(Signature of "Franking Officer.")	By........

TO: 15 Corps, 30 Div, 40 Div

Sender's Number.	Day of Month.	In reply to Number.	AAA
* G.O. 54	5		

Continuation		G.O. 53	aaa
30	prisoners	taken	15th
I.R.	38	Div	AAA
Also	Corps	reports	flank
divisions			

G.O.C.
G.S.O 1
G.S.O.2
G.S.O 3

From 14 Div
Place
Time [illegible]

The above may be forwarded as now corrected. (Z)

Censor. Signature of Addressor or person authorised to telegraph in his name.

* This line should be erased if not required.

(4715) Wt. W3253/P522 2,525,336 Shts. 2/18 C. & Co. (534)

22

"C" FORM.
MESSAGES AND SIGNALS.

Army Form C. 2123.
(In books of 100.)
No. of Message...........

ARMY SIGNALS

Prefix A O Code 0915 Words 96

Received from Vaki By G/At

Sent, or sent out. Office Stamp.

At .... m.

To ....

By ....

Service Instructions

Urgent Operations Priority

Handed in at Vaki Office 0915 m. Received 0934

G.O.C.
G.S.O. 1
G.S.O. 2
G.S.O. 3

TO 14th Div

*Sender's Number.	Day of Month.	In reply to Number.	AAA
GS3	5		

DIO report aaa Prisoners taken between V24B55 and U30C belong to 1st ~~[illegible]~~ Coy 95 IR and 1 and 2 Coys 96 IR aaa order of battle N. to S. 95 96 94 aaa Coy strengths 40 to 45 aaa Two Bns each three Coys aaa 1/96th Relieved 3/96 in line 2/3 aaa 3/96 support at CELLES aaa Three Coys in line aaa orders to withdraw to MAIN LINE resistance running through POTTES NE and SW if attacked aaa Know of no intention to withdraw aaa added 2nd army rptd all concerned

09.36

FROM 10 14 Div

PLACE & TIME

* This line, except AAA, should be erased, if not required.

(3287) Wt. W54/P738. 691,000 Pads. 3/18. A.P.Ltd. (E3013)

V24B55

"C" FORM.
MESSAGES AND SIGNALS.

Army Form C. 2123.
(In books of 100.)
No. of Message ....

Prefix SB Code 1600 Words 34	Sent, or sent out.	Office Stamp.
Received from vaki By Rapter	At .... m.	
Service Instructions vaki Priority	To	
	By	

Handed in at .... Office 1600 m. Received 1613 m.

TO Gotha

G.O.C.
G.S.O.1
G.S.O.2
G.S.O.3

* Sender's Number.	Day of Month.	In reply to Number.	AAA
210	5/11/18		

Evening	wire	aaa	Situation
fairly	Quiet	enemy	artillery
active	in	vicinity	of
U16B	and	D	U23A
and	U22A	aaa	our
artillery	active	in	retaliation
aaa wind	SW	fresh	rain
aaa			

FROM vaki
PLACE & TIME

* This line, except AAA, should be erased, if not required.
(3287) Wt. W34/P736. 691,000 Pads. 3/18. A.P.Ltd. (E3913)

"A" Form

MESSAGES AND SIGNALS.

Army Form C. 2121
(In pads of 100.)

No. of Message..............

Prefix.............. Code..............m | Words. | Charge.

Office of Origin and Service Instructions

Priority

15 Corps

Sent

At..................m.

To..................

By..................

This message is on a/c of: G.S.O. / G.S.O. 1 / G.S.O. 2 / G.S.O. 3

Service.

(Signature of "Franking Officer.")

Recd. at..........m.

Date..................

From..................

By..................

TO			
30 Div.			
40 Div.			

Sender's Number.	Day of Month.	In reply to Number.	AAA
G.O. 58	5		

Evening	Report	AAA	Enemy
artillery	active	in	vicinity
U 16 B	and D	U 23 A	and
U 22 A	AAA	our	artillery
active	in	retaliation	AAA
Captures	21	prisoners	and
5 Eng.R.	M.G.	AAA	Added
Corps	ref (?)	flank	divisions

From 14 Div.

Place

Time

The above may be forwarded as now corrected.

(Z) [signature] Capt

Censor.

Signature of Addressor or person authorised to telegraph in his name.

* This line should be erased if not required.

(4325) Wt. W.....
C. & Co. (.034)

GENERAL STAFF, 14TH DIVISION.
No.......
Date 4-11-18
File G.9.

G.O.C.
G.S.O.1
G.S.O.2
G.S.O.3

SECRET & URGENT. Copy No 9.

41st INFANTRY BRIGADE ORDER No.35.

4th November, 1918.

Refce. Map Sheets 29 S.W. 1/20,000.
29 S.E. "
37 N.W. "

1. On night 4th/5th Novr., 1918, 33rd London Regt., R.B., in conjunction with 61st Field Coy., R.E. will cross L'ESCAUT between U 30 c 40.00 and U 24 b 6.6 and establish posts on E bank of the River.

2. At zero 61st Field Coy., R.E., will throw bridges across L'ESCAUT at following points :-
(a) U 30 c 40.50 No.1 bridge.
(b) U 30 c 80.95 No.2 bridge.
(c) U 24 b 60.60 No.3 bridge.

3. As soon as the above bridges have been constructed 33rd L.R.B. will cross L'ESCAUT as follows :-

(a) 1 Platoon will cross No.1 bridge and will establish a strong post at or near U 30 c 40.15 to cover approach to bridge from S.E. direction. The remainder of the platoon will proceed N along E bank of L'ESCAUT and join up with platoon crossing by No.2 bridge, having established posts along the river between No.1 & No.2 bridges.

(b) 1 Platoon will cross at No.2 bridge and will establish a post at or near U 30 c 80.80. The remainder of the platoon will then proceed N along E bank of L'ESCAUT and establish posts, finally gaining touch with platoon crossing by No.3 bridge.

(c) 1 Platoon will cross at No.3 bridge and will establish a post at or near U 24 b 7.7 and then proceed S along E bank of L'ESCAUT, establishing posts and finally joining up with platoon from bridge No.2.

(d) To avoid delay in crossing in the event of any one of the bridges being destroyed or not being thrown across Reserve platoons will be located in following areas so that if required they can immediately reinforce the platoons who have been able to effect a crossing.
(i) 1 Platoon at approximately U 29 b to reinforce either bridges Nos. 1 or 2.
(ii) 1 Platoon at approximately U 24 a to reinforce bridge No.3.

4. 33rd London Regt. R.B. will arrange for each platoon to have a distinctive signal either by whistle or any other suitable instrument so that the progress made by each platoon can be followed. By this means the possibility of one platoon mistaking another for the enemy should be obviated.

5. 33rd London Regt. will also arrange with Battalion on left flank to engage hostile posts in U 24 b 9.9 with Lewis gun and rifle fire.

6. 46th & 47th Bdes., R.F.A., will co-operate as arranged at conference to-day.

7. Left Coy. of 14th M.G.Battn. will also co-operate as arranged.

8. D.T.M.O. will arrange to fire as under :-
From Z - 10 to Zero along E bank of L'ESCAUT in U 30 c.
Z - 10 to Z plus 25 on GUERMIGNIES in C 6 a.

9. 41st T.M.Bty. will also co-operate under instructions to be detailed by 33rd L.R.B.

2230.

10. Zero will be at 23.00 on 4th November, 1918.

11. Units taking part in above operation will each send an Officer to Advanced Bde. H.Qs. TROIS FERMES, U 20 c 6.4 at 17.00 to synchronise watches with Bde. Signal Officer.

12. Completion of operation to be wired to Bde. H.Qs. employing code word YES UNCLE!

13. Acknowledge. 9R.433

Issued to Sigs. at

A.W. Watson Capt.
Captain,
Brigade Major,
41st Infantry Brigade.

Copies to:
1. 18th Y. & L.
2. 29th D.L.I.
3. 33rd L.R.B.
4. 41st T.M.B.
5. 61st Field Coy.R.E.
6. A Coy. 14th M.G.Bnm
7. D Coy. 14th M.G.Bn.
8. D.T.M.O.
9. 14th Div. "G".
10. 14th D.A.
11. 46th F.A.Bde.
12. 47th F.A.Bde.
13. 36th Bde.R.G.A.
14. 14th M.G.Battn.
15. 121st Inf. Bde.
16. 90th Inf. Bde.
17. A.D.S. 44th Field Amb.
18. B.G.C.
19. S.C.
20. B.I.O.
21. B.S.O.
22. File.
23. W.D.

J.B.1.

Ref. Map Sheet 29 S.W.

G.O.C.
G.S.O.1
G.S.O.2
G.S.O.3

Adjt. MEZI.

Report on operations carried out on night Novr. 4th/5th, 1918, on front bounded by the two points U 30 c 4.5 and U 24 b 6.6.

The object of this operation was to establish line of posts E of L'ESCAUT covering the following bridgeheads made by R.E., after providing covering parties whilst R.E. did the bridging:-

1. U 30 c 4.5.
2. U 30 a 80.15.
3. U 24 b 6.8.

Zero hour was at 23.30 after barrage of 10 minutes duration had lifted. The R.Es. then started walking the bridges forward and getting them launched under cover of one platoon at each bridge.

Dispositions of B Coy.

No.8 Platoon was detailed to cross No.1 bridge, No.7 platoon No.2 bridge, No.5 No.3 bridge.

No.6 platoon was in support at U 30 a 50.35.

The platoons detailed for Nos. 1 and 3 bridges got over without much difficulty though meeting considerable opposition on extending on the far side. No.2 bridge was not successfully thrown over at the appointed time. Accordingly No.7 platoon was ordered to cross by No.1 bridge, which it succeeded in doing. Meanwhile a L.G. team of No.7 platoon had succeeded in getting across No.2 bridge in spite of the fact that it was not properly secured and the water was lapping over it to a depth of 3 ft in the middle. This section worked 100yds. South under cover of the bank, and established itself, engaging a German machine gun which was located at U 30 d 1.7.

Under orders, it then went back to bridgehead to establish post there and then found that the R.E. had succeeded in getting the bridge in working order.

No.8 platoon managed to make its dispositions as ordered, after encountering heavy M.G. fire from its left and considerable opposition on its right.

No.7 platoon which was now across L'ESCAUT and then turned left working along river bank towards positions allotted to them. They encountered heavy M.G. fire but on approaching same theorem fields But one section who followed this cannot now be located. This platoon now got to its own bridgehead.

No.6 platoon (support platoon) was now ordered to go forward over No.2 bridge as the gap between Nos. 5 & 7 platoons was considered too large. This platoon encountered several of the enemy and had difficulty in pushing to its left flank.

No.5 platoon crossed the river at about 2400 when the bridge was across and met opposition from both flanks, particularly on the right A Lewis gun team came to point blank range connection with a German M.G. post on the river bank. After killing four of the crew of this post, the Lewis gun was put out of action by a bullet through the barrel. This platoon established all its posts as ordered, but was not in touch with No.6 platoon. This platoon captured three machine guns and prisoners.

A section of D Coy. was now ordered to work along river bank and establish connection with No.6 platoon. It did so, finding at every 50 to 100yds. a German post consisting of 1, 2 or 3 men. Many of these posts were already vacated as there were two already killed by shell or L.G. fire. All these posts surrendered with exception of one man who was shot. Liaison was thereby established with No.6 platoon and five prisoners captured. Posts were established approximately as follows:

1. U 30 c 55.10.
2. U 30 c 40.30.
3. U 30 d 10.70.
4. U 30 b 05.15.
5. U 30 b 15.25.
6. U 30 b 35.70.
7. U 24 d 85.20.
8. U 24 d 85.50.
9. U 24 b 90.05.
10. U 24 b 95.90.

Company H.Qs. is now established at U 29 b 50.65.

Bridgeheadz parties were established at all bridges on the far bank.

It seems that the enemy was holding this position strongly, not only by the fact that posts were so near together, but by the statement volunteered by a prisoner that a whole company was billeted in the Northern end of POTTES.

At 06.30 hours the enemy was shelling somewhat heavily 200 yds. in advance of our established posts as also on river bank. He also shelled this side of the river bank slightly. This was chiefly with 4.2 and 77mm. His Very lights were being sent up well the further side of GRAND COURANT Canal. These were of all colours.

10.42.
5/11/18.

(Sd) J.E.B. GRAY Capt.
O.C. B Coy., MEZI.

Operation Report. 4/11/18.

Carried out by 13 Platoon & 2 L.G. Sections of 16 platoon and by O.C. Coy.

We established posts on the Southern side of R.SCHELDT, and after consolidating sent out a rec' patrol which worked 250yds. to our left, reporting that they had been fired on by a M.G.

We pushed forward with 2 rifle sections along River Bank, occupying and establishing posts in houses, making our right the sluice and our left the road about 600yds. to the left of it. The Bosche during the night of the 3/11/18 sent about 6 Very lights up and had a M.G. very active about 70yds. in front of our left post. We withdrew into the houses during the day.

During the day 4/11/18 hostile guns and T.Ms. got four direct hits on our right billet. At 19.00 a party of 20 Bosche were seen in front of our left post and were dispersed by rifle fire. At 4 pm. a party of 5 Bosche were seen and my sentry fired at by them, they were dispersed by rifle fire, one apparently being hit.

At 6.30 pm. my left post was bombed by a party of about 12 Bosche. These were dispersed by L.G. fire.

At 7.15 pm. relieved by Y. & Ls.

The Bosche evidently evacuated the posts as we advanced, the latter showing signs of very recent occupation.

(Sd) F.H. FULLER 2/Lieut.
4/11/18. O.C. 13 Platoon, D Coy. MEZI.

Patrol Report from O.C. "D" Coy. Nov.5th/18.

I reconnoitred the ground in front of our positions to ascertain the best means of getting the information asked for. It was not possible to send out a patrol down the road from our No.5 post at C 5 b 4.6 as it was covered by two enemy M.Gs. firing straight down the road into our post. This enemy position is held by these 2 guns and a number of riflemen at a distance of about 75 yards from ours. He continually sent up lights which dropped on us. I then reconnoitred the other end of the track at the sluice. There I found a dyke filled with water about 4'6" deep and 6' across.

After some little work, I collected enough wood from the canal to construct a bridge.

I then sent 2/Lieut. Jackson out and 5 O.R. from our post at C 5 a 20.05 and he proceeded eastwards along the track for about 60 yards when the track is under water knee deep. He continued almost to the road, wading knee deep. He then returned and examined the conduit which is in quite good condition and the track from there westwards is also good. The patrol returned to the canal from about C 4 d 6.9.

I commenced the first reconnaissance at 01.45, but after several efforts, it was 03.40 before the patrol got into the track. Good progress was then made and the patrol reached our lines again at 04.45.

From 03.20 until 03.50 the enemy bombarded the whole front heavily, and trench mortars fell all round the post and track being reconnoitred.

(Sd) R.J. RILEY Capt.
Nov.5th O.C. "D" Coy. ~~MEZI.~~ MERA
05.30.

Report on Operations on Right Coy. front (MEZI)
night 3rd/4th.

41st Inf. Bde.
B.21 4th.
Ref. B.M.273.

1. Party consisting of 1 officer, 2/Lieut. FULLER and 30 O.R. crossed bridge at C 4 b 9.4 shortly after 1700hrs. Novr. 3rd.

2. They established posts on RIGOLE D'ASSECHEMENT at Sluice C 5 a 2.4 and on road at C 5 a 20.05 with a post to keep touch with post in vicinity of bridge C 4 b 9.4.

3. Patrols were pushed forward from this point E along River ESCAUT and at about 2400 reinforcements, 1 officer and 20 O.R., were sent and posts were pushed forward to houses at C 5 a 80.40 and C 5 b 30.45.

4. Reconnaissance was made of ground S of river to marshes.

5. Opposition was strongest at houses C 5 b 30.45.

6. Fuller details of operations are contained in attached report.

(Sd) J. McGAVIN GREIG Major,
Commdg. 33rd L.R.B.

To Adjt. MEZI.

In compliance with instructions I crossed the River L'ESCAUT at 17.55 (having been delayed at bridge by heavy gas shell fire) with 2/Lieut. FULLER, 1 platoon and 1 L.G. section, and established a post at C 5 a 0.4. I then split party into two fighting patrols under 2/Lieut. FULLER and myself.

I got within a few yards of sluice bridge at river and rushed it finding no Bosche. The bridge was heavily wired, we cut through this, and worked up W bank of sluice and to assist other patrols. In the meantime they had established themselves at bridge where sluice runs into marsh. I then took forward 1 rifle section and 1 L.G. team, and got into house at C 5 a 7.5, the Bosche had evidently cleared out first before we entered, and we found rifle and ammunition there.

I reported progress and received instructions to go on and establish posts at C 5 b 1.2 and C 5 b 3.6. We rushed the house at C 5 b 3.6, and established a post there, the Bosche clearing out as we arrived. I immediately took a party out to C 5 b 1.2, the Bosche observed us, and opened up with M.Gs. and rifle fire at about 50 yards range, to which we replied from the post established at C 5 b 3.6, and under cover of this withdrew. There was absolutely no cover of any kind at C 5 b 1.2 and therefore as the Bosche had a post strongly held at C 5 b 75.20 and we were in full view I withdrew. The posts which are established at C 5 b 3.6 and the house marked on sketch cover this pathway entirely.

The operation thus finished for the night and posts are now established as marked on enclosed sketch.

(Sd) J.S.OSBORNE Lieut.
O.C. D Coy., MEZI.

4/10/18.

G.O.C.
G.S.O.1
G.S.O.2
G.S.O.3

Copy No. 24

S E C R E T.

5th November, 1918.

14th Divisional Order No. 238.

Reference Sheet 29 S.E. 1/20-000.

1. (a) On the night of 6th/7th November, the 14th Division will hand over to the 30th Division that part of the Divisional front North of U.30.c.central. Relief to be complete by 0001 November 7th.

(b) The Bridge at U.30.c.central will be inclusive to 14th Division.

2. All arrangements will be made by G.Os. C. concerned.

3. C.R.A. and O.C. 14th Machine Gun Battalion will arrange with 30th Division for the relief of guns and machine guns covering that part of the front.

4. Command of that part of the line from U.30.c.central to U.24.b.5.5 will pass to G.O.C. 30th Division on completion of relief.

5. ACKNOWLEDGE.

J.S. Beaumont Capt.
for Lieut-Colonel,
General Staff,
14th Division.

Issued at 20.00 hrs.

Copies to :-
No. 1 - 41st Infantry Brigade.
2 - 42nd Infantry Brigade.
3 - 43rd Infantry Brigade.
4 - C.R.A.
5 - C.R.E.
6 - 15th L.N. Lancs. Regt. (Pioneers).
7 - 14th Machine Gun Battalion.
8 - 14th Div. Signal Coy.
9 - 14th Divisional Train.
10 - S.S.O.
11 - 14th Div. M.T. Coy.
12)
13) - A & Q.
14 - A.D.M.S.
15 - D.A.D.V.S.
16 - D.A.D.O.S.
17 - D.A.P.M.
18 - D.G.O.
19 - XV Corps "G".
20 - XV Corps "A".
21 - XV Corps H.A.
22 - 40th Division.
23 - 30th Division.
24 - War Diary.
25 - File.

Appendix A (6)

14th Division - General Staff.

War Diary - Nov. 1918.

VOL. XLV.

Operations - 6 Nov. 1918

Army Form C. 2123.
(In books of 100.)

"C" FORM.

MESSAGES AND SIGNALS.

No. of Message............

Prefix SB Code 0400. Words 29

Received from BDa By Green. T

Service Instructions 3 adds pty

Sent, or sent out. At ......m. To ...... By ......

Office Stamp.

Handed in at VAKI Office 0400 m. Received 0409 m.

TO GOKA

G.S.O.
G.S.O.1
G.S.O.2
G.S.O.3

*Sender's Number.	Day of Month.	In reply to Number.	AAA
I 11	6/11/18		
morning	wire	aaa	Situation
fairly	quiet	enemy	artillery
active	aaa	our	LG
post	at	C5B4.5	has
been	attacked	no	further
news	to	hand	yet
aaa			

FROM VAKI

PLACE & TIME

* This line, except AAA, should be erased, if not required.

(3287) Wt. W54/P738. 691,000 Pads. 3/18. A.P.Ltd. (E3013)

"A" Form.

MESSAGES AND SIGNALS.

Army Form C. 2121.
(In pads of 100.)

No. of Message..........

Prefix......... Code.......... m.	Words.	Charge.	This message is on a/c of:	Recd. at....... m.
Office of Origin and Service Instructions.	Sent		..................Service.	Date..........
Priority to XV Corps	At.......... m.			From
	To		G.O.C. / G.S.O. 1 / G.S.O. 2 / G.S.O. 3	
	By		(Signature of "Franking Officer.")	By

*TO 15 Corps
30 th Division
40 th Division

Sender's Number.	Day of Month.	In reply to Number.	AAA
* G.O. 62	6th		

Situation Report aaa Situation fairly quiet but enemy Arty active aaa Our LG post at C.5.b.45 has been attacked aaa Details ~~will~~ will follow

From 14th DIVN.

Place

Time 0435

The above may be forwarded as now corrected. (Z) W. P. Fletcher [illegible]

Censor. Signature of Addressor or person authorised to telegraph in his name.

* This line, except **A A A**, should be erased if not required.

Wt. W 3253/P511. 500,000 Pads. 1/18. B. & S. Ltd. (E2389.)

"A" Form.
MESSAGES AND SIGNALS.

Army Form C. 2121.
(In pads of 100.)
No. of Message ....

Prefix .... Code .... m. | Words. | Charge.

Office of Origin and Service Instructions.

Sent
At .... m.
To ....
By ....

This message is on a/c of:
G.O.C.
G.S.O.1
Service.
G.S.O.2
G.S.O.3
(Signature of "Franking Officer.")

Recd. at .... m.
Date
From
By

TO 41st Inf. Bde.

Sender's Number.	Day of Month.	In reply to Number.	
* G.O.76	6th		AAA

~~Following from 89th Field Coy. R.E. begins aaa~~
SLUICE CHANNEL cleared of debris 0130 hours aaa
Gates will not open aaa Passage for water made
under gate aaa W.L. east of gates 18 to 24
inches above river level aaa Passage opened aaa
Waterflowing rapidly thro aaa ends

From 14th Divn G.
Place
Time

The above may be forwarded as now corrected.
Censor.

(Z)
Signature of Addressor or person authorised to telegraph in his name.

* This line, except **A A A**, should be erased if not required.

Wt. W 3253/P511. 500,000 Pads. 1/18. B. & S. Ltd. (E2380.)

"A" Form.

Army Form C. 2121.
(In pads of 100.)

MESSAGES AND SIGNALS.

No. of Message ....

Prefix .... Code .... m. | Words. | Charge.

Office of Origin and Service Instructions.

Sent
At .... m.
To ....
By ....

This message is on a/c of:

.... *Service.*

(Signature of "Franking Officer.")

Recd. at .... m.
Date ....
From ....
By ....

G.O.C.
G.[illegible]
G.S.O.
C.[illegible]

TO: CRA
Q

Sender's Number.	Day of Month.	In reply to Number.	
* G.O. 66	6		AAA

Continuation G O 65 AAA
96th Brigade RFA will
withdraw to wagon lines
N 16 tonight marching to
HERSEAUX tomorrow

From: III Div
Place:
Time: 1530

The above may be forwarded as now corrected.

.... *Censor.*

(Z) [illegible] Capt.

Signature of Addressor or person authorised to telegraph in his name.

* This line, except **A A A**, should be erased if not required.

Wt. W 3253/P511. 500,000 Pads. 1/18. B. & S. Ltd. (E2389.)

Army Form C. 2123.
(In books of 100.)

"C" FORM.

MESSAGES AND SIGNALS.

No. of Message ....

Prefix Sm Code 15 05 Words 36T

Received from Vk By Cam

Service Instructions

Sent, or sent out. At ......m. To ...... By ......

Office Stamp. ARMY SIGNALS ... 6 .1. 18

Handed in at PCO Office 1503 m. Received 1520 m.

G.O.C. G.S.O 1 G.S.O 2 G.S.O 3

TO 14th Division

*Sender's Number.	Day of Month.	In reply to Number.	AAA
G212	6th		

Reference badger wire G211 aaa 96th RUFF will withdraw to wagon line N16 tonight marching to BOURTON tomorrow and addsd 14 Division repld 10th Corps and GOCRA and Q.

retd CRA Q 6/1 15 2/6

FROM
PLACE & TIME 15th Corps 1500

* This line, except AAA, should be erased, if not required.

(2853) Wt. W544/P738. 601,000 Pads. 3/18. A.P.Ltd. (E.2064)

G.O.C.
G.S.O 1
G.S.O.2
G.S.O 3

C.R.A.
Q.

G.O. 65 6

96th	Brigade	RFA	will
be	withdrawn	from	action
tonight	under	arrangements	of
X Corps	to	HERSEAUX.	AAA
Coming	under	orders	of 14th
Division	on	arrival	AAA
Billets	from	Area	Cdt
HERSEAUX	AAA	NO	route
restrictions			

aaa Brigade should arrive at HERSEAUX about 1300 on 9th

14th Division.

[illegible] G.S.

27

"C" FORM.
Army Form C. 2123.
(In books of 100.)

MESSAGES AND SIGNALS. No. of Message ....

Prefix .... Code .... Words ....

Sent, or sent out — Office Stamp.

At .... m.

To ....

By ....

ARMY SIGNALS ... XI. 18

Received from .... By ....

Service Instructions

Handed in at ..... PCo ..... Office 12.30 p.m. Received 12.41 p.m.

G.S.O. 1
G.S.O. 2
G.S.O. 3

TO 14th Divn.

*Sender's Number.	Day of Month.	In reply to Number.	AAA
G 211	6th		
96th	Bde RFA RUFF	will	be
withdrawn	from	action	tonight
under	arrangements	of 11 Corps	HARRIET
to	BOURTON Herseaux	aaa	Coming
under	orders	of	TENCH
on	arrival	aaa	Billets
from	area	Comdt	BOURTON
aaa	No	Route	restriction
aaa	added	14th	Divn
Reptd	15th	Corps	GOC
RA	and	"Q"	

12.48

Confirmation of attached telephone msg.

FROM
PLACE & TIME — 15th Corps 1205

* This line, except **A A A**, should be erased, if not required.

CRA Q

TELEPHONE MESSAGE

Date 6. 11. 18 Time 11.40

Office ~~ringing~~ or rang up. XV Corps G.

Officer spoken to. A/G S O 3

MESSAGE

96th Bde. A. F. A. are moving from BOSSUYT area tonight & wish to billet in HERSEAUX. On arrival they come under G.O.C. 14th Div.

Q say they can fit them in but will be very scattered. They have informed Area Commandant HERSEAUX.

Action taken. Informed Corps what Q say. Said there would be no restrictions as to route. BMRA informed verbally.

W. J. Fitzgerald ....Signature
Capt

60

"C" FORM.
MESSAGES AND SIGNALS.

Army Form C. 2123.
(In books of 100.)
No. of Message ......

Prefix ...... Code ...... Words ......
Received from ...... By ......
Service Instructions ...... 1 NOV

Sent, or sent out. At ......m. To ...... By ......
Office Stamp. SIGNALS

Handed in at Vaki Pty Office 1543 m. Received 1614 m.

TO Broka

G.S.O. / G.S.O. 1 / G.S.O. 2 / G.S.O. 3

*Sender's Number.	Day of Month.	In reply to Number.	AAA
Bm 284	6		
situation	unchanged	enemy	
artillery	very	active	from
0930	to	1000	on
U28B	and	D	and
HELCHIN	with	4.2	U21A
and	B	shelled	with
77	mm	and	4.2
from	1320	to	1340
aaa	DOTTIGNIES	shelled	by
HV	at	1510	enemy
and	our	MGs	firing
occasional	bursts	material	and
prisoners	captured	NIL	visib
bad			

FROM VAKI
PLACE & TIME

* This line, except AAA, should be erased, if not required.

(8287) Wt. W54/P738. 691,000 Pads. 3/18. A.P.Ltd. (E3013)

"A" Form. Army Form C. 2121. (In pads of 100.)

MESSAGES AND SIGNALS.

No. of Message ....

Prefix .... Code .... m. | Words. | Charge.

Office of Origin and Service Instructions.

Priority
to XV Corps

Sent
At .... m.
To ....
By ....

This message is on a/c of: .... *Service.*

(Signature of "Franking Officer.")

Recd. at .... m.
Date ....
From ....
By ....

G.S.O.
G.S.O. 1
G.S.O. 2
G.S.O. 3

TO
15 Corps
30 Division
40 Div.

Sender's Number.	Day of Month.	In reply to Number.	AAA
G.O. 67	6		

Evening	Report	AAA	Enemy
artillery	active	0920	to
1000	on	HELCHIN	and
area	EAST	of	HELCHIN.
with ~~AAA~~	105 mm	AAA	U21 a
and	c	shelled	1320
to	1340	with	77 mm
and	105 mm	AAA.	DOTTIGNIES
shelled	with	H.V.	gun
1570.	AAA	prisoners	Capt.
24 hrs	nil	~~A~~ since	Nov. 1st
21.	AAA	attached	XV Corps
right	flank	Divns	

From 14 Div.
Place
Time

The above may be forwarded as now corrected. (Z)

Censor. Signature of Addressor or person authorised to telegraph in his name.

* This line, except **A A A**, should be erased if not required.

Wt. W 3253/P511. 500,000 Pads. 1/18. B. & S. Ltd. (E2380.)

7

Appendix A (7)

14th Division - General Staff

War Diary - Nov. 1918

VOL. XLV

Operations 7 Nov. 1918

"C" FORM.
MESSAGES AND SIGNALS.

Army Form C. 2123. 15
No. of Message

Prefix SB Code 0844 Words 20

Sent, or sent out. Office Stamp.

7. XI. 18
SIGNALS

Received from PCO By Cown

At ... m.

Service Instructions
Priority
Urgent Operations

To

By

Handed in at PCO Office 08 44 m. Received 0846 m.

TO 14 Div

*Sender's Number.	Day of Month.	In reply to Number.	A A A
G225	7		

Please report early as possible extent of rise in level of ESCAUT and inundations

G.O.C.
G.S.O. 1 ✓
G.S.O. 2
G.S.O. 3

08-50

FROM
PLACE & TIME 15 Corps 08 35

* This line, except A A A, should be erased, if not required.

"A" Form.
Army Form C. 2121.
(In pads of 100.)

MESSAGES AND SIGNALS.

No. of Message..........

Prefix......... Code.......... m. | Words. | Charge.
Office of Origin and Service Instructions.

Sent
At.......... m.
To
By

This message is on a/c of:
.... Service.
(Signature of "Franking Officer.")

Recd. at......... m.
Date
From
By

G.O.C.
G.S.O.1
G.S.O.2
G.S.O.3

TO C.R.E. 41st Inf. Bde.

Sender's Number.	Day of Month.	In reply to Number.	
* G.O.73	7th		AAA

Report early as possible extent of rise in level of ESCAUT and inundations

From 14th Divn.
Place
Time

The above may be forwarded as now corrected. (Z)
Censor.
Signature of Addressor or person authorised to telegraph in his name.

* This line, except **A A A**, should be erased if not required.

Wt. W 3253/P511. 500,000 Pads. 1/15. B. & S. Ltd. **(E2339.)**

"A" Form
MESSAGES AND SIGNALS.

Army Form C. 2121
(In pads of 100.)

No. of Message..............

Prefix.......... Code..........m Office of Origin and Service Instructions	Words. Charge. Sent At..........m. To.......... By..........	*This message is on a/c of:* .... *Service.* .... (Signature of "Franking Officer.")	Recd. at..........m. Date.......... From.......... By..........

TO { 15 Corps

Sender's Number.	Day of Month.	In reply to Number.	AAA
*G079	7	G225	

General	rise	of	from
10	to	18	inches
noted			

G.O.O.
G.S.O.1
G.S.O.2
G.S.O.3

From 14 Div.
Place
Time

The above may be forwarded as now corrected. (Z)
.... Censor.
Signature of Addressor or person authorised to telegraph in his name.

* This line should be erased if not required.

(4715) Wt. W3253/P511 1,113,336 Shts. 2/18 C. & Co. (.684)

58

Army Form C. 2123.
(In books of 100.)

"C" FORM.
MESSAGES AND SIGNALS.

No. of Message..........

Prefix ..... Code 1550 Words 14	Sent, or sent out.	Office Stamp.
Received from .... By Ja	At ......m.	
Service Instructions	To	
Vaki	By	

Handed in at .... Office 1550 m. Received 1556 m.

TO Goka

*Sender's Number.	Day of Month.	In reply to Number.	AAA
Bm 293	7	GO 73	
General	Rise	of	from
10	to	18	inches
noticed			

Repeated to C.R.E.

G.O.C.
G.S.O.1
G.S.O.2
G.S.O.3

FROM
PLACE & TIME Vaki

* This line, except AAA, should be erased, if not required.

(3287) Wt.W54/P738. 691,000 Pads. 3/18. A.P.Ltd. (E3013)

16

Army Form C. 2121.
(In books of 100.)

"C" FORM.

MESSAGES AND SIGNALS. No. of Message

ARMY SIGNALS
YN ... VII. 18

Prefix ... Code ... Words ...	Sent, or sent out. At ... m. To ... By ...
Received from ... By ...	Office Stamp.
Service Instructions	

Handed in at Vakr Office 0937 m. Received 0940 m.

TO CRE Tioth

G.O.C.
G.S.O 1
G.S.O 2
G.S.O 3

*Sender's Number.	Day of Month.	In reply to Number.	AAA
R1	7		
SLUICE	CHANNEL	cleared	of
debris	0130	hours	aaa
Gates	will	not	open
aaa	Passage	for	water
made	under	gate	aaa
WL	east	of	gates
18	to	24	inches
above	river	level	aaa
Passage	opened	aaa	Water
flowing	rapidly	thro	aaa
Urgent			

Ref 90.76

FROM PLACE & TIME: Dezu 6th Field Coy.

* This line, except AAA, should be erased, if not required.

(3287) Wt. W54/P738. 691,000 Pads. 2/18. A.P.Ltd. (E2612)

"A" Form.

MESSAGES AND SIGNALS.

Army Form C. 2121.
(In pads of 100.)

No. of Message...........

Prefix.........Code..........m. | Words. | Charge.

Office of Origin and Service Instructions.

Sent
At..........m.
To..........
By..........

This message is on a/c of:
..........*Service.*
(Signature of "Franking Officer.")

Recd. at......m.
Date......
From......
By......

G.O.C.
G.S.O.1
G.S.O.2
G.S.O.3

TO ORA CRE

Sender's Number.	Day of Month.	In reply to Number.	AAA
G.O.101	7		

"It is probable in the event of the enemy retiring that delay action mines will be left in the causeways over the marshes at LE RIVAGE and HERINNES aaa The bridge at I.3.a.3.4 has not yet blown up and should be examined as soon as possible.

From 14th Divn.
Place
Time 09.15

The above may be forwarded as now corrected. (Z)

Censor.

Signature of Addressor or person authorised to telegraph in his name.

Capt

* This line, except AAA, should be erased if not required.

Wt. W 3253/P511. 500,000 Pads. 1/18. B. & S. Ltd. (E2389.)

XV Corps
No. I.G. 116/8.

14th Division. ✓

40th Division.

G.O.C.	
G.S.O.1	
G.S.O.2	
G.S.O.3	

It is probable in the event of the enemy retiring that delay action mines will be left in the causeways over the marshes at LE RIVAGE and HERINNES.

The bridge at I.3.a.3.4 has not yet blown up and should be examined as soon as possible.

telephoned to 43 Bde at 0905

R W Brooke Major.
for Brigadier-General,
General Staff.

XV Corps,
8.11.18.

Repeated to CRE & CRA
G.O. 101

GENERAL STAFF.
14TH
DIVISION.
No.
Date 9.11.18
File I 20

C. 2121.
(In pads of 100.)

…AGES AND SIGNALS. No. of Message……………

Prefix……… Code……………m. | Words. | Charge.

Office of Origin and Service Instructions.

Sent
At……………m.
To……………
By……………

This message is on a/c of:

……………………*Service.*

(Signature of "Franking Officer.")

Recd. at………m.
Date……………
From……………
By……………

TO 41/43 Inf. Bdes. CRA. CRE.

Sender's Number.	Day of Month.	In reply to Number.	AAA
G.O.94	7th		

No parlementaires are to be expected on British front aaa They will pass through the French lines

G.O.C.	
G.S.O.1	✓
G.S.O.2	
G.S.O.3	

From
Place 14th Divn
Time

The above may be forwarded as now corrected. (Z)

Censor. Signature of Addressor or person authorised to telegraph in his name.

* This line, except **AAA**, should be erased if not required.

Wt. W 3253/P511. 500,000 Pads. 1/18. B. & S. Ltd. **(E2388.)**

"A" Form

Army Form C. 2121
(In pads of 100.)

MESSAGES AND SIGNALS.

No. of Message..............

Prefix.............. Code..............m | Words. | Charge.

Office of Origin and Service Instructions

Sent

At..................m.

To....................

By....................

This message is on a/c of: .... Service.

(Signature of "Franking Officer.")

Recd. at..........m.

Date....................

From....................

By....................

G.S.O.1
G.S.O.2
G.S.O.3

TO 41/43 Infy Bde. C.R.A.
14 M.G.Bn.

Sender's Number.	Day of Month.	In reply to Number.	AAA
G.O.78	7		

If an Officer bearing a flag of truce should present himself at any point on the Corps front he will be conducted to the nearest Divl. H.Q. and detained there pending instructions from G.H.Q. aaa G.H.Q. will be immediately informed of his arrival

From
Place 14th Division.
Time

The above may be forwarded as now corrected. (Z)

Censor. Signature of Addressor or person authorised to telegraph in his name.

* This line should be erased if not required.

(4715) Wt. W3253/P511 1,113,336 Shts. 2/18 C. & Co. (.084)

27

"C" FORM.
MESSAGES AND SIGNALS.

Army Form C. 2121 (In books of 100.)
No. of Message ....

Prefix SB Code 11.02 Words 57

Received from PCO By Owen

Sent, or sent out. At .... m. To .... By ....

Office Stamp: ARMY SIGNALS

Service Instructions
Priority

Handed in at PCO Office 11.2 m. Received 11.11

G.O.C.
G.S.O. 1
G.S.O. 2
G.S.O. 3

TO 14 Divn

* Sender's Number.	Day of Month.	In reply to Number.	AAA
G.228	7	G.0.75	

If an officer bearing a flag of truce should present himself at any point on the corps front he will be conducted to the nearest Divn HQ and detained there pending instructions from GHQ aaa GHQ will be immediately informed of his arrival aaa Added 14 and 40 Divs aaa acknowledge

11.15

G.R. 11.44

CRA.
M.G.
41 Bde

FROM
PLACE & TIME
15 Corps 11.35

* This line, except AAA, should be erased, if not required.

(3227) Wt. W54/P738. 691,000 Pads. 2/18. A.P.Ltd. (E.2613)

"C" FORM.

MESSAGES AND SIGNALS. No. of Message

Prefix .... Code .... Words ....

Received from .... By ....

Service Instructions

Sent, or sent out. At .... m. To -8. XI. 13. By ....

Office Stamp. 116

Handed in at P Co Office .... m. Received 2026 m.

TO 14th Divn

G.8.0.1

G.8.0.2

G.8.0.3

*Sender's Number.	Day of Month.	In reply to Number.	AAA
Y 257	8th		
Ref	15th	Corps	RA
F16/121	of	today	aaa
Corps	HA	will	notify
Divns	at	once	of
exact	Areas	to	be
Bombarded	aaa	Troops	to
be	Warned	aaa	Added
Corps	HA	Divns	Reptd
GOCRA			
			2035
			20.35

FROM PLACE & TIME 15th Corps 2015

* This line, except AAA, should be erased, if not required.

(3287) Wt. W54/P738. 691,000 Pads. 2/18. A.P.Ltd. (E3013)

S E C R E T   XV Corps R.A. [illegible]/121

G.O.C.
G.S.O 1 ✓
G.S.O.2
G.S.O 3

XV Corps H.A.
C.B.S.O.

1. XV Corps Heavy Artillery will bombard known enemy Gun positions, tonight, from 1900 - 2200 hours, with B.B. gas.

Only those battery positions will be engaged which are more than 1 mile outside the final objective.

2. Acknowledge.

8/11/1918

(sd). R.N.DUKE
Major R.A
S.O., R.A. XV Corps

14th Division
S.G.1492

41/43 Inf.Bdes.
C.R.A.
C.R.E. /

For information.

8/11/1918

Lieut.Colonel G.S.
14th Division

GENERAL STAFF,
14TH DIVISION.
Ref. G 1492
Date 8-11-18
File 00

S E C R E T.

XV Corps R.A. No. F.16/121.

XV Corps Heavy Artillery.
Counter Battery Staff Officer.

1. XV Corps Heavy Artillery will bombard known enemy Gun Positions, to-night, from 1900 - 2200 hours, with B.B. Gas.
Only those Battery Positions will be engaged which are more than 1 mile outside the final objective.

2. ACKNOWLEDGE.

G.O.C.	
G.S.O.1	[illegible]
G.S.O.2	
G.S.O.3	

[signature]
Major R.A.,
S.O., R.A., XV Corps.

8/11/18.

Copies to :- XV Corps "G".
XV Corps "Q".
14th Division. ✓
40th Division.
14th Divisional Artillery.
40th Divisional Artillery.

G.1492

Copy to 41st Bde R.F.A.
42nd Bde R.F.A.
CRA
CRE

8/11/18

For info.

(sd) G.M.P. Fitzgerald Capt for G.S.

G.O.C.	
G.S.O 1	
G.S.O.2	
G.S.O.3	

C.R.E.

G.O. 98 8

Wire from 41 Infantry Bde. begins AAA

Patrol reports GRAND COURANT in U 30 c much swollen and at present 30 to 40 feet broad and of considerable depth AAA Enemy M.Gs. and T.Ms. active on MESO front no shelling reported AAA Ends

---

14 Division

Hammond Capt

G.S.

123

Army Form C. 2123.
(In books of 100.)

"C" FORM.

MESSAGES AND SIGNALS. No. of Message..........

Prefix Am Code 2042 Words 37		Sent, or sent out.	Office Stamp.
Received from Vaki	By Raf	At .... m.	8 XI. 18
Service Instructions Vaki		To N	
		By	

Handed in at .... Office 2032 m. Received 2045 m.

TO Joka

G.S.O.1
G.S.O.2
G.S.O.3

*Sender's Number.	Day of Month	In reply to Number.	AAA
Bm 299	8		

Patrol	reports	GRAND	COURANT
in	U30C	much	swollen
and	at	present	30
to	40	ft	broad
and	of	considerable	depth
aaa	enemy	mgs	and
TMS	active	on	MESO
front	no	Shelling	reported

G.O 92

2055

Repeated to CRE

FROM Vaki

PLACE & TIME

* This line, except AAA, should be erased, if not required.

(3287) Wt. W54/P738. 691,000 Pads 1/18 A.F.Ltd (E3013)

TELEPHONE MESSAGE.

Date. 8. 11. 18 Time. 0925

Office ringing or rang up. Corps G.

Officer spoken to. GSO3.

MESSAGE

Fifth Army report enemy evacuated front opposite their centre Corps early this morning, & civilians coming from TOURNAI report town evacuated by the enemy.

Action taken. GOC & BGC 41 Bde informed.

[illegible] Signature
Capt

"A" Form.

MESSAGES AND SIGNALS.

No. of Message

Prefix ...... Code ...... m.	Words.	Charge.	This message is on a/c of:	Recd. at ...... m.
Office of Origin and Service Instructions.	Sent		G.O.C.	Date
	At ...... m.		G.S.O.1 Service.	From
	To		G.S.O.2	By
	By		(Signature of "Franking Officer.") G.S.O.3	

TO 41/43 Inf. Bdes. C.R.A.

Sender's Number.	Day of Month.	In reply to Number.	AAA
* G.O.88	8th		

Following from 40th Division begins aaa Patrol of POPA crossed river at PECQ bridge 1130 hrs aaa Fired on 11.40 hrs from house at I.3.a.8.3 aaa ends

From

Place 14th Divn.

Time

The above may be forwarded as now corrected. (Z) W Beaumont Capt

Censor.

Signature of Addressor or person authorised to telegraph in his name.

* This line, except A A A, should be erased if not required.

Wt. W 3253/P511. 500,000 Pads. 1/18. B. & S. Ltd. (E2380.)

75

"C" FORM.
MESSAGES AND SIGNALS.

Army Form C. 2121
(In books of 100.)

No. of Message

Prefix Sm Code 1415 Words 33

Received from PCQ By Green

Service Instructions

Sent, or sent out.
At m.
To
By

Office Stamp.
ARMY
YN 8 XI 18

Handed in at YBz Office 1415 m. Received 1448 m.

TO 14 Div

*Sender's Number.	Day of Month.	In reply to Number.	AAA
GS363	8th.		
Patrols	of	POPA	crossed
river	at	PECQ	bridge
1130	hours	aaa	Fired
on	11·40	hrs	from
house	at	J3a8.3	aaa
adsd	15	Corps	repd
flank	divs	and	CRA

G.O.C. ✓
G.S.O. 1 ✓
G.S.O. 2
G.S.O. 3

Repeat 41st 43 Bdes CRA

FROM 40 Div

PLACE & TIME

* This line, except AAA, should be erased, if not required.

(2987) Wt. W54/P738. 691,000 Pads. 3/18. A.P.Ltd. (E3413)

Army Form C. 2121
(In pads of 100.)

"A" Form
MESSAGES AND SIGNALS.

No. of Message..............

Prefix.............. Code..............m Office of Origin and Service Instructions	Words. Charge. Sent At..................m. To.................... By....................	This message is on a/c of: G.S.O. G.S.O.1 G.S.O.2 G.S.O.3 .... Service. (Signature of "Franking Officer.")	Recd. at...........m. Date.................. From .... By....................

TO { 41st Infy Bde — 43rd Infy Bde
C.R.A.

Sender's Number.	Day of Month.	In reply to Number.	AAA
* G.O.89	8		

Air observers report small bodies enemy still in HERINNES aaa Rifle fire heavy from I 4 ~~d~~ and C 28 and on General line 2000 yards east of river aaa Enemy post of six men at I 3 a 30.40 in crater aaa A.A. very far back.

From
Place 14th Div.
Time

The above may be forwarded as now corrected. (Z)

Censor. Signature of Addressor or person authorised to telegraph in his name.

* This line should be erased if not required.

(4715) Wt. W3253/P511 1,113,336 Shts. 2/18 C. & Co. (.634)

"C" FORM.
MESSAGES AND SIGNALS.

Army Form C. 2123.
(In books of 100.)
No. of Message ....

Prefix Sm Code 1445 Words 54

Received from Pco By Green T.

Service Instructions

Sent, or sent out. At ....m. To .... By ....

Office Stamp. A.R. ... 8.XI.18 ... SIGNALS

G.O.0 / O.S.O.1 / G.O.2 / G.O.3

Handed in at Pco Office 1445 m. Received 1501 m.

TO 14 Divs

*Sender's Number.	Day of Month.	In reply to Number.	A A A
Lg 816	8.		
Air	observers	report	small
bodies	enemy	still	in
HERINNES	aaa	Rifle	fire
heavy	from	I. 4	and
C. 28	and	on	general
line	2000	yards	east
of	river	aaa	enemy
post	of	six	men
at	I 3 a 30.	40 in	crater
aaa	aa	very	far
back	aaa	addsd	14th
and	40th	divs	

~~Repeat 40th 14th Bde~~
CRA

FROM 15 Corps.

PLACE & TIME 14 30.

* This line, except A A A, should be erased, if not required.

(2287) Wt.W54/P738. 691,000 Pads. 3/16. A.P.Ltd. (E.2612.)

MESSAGES and SIGNALS.

G.O.C.	
G.S.O.1	
G.S.O.2	
G.S.O.3	

41 Inf.Bde. C.R.A.
42 Inf.Bde. C.R.E.
43 Inf.Bde.
14 M.G.Bn.
16 L.N.Lancs.

G.O. 96 6 AAA

Add to my G.O. 95 the locality D 26 d 08

AAA Added all recipients

---

14 Division

Eric Smither
Lieut
for G.S.

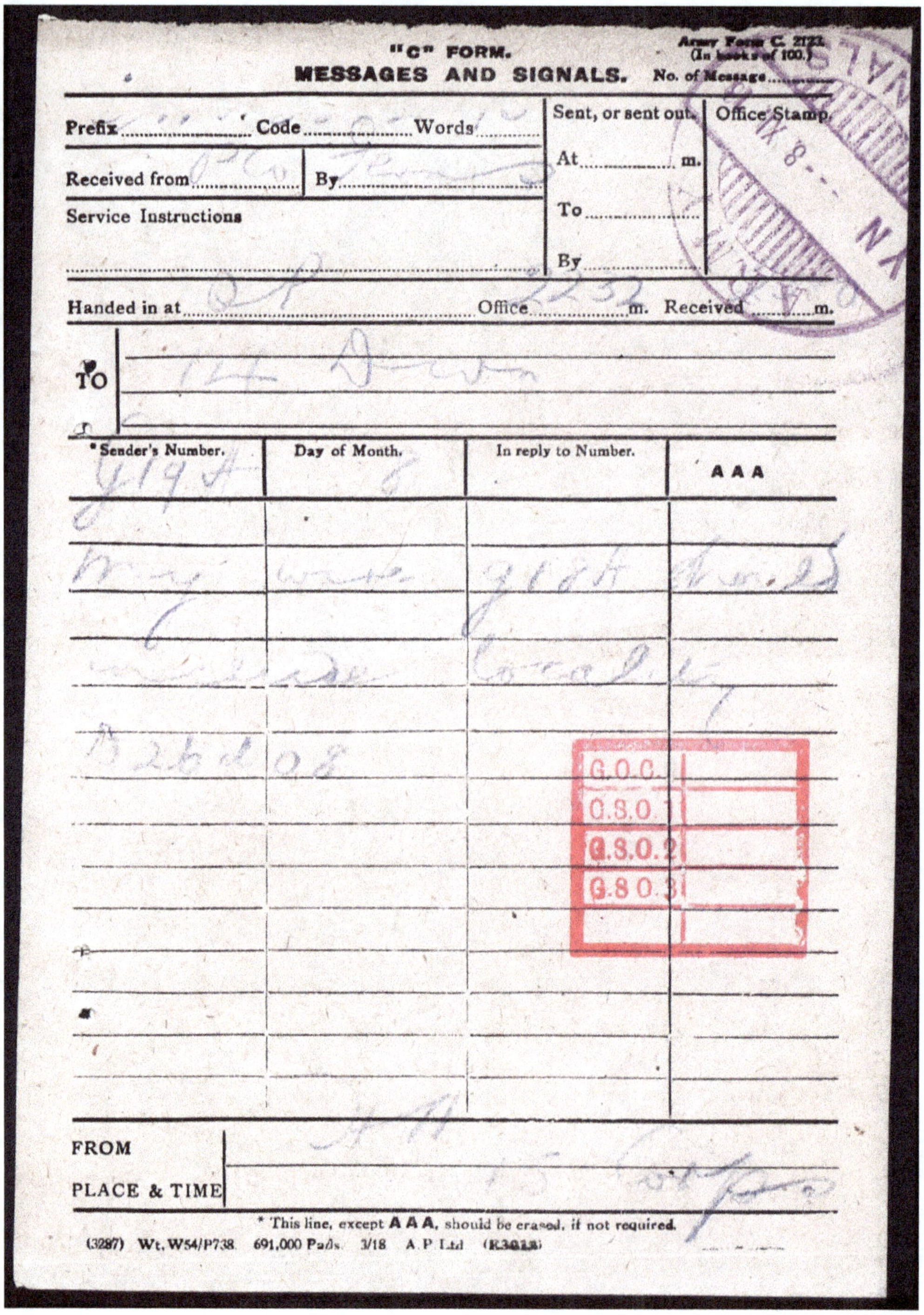

"C" FORM.
MESSAGES AND SIGNALS.

Army Form C. 2123.
(In books of 100.)
No. of Message..........

Prefix .... Code .... Words .... Received from .... By .... Service Instructions	Sent, or sent out. At ....m. To .... By	Office Stamp. 8 XI

Handed in at .... Office 2232 m. Received ....m.

TO

*Sender's Number.	Day of Month.	In reply to Number.	AAA
G194	8		

B26d08

G.O.C.
G.S.O.1
G.S.O.2
G.S.O.3

FROM
PLACE & TIME

* This line, except **A A A**, should be erased, if not required.

(3287) Wt. W54/P738. 691,000 Pads. 3/18 A.P. Ltd (E3018)

G.O.C.	
G.S.O.1	
G.S.O.2	
G.S.O.3	

MESSAGES and SIGNALS.

41 Inf.Bde.
42 Inf.Bde.
43 Inf.Bde.
C.R.A.
C.R.E.
14 M.G.Battn.
15 L.N.Lancs.(Pnrs).

G.O. 93.   8   AAA

Localities shown below have been gassed with BB and should be avoided in event of an advance AAA D 26 c 73 D 26 b 9850 J 1 b 51 J 2 b 66 J 2 b 03 Addsd. VAKI VANO VATE LOLA GOTU PAGI MEVA

14 Division

J W Beaumont Capt
G.S.

129

Army Form C. 2123 (In books of 100.)

"C" FORM.
MESSAGES AND SIGNALS.

No. of Message ....

Prefix .... Code .... Words	Sent, or sent out.	Office Stamp.
Received from .... By	At .... m.	
Service Instructions	To	
	By	

Handed in at .... Office 2115 m. Received 2131

TO QP
14 Divn

G.O.C.
G.S.O.1
G.S.O.2
G.S.O.3

*Sender's Number.	Day of Month.	In reply to Number.	AAA
G18H	8		

Localities shown below have been gassed with BB and should be avoided in event of an advance D26C73 D26B9850 J1B51 J2B66 J2B03 added Division Repld Corps RA

Repeat
3 45th B.B.S.
CRA
CRE
MGB
Pioneers

G.Q. 93

FROM
PLACE & TIME HA 15 Corps

* This line, except A A A, should be erased, if not required.

[illegible]

Appendix A(8)

14th Division - General Staff.

War Diary - Nov. 1918

VOL. XLV

Operations - 8 Nov. 1918

G.O.C.	
G.S.O.1	
G.S.O.2	✓
G.S.O.3	

SECRET

Copy No. 26

14th DIVISION ORDER No. 240.

Ref. Sheets
29 and 37, 1/40,000

7 Nov. 1918.

1. (a). On the night 8/9th November, the 43rd Infantry Brigade will relieve the 41st Infantry Brigade in the line. Relief to be complete by 0001 on 9th November.

(b). Two battalions of 43rd Infantry Brigade now at EVREGNIES and QUEVAUCAMP will be clear of present billets by 1600 hrs.

(c). Battalion of 43rd Infantry Brigade from PETIT AUDENARDE - ESTAMPUIS area will be clear of Railway crossing A 12 d 42 by 1500 hrs

(d). All other details of relief will be arranged by B.Gs. C concerned.

(e). Command of front will pass to B.G.C. 43rd Infantry Brigade on completion of relief.

2. On November 8th, 42nd Infantry Brigade will move into area vacated by 43rd Infantry Brigade. Not to enter billets in EVREGNIES and QUEVAUCAMP before 1600.

3. (a). On relief 41st Infantry Brigade will move into HERSEAUX area vacated by 42nd Infantry Brigade.

(b). Battalion now in reserve in DOTTIGNIES will be clear of billets by 1600, and will march via CROMBION and MALCENSE to HERSEAUX - not to enter HERSEAUX before 1530.

4. All movement E. of a line ESTAMPUIS - CROMBION will be by platoons at 200 yds.

5. Completion of moves to be reported to this office.

6. ACKNOWLEDGE.

H.S. Beaumont Capt
for Lieut.Colonel
General Staff
14th Division.

Issued at 15-45

Copies to -

No. 1 - 41 Inf.Bde.
2 - 42 Inf.Bde.
3 - 43 Inf Bde.
4 - C.R.A.
5 - C.R.E.
6 - 15th L.N.Lancs.
7 - 14th M.G.Bn.
8 - 14th Div.Sig.Coy.
9 - 14th Div. Train.
10 - S.S.O.
11 - 14th Div. M.T.Co.
12 & 13 - A.Q.
14 - A.D.M.S.
15 - D.A.D.V.S.
16 - D.A.D.O.S.
17 - D.A.P.M.
18 - D.G.O.
19 - 14th Div.Reception Camp
20 - XV Corps G.
21 - XV Corps Q.
22 - XV Corps H.A.
23 - 29th Division
24 - 40th Division
25 - War Diary.
26 - File.

Appendix B.

14th Division - General Staff

War Diary - Nov 1918

Vol. XLV

Adjustment of Div. Areas.
Nov. 1918

G.O.C.	
G.S.O 1	✓
G.S.O.2	
G.S.O.3	

SECRET.

Copy No. 2

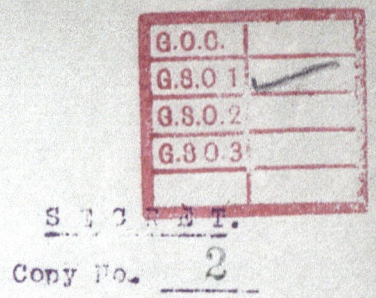

XV CORPS ORDER No. 258.

Ref. Sheet
29. 1/40,000 and Attached Map. 2nd November, 1918.

1. The XV Corps front has been extended Northwards, 14th Division taking over from 30th Division up to U.24.b.6.3.

2. (1) Boundaries as shewn on attached Map will come into force forthwith.

(2) The Reserve Division, XV Corps, will be accommodated in the Army Area.

(3) Certain Units at present located outside the areas now allotted to the XV Corps will be required to move. Instructions will be issued.

3. ACKNOWLEDGE. ✓ GR 429

Brigadier-General,
General Staff.

Issued at 1545

Copy No.		
	1	A.D.C. to Corps Commander.
	2 - 3	14th Division.
	4 - 5	29th Division.
	6 - 7	40th Division.
	8 - 10	G.O.C., R.A.
	11	D.A. & Q.M.G.
	12	"Q".
	13	"A".
	14	C.E.
	15	A.D.A.S.
	16	D.D.M.S.
	17	O.C., 2nd Wing, R.A.F.
	18	4th Squadron, R.A.F.
	19	A.P.M.
	20	X Corps.
	21	XI Corps.
	22	XV Corps Cyclist Battalion.
	23	No. 6 Balloon Company.
	24 - 25	Second Army.
	26 - 33	G.S. and File.
	34	War Diary.

GENERAL STAFF.
14TH
DIVISION.
No.
Date 2. 11. 18
File O. 9

Copy to Q

G.O.C.	
G.S.O.1	
G.S.O.2	
G.S.O.3	

S E C R E T.

XV Corps No. G.S.2/156 G.
dated 3/11/18.

14th Division.

Reference XV Corps Order No. 258, para. 2 (c).

1. Units of your Division (less Divisional H.Q.) will move to your new area and be clear of MOUSCRON by 1100 3rd instant.

2. Divisional H.Q. only, will move into TOURCOING and will be clear of MOUSCRON by 1100 4th instant.

ACKNOWLEDGE.

G.R. 429

XV Corps,
2/11/1918.

Brigadier-General,
General Staff.

Copies to :- 39th Division.
40th Division.
G.O.C.,R.A.
D.A. & Q.M.G.
"Q".
"A".
C.E.
A.D.A.S
D.D.M.S.
O.C., 2nd Wing, R.A.F.
4th Squadron R.A.F.
A.P.M.
X Corps.
XI Corps.
XV Corps Cyclist Battalion.
No. 6 Balloon Company.
Second Army.

GENERAL STAFF.
14TH DIVISION.
No.
Date 2-11-18
File

Copy to Q
JMB

Issued with
XV Corps Order No 258
dated
X
XV
Army Area
COURTRAI
ROUBAIX
TOURCOING
LILLE
TOURNAI
RENAIX
MENIN

G.O.C.	
G.S.O.1	
G.S.O.2	
G.S.O.3	

S E C R E T.

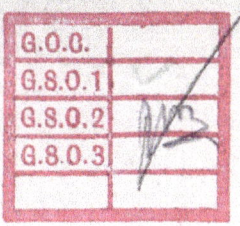

XV Corps No.G.S.2/157
2nd November 1918.

29th Division.
G.O.C.,R.A.

Reference XV Corps Order No. 256, dated 2nd November 1918, paragraph 2 (3).

1. On 3rd November, the moves shewn on Table overleaf will be carried out.

2. Billets will be arranged for with XV Corps "Q".

3. Traffic regulations will be observed throughout as laid down in S.S.724.

4. ACKNOWLEDGE.

J. Morrison, Capt
for Brigadier-General.
General Staff.

XV Corps,
2/11/1918.

Copies to:- 14th Division.
40th Division.
D.A. & Q.M.G.
"Q".
"A".
C.E.
A.D.A.S.
D.D.M.S.
O.C.,2nd Wing, R.A.F.
4th Squadron, R.A.F.
A.P.M.
II Corps.
X Corps.
XI Corps.
XV Corps Cyclist Battalion.
No. 6 Balloon Coy.
Second Army.

GENERAL STAFF,
14TH
DIVISION.
No.........
Date 3.11.18
File 20

/ P.T.O.

MARCH TABLE ISSUED WITH XV CORPS No. G.S. 2/157.

Serial No.	Unit.	From	To	Route.	Remarks.
1.	29th Divl. Arty.	RONCQ.	TOURCOING, area in F.3. and 9.	LE BLANC FOUR - F.3.a.5.2.	To be clear of cross roads X.20.d.0.2. by 0900.
2.	45th Bde., R.G.A.	LINSELLES.	TOURCOING area, F.9. and 10.	CROIX BLANCHE - F.14.a.6.9.	To be clear of LINSELLES by 0900.
3.	33rd Bde., R.G.A.	RONCQ.	Do.	Any.	Not to cross CROIX BLANCHE - BETHLEEM (X.9.d.) Road before 1000.
4.	64th Bde., R.G.A.	Do.	Do.	Do.	Not to cross CROIX BLANCHE - BETHLEEM (X.9.d.) Road before 1100.

G.O.C.
G.S.O.1
G.S.O.2
G.S.O.3

SECRET.

Copy No 26

14th DIVISION ORDER No. 237

Ref. Sheets. 29 and 37 1/40,000
and TOURNAI. 1/100,000.

2nd November 1918

1. The Divisional Boundary has been extended Northwards to U.24.b.6.3.

2. The Northern Boundary runs as follows :-

U.24.b.5.5 - U.4.a.0.0 - A.3.d.0.0.

Southern Boundary. ESPIERRES Canal (inclusive) to B.23.a.6.6 thence along North bank of Canal to Railway A.27.a.2.6.

3. Troops of 14th Division at present outside these boundaries will move in accordance with attached March Table.

4. Refilling Point for Nos. 2 and 4 Coys. Divisional Train will be in the Square WATTRELOS at 15.00 hours Nov. 3rd.

5. Divisional H.Q. will close at MOUSCRON at 11.00 on 4th. inst. and re-open at TOURCOING at the same hour.

6. ACKNOWLEDGE.

Lieut-Colonel.
General Staff.
14th Division.

Issued at 20.00.

Copies to - No.
1 - 41st Inf. Bde.
2 - 42nd Inf. Bde.
3 - 43rd Inf. Bde.
4 - C.R.A.
5 - C.R.E.
6 - 15th L.N.Lancs.Regt. Pioneers.
7 - 14th Machine Gun Bn.
8 - 14th Signal Coy.
9 - 14th Div. Train.
10 - S.S.O.
11 - 14th Div. M. T. Coy.
12) 13) - AQ Branch.
14 - A.D.M.S.
15 - D.A.D.V.S.
16 - D.A.D.O.S.
17 - D.A.P.M.
18 - D.G.O.
19 - O.C. 14th Div.Reception Camp.
20 - XV Corps G.
21 - XV Corps Q.
22 - XV Corps H.A.
23 - 30th British Division
24 - 40th British Division.
25 - War Diary.
26 - File.

SECRET

MARCH TABLE TO ACCOMPANY 14th DIVISION ORDER NO. 237.

Serial No.	Date.	Unit.	From	To	Route	Remarks
1.	Nov. 3	Battn. 42 Inf.Bde.	LUINGNE	WATTRELOS	HERSEAUX - PETIT AUDENARDE	To be clear of LUINGNE by 10.00. Billets from Area Cmdnt. WATTRELOS.
2	Nov. 3	Battn. 42 Inf.Bde.	LUINGNE	PETIT AUDENARDE - ESTAMPUIS area	HERSEAUX PETIT AUDENARDE	Available accommodation in Sqs A 12 c & d, A 18, B 7, B 12. Not to move before 10.00 and to be clear of LUINGNE by 11.00.
3	Nov. 3	14th M.G.Bn. H.Q.	LUINGNE	HERSEAUX		Billets from Area Cmdnt HERSEAUX
4	Nov. 3	No. 4 Coy. Div. Train.	28/ X 17 c 87.	WATTRELOS	No. restrictions	Billets from Area Cmdnt. WATTRELOS.
5	Nov. 3	No. 2 Coy. Div. Train	29/ S 22 d 8540	PETIT AUDENARDE - ESTAMPUIS area		Billets to be arranged by O.C. Div. Train in conjunction with 43 Infantry Bde.
6	Nov. 4	Divisional H.Q.	MOUSCRON	TOURCOING		To be clear of MOUSCRON by 11 00.

41 Inf.Bde.	14 M.G.Bn.	14 Div.Gas Officer
42 Inf.Bde.	14 Div.Sig Coy	A.D.M.S.
43 Inf.Bde.	14 Train	D.A.D.V.S.
C.R.A.	S.S.O. 14 Div.	D.A.D.O.S.
C.R.E.	14 M.T.Coy.	D.A.P.M.
15 L. [illegible].Lancs.	14 Div.Recep.Camp	AQ.
15 Corps G.	30 Division	15 Corps H.A.
15 Corps Q.	40 Division	

G.O.C.
G.S.O. 1
G.S.O. 2
G.S.O. 3

G.O. 30   2   AAA

Amend serial No. 2 of March table issued with my order 237 AAA For 42 read 43 Inf. Bde. AAA Added. all recipients

---

14 Division

[illegible] Beaumont Capt.

G. S.

"A" Form
MESSAGES AND SIGNALS.

Army Form C. 2121
(In pads of 100.)

No. of Message..............

Prefix.............. Code..............m | Words. | Charge. | This message is on a/c of: | Recd. at..........m.

Office of Origin and Service Instructions

Sent
At..................m.
To..................
By..................

.... Service.

(Signature of "Franking Officer.")

Date..................
From..................
By..................

G.O.C.
G.S.O.1
G.S.O.2
G.S.O.3

TO 15 Corps

Sender's Number.	Day of Month.	In reply to Number.	AAA
* 9048	4		

DHQ Opened at TOURCOING 11 am

From 14 Div.
Place
Time

The above may be forwarded as now corrected. (Z)
.... Censor.

Signature of Addressor or person authorised to telegraph in his name.

* This line should be erased if not required.

(4715) Wt. W3253/P352 ... Shts. 9/18 C. & Co. (534)

Appendix C

14th Division - General Staff
War Diary - November 1918

Volume

Extension of front on L'Escaut
6/7 November 1918

Army Form C. 2123
(In books of 100.)

MESSAGES AND SIGNALS. No. of Message..............

Prefix Sm Code 1810 Words 34	Sent, or sent out.
Received from PCO By Conn	At .... m.
Service Instructions	To ....
	By

Office Stamp.

Handed in at PCO Office 1810 m. Received 8.16 m.

G.O.C. / G.S.O 1 ✓ / G.S.O 2 / G.S.O 3 / A A A

TO 14th Division

* Sender's Number.	Day of Month.	In reply to Number.	AAA
G199	5th		

Hand over front north of U 30 b Central to 30th Division on night 6th/7th aaa Bridge at U 30 b Central to 14th Division aaa Acknowledge aaa Added 14 Div repeated 14th Corps

GR 436

FROM PLACE & TIME 15th Corps 1800

* This line, except AAA, should be erased, if not required.

(3287) Wt. W54/P738 691,000 Pads. 3/18. A.P.Ltd. (E3012)

G.O.C.	
G.S.O.1	
G.S.O.2	
G.S.O.3	

SECRET.

Copy No. 2

XV CORPS ORDER No. 259.

6th November, 1918.

Reference Sheets 29 and 37,
1/40,000.

1. The following transfers and re-adjustments of the Corps front will take place on the dates given :-

(1) The 29th Division will be transferred forthwith to, and will move under the orders of the Xth Corps, coming under the orders of that Corps on arrival in their area.

(2) The 70th Brigade, R.G.A., will be transferred to the Xth Corps at 0800, 6th November.

2. On the night of the 6th/7th November, the 14th Division will hand over to the 30th Division that portion of the front from U.24.b.6.3. to U.30.c.5.5.

The bridge at U.30.c.central will be inclusive to 14th Division.

Details of relief to be arranged direct between Divisions concerned, command of the new front passing to 30th Division at 0600, 7th November.

3. On completion of this relief, the Northern Corps Boundary will run from U.30.c.5.5. to U.8.b.2.8., thence South-West along present boundary.

4. On the night of the 7th/8th November, the 14th Division will take over from the 40th Division the front from the ROUBAIX - ESPIERRES Canal to C.15.c.7.3. Details of relief to be arranged between Divisions concerned, command of the new front passing to 14th Division at 0600 on 8th November.

5. On the completion of this relief, the Inter-Divisional Boundary will run from C.15.c.7.3. to Bridge B.18.c.5.9. (inclusive to 14th Division) and thence along present boundary.

6. The redistribution of Divisional Artilleries to cover the front will be arranged between Divisions concerned.

7. Completion of reliefs to be reported to XV Corps Headquarters.

8. ACKNOWLEDGE.

Brigadier-General,
General Staff.

Issued at 0600.

GENERAL STAFF,
14TH
DIVISION.
No.
Date 6-11-18
File

P.T.O.

Copy No.	1	A.D.C. to Corps Commander.
	2 - 3	14th Division.
	4 - 5	29th Division.
	6 - 7	40th Division.
	8 -10	G.O.C. R.A.
	11	D.A. & Q.M.G.
	12	"Q".
	13	"A".
	14	C.E.
	15	A.D.A.S.
	16	D.D.M.S.
	17	4th Squadron, R.A.F.
	18	O.C. 2nd Wing, R.A.F.
	19	A.P.M.
	20	"J" A.A. Battery.
	21	XV Corps Cyclist Battalion.
	22	No. 6 Balloon Company.
	23	Xth Corps.
	24	XI Corps.
	25-26	Second Army.
	27-34	G.S. and File.
	35	War Diary.

"C" FORM.
MESSAGES AND SIGNALS.

Army Form C. 2123.
(In books of 100.)
No. of Message.........

Prefix .... Code .... Words	Sent, or sent out.
Received from .... By	At .... m.
Service Instructions	To ....
	By ....

Office Stamp. (stamp: R... SIGNA... XI.)

Handed in at P C O Office 1020 m. Received 1050 m.

TO 14th Divn

Sender's Number.	Day of Month.	In reply to Number.	AAA
G 210	6th		
Order	no	259	modified
as	follows	aaa	SMELT 40th Div
will	tonight	readjust	front
with	TENCH 14th Div	aaa	Readjust-
of	front	of	TENCH 14th Div
with	HARRIET X Corps	will	take
place	night	7/8th	aaa
Added	14th	and	40th
Divn	Repted	all	recipients
of	Order	no	259

Arranged by phone with 40th Div 10.55 + 41 Bde

G.O.C.
G.S.O. 1
G.S.O. 2
G.S.O. 3

FROM 15th Corps
PLACE & TIME 1020

* This line, except AAA, should be erased, if not required.
(362) Wt. W5417P72. 691,000 Pads. 2/15. A.P.Ltd. (E2635)

GENERAL STAFF. 14TH DIVISION.
No.
Date.
File

G.O.C. | CD
G.S.O 1
G.S.O 2 | WS
G.S.O 3

SECRET.

Copy No. 25

6th November, 1918.

14th Division Order No. 239.

Reference Sheet 37 N.W. - 1/20,000.

1. On the night of 6th/7th November, the 14th Division will take over from the 40th Division the front from the present Southern Boundary to C.15.c.7.3.

Relief will be complete by 0001 November 7th.

2. All arrangements will be made by B.Gs. C. concerned.

3. C.R.A. and O.C. 14th Machine Gun Battalion will make the necessary arrangements to cover the new front.

4. On completion of relief the Southern Boundary will run from C.15.c.7.3 to Bridge B.18.c.5.9 (inclusive to 14th Division) thence along present Boundary.

5. Command of the new front will pass to G.O.C. 14th Division ~~on completion of relief~~. — 0600 Nov. 7th.

6. ACKNOWLEDGE.

[signature] Capt
for Lieut-Colonel,
General Staff,
14th Division.

Issued at 14.00 hrs.

Copies to :-

No. 1 - 41st Infantry Brigade.
2 - 42nd " "
3 - 43rd " "
4 - C.R.A.
5 - C.R.E.
6 - 15th L.N.Lancs.Regt.(Pnrs).
7 - 14th Machine Gun Battn.
8 - 14th Div. Signal Coy.
9 - 14th Divisional Train
10 - S.S.O.
11 - 14th Div. M.T. Coy.
12)
13) - A & Q.
14 - A.D.M.S.
15 - D.A.D.V.S.
16 - D.A.D.O.S.
17 - D.A.P.M.
18 - D.G.O.
19 - XV Corps "G".
20 - XV Corps "Q".
21 - XV Corps H.A.
22 - 40th Division.
23 - 30th Division.
24 - War Diary.
25 - File.

Addendum to 14th Division Order No. 238 dated 5th Nov. 1918.

On completion of relief the Northern Divisional Boundary will run from U.30.c.5.5 to U.8.b.2.8 - thence South-West along present boundary.

"A" Form.

Army Form C. 2121.
(In pads of 100.)

MESSAGES AND SIGNALS.

No. of Message..........

Prefix......... Code........... m.	Words.	Charge.	This message is on a/c of:	Recd. at .... m.
Office of Origin and Service Instructions.	Sent		Service.	Date
	At .... m.			From
	To			
	By		(Signature of "Franking Officer.")	By

G.O.C.
G.S.O. 1
G.S.O. 2

TO 15 CORPS

Sender's Number.	Day of Month.	In reply to Number.	
* GO 74	7		AAA

Relief with 40 DIV
Complete at 0350

From 14 DIV
Place
Time

The above may be forwarded as now corrected. (Z)
Censor. Signature of Addressor or person authorised to telegraph in his name.

* This line, except AAA, should be erased if not required.

Wt. W 3253/P511. 500,000 Pads. 1/18. B. & S. Ltd. (E2380.)

"A" Form.
MESSAGES AND SIGNALS.

Army Form C. 2121.
(In pads of 100.)
No. of Message..........

Prefix....... Code..........m.	Words.	Charge.	This message is on a/c of:	Recd. at.......m.
Office of Origin and Service Instructions.	Sent		..........Service.	Date..........
	At..........m.			From
	To			
	By		(Signature of "Franking Officer.")	By

40th Divn. 41st Inf. Bde. 14 M.G.Bn.
CRA. CRE. Q.

Sender's Number.	Day of Month.	In reply to Number.	AAA
[illegible]	8		

Amend D.O.230 para. 8 sea Command to pass
06.00 Nov. 7th

G.O.C.	
G.S.O 1	
G.S.O 2	
G.S.O 3	

From
Place 14th Divn.
Time

The above may be forwarded as now corrected. (Z)
Censor. Signature of Addressor or person authorised to telegraph in his name.

* This line, except AAA, should be erased if not required.

Wt. W 3253/P511. 500,000 Pads. 1/18. B. & S. Ltd. (E2380.)

"C" FORM.
MESSAGES AND SIGNALS. No. of Message

Army Form C. 2123 (In books of 100.)

Prefix	Code	Words	Sent, or sent out.	Office Stamp.
Received from	By		At ... m. To ... By ...	ARMY SIGNALS YN 7. XI. 18

Service Instructions

Handed in at VAKI Office 0350 m. Received 0400 m.

TO GO KA G

G.O.C. / G.S.O.1 / G.S.O.2 / G.S.O.3

* Sender's Number.	Day of Month.	In reply to Number.	AAA
SC 65	7		
DO	839	Complied	with

0435

FROM VAKI
PLACE & TIME 0330

* This line, except A A A, should be erased, if not required.

[illegible]

Appendix D

14th Division - General Staff

War Diary - Nov 1918

VOL. XLV

Extension of Front - 7/8 Nov. 1918

G.O.C. |
G.S.O.1 |
G.S.O.2 | ✓
G.S.O.3 |

SECRET.

14th DIVISION ORDER 238/1.

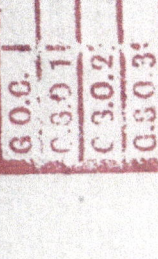

1. Reference 14th Division Order No. 238.

Delete para 1 (a) and substitute "On the night 7th/8th Nov. 14th Division will hand over to the 29th Division that part of the Divisional Front North of U.30.c.central. Relief to be complete by 0001 November 8th."

2. Reference para. 4. Command will pass to G.O.C. 29th Division at 06.00 8th November.

J.S. Beaumont Capt.
for Lieut-Colonel.
General Staff.
14th Division.

3/11/1918.

Copies to all Recipients D.O. 238.

G.O.C.	
G.S.O 1	
G.S.O.2	MB
G.S.O 3	

MESSAGES and SIGNALS.

41 Inf.Bde.
C.R.A.
C.R.E.
14 M.G.Battn.

14 Signal Coy.
Q.
30 Division.

½ G.O. 64 6 AAA

Ref. D.O. 238 para. 1 (a) AAA For night 6/7 Nov substitute 7/8 Nov. AAA VAKI (41st Bde) LOLA (DA) and PAGI (MG Bn) to acknowledge AAA Addsd. VAKI LOLA and PAGI reptd. YORI (30th Div) GOTU GEQA and Q.

---

14 Division

1130

[signature]
Capt.
for G.S. 14 Div.

S E C R E T. Copy No. 25

6th November, 1918.

14th Divisional Order No. 238.

Reference Sheet 29 S.[illegible]. 1/20-000.

1. (a) On the night of 6th/7th November, the 14th Division will hand over to the 30th Division that part of the Divisional front North of U.30.c.central. Relief to be complete by 0001 November 7th.

(b) The Bridge at U.30.c.central will be inclusive to 14th Division.

2. All arrangements will be made by B.Gs. C. concerned.

3. C.R.A. and O.C. 14th Machine Gun Battalion will arrange with 30th Division for the relief of guns and machine guns covering that part of the front.

4. Command of that part of the line from U.30.c.central to U.24.b.5.5 will pass to G.O.C. 30th Division on completion of relief.

5. ACKNOWLEDGE.

J.S. Beaumont Capt

for Lieut-Colonel,
General Staff,
14th Division.

G.O.C.
G.S.O.1 ✓
G.S.O.2
G.S.O.3

Issued at 20.00 hrs.

Copies to :-

No. 1 - 41st Infantry Brigade.
2 - 42nd Infantry Brigade.
3 - 43rd Infantry Brigade.
4 - C.R.A.
5 - C.R.E.
6 - 15th L.N. Lancs. Regt. (Pioneers).
7 - 14th Machine Gun Battalion.
8 - 14th Div. Signal Coy.
9 - 14th Divisional Train.
10 - S.S.O.
11 - 14th Div. M.T. Coy.
12) - A & Q.
13)
14 - A.D.M.S.
15 - D.A.D.V.S.
16 - D.A.D.O.S.
17 - D.A.P.M.
18 - D.G.O.
19 - XV Corps "G".
20 - XV Corps "A".
21 - XV Corps H.A.
22 - 40th Division.
23 - 30th Division.
24 - War Diary.
25 - File.

SECRET

S.G. 1472

G.O.C.
C.S.O. 1
C.S.O. 2
C.S.O. 3

41st Infantry Bde.

6/7

Your Brigade will night of 7/8th take over front down to approximate boundary shewn in Blue on attached map.

Existing posts of 40th Division and Bridge shewn in black.

A reconnaissance of the area shewn in red, as to its practicability for the movement of troops in a South Easterly direction is required, i.e., whether flooded, swampy only, or absolutely impracticable.

Information as to the Rigola D'Asschement, in this area, i.e. width, whether full of water, height of banks above water level, etc., also is required.

The location of any enemy posts in the neighbourhood is also of much importance

Enemy post presumed to exist at SLUICE, C 21 b 28 but there may be another post still further north along track hence ~~torwar~~ towards C 15 central.

Posts of 40th Division at C 15 central and C 15 d may be able to give information about this.

Please send patrols tonight to obtain the information required.

G.O.C. 40th Division agrees, but please arrange with Brigadier on your right details, as to time, route, etc

The information is important and must be obtained if possible, but no "enterprise" nor fighting are required: it is the information only that is wanted.

(sd) P.C.B.SKINNER
Major-General
Commanding 14th Division

6/11/1918

GENERAL STAFF,
14TH
DIVISION,
No.
Date.
File.

EDITION 3A (LOCAL) PROVISIONAL ISSUE. SHEET

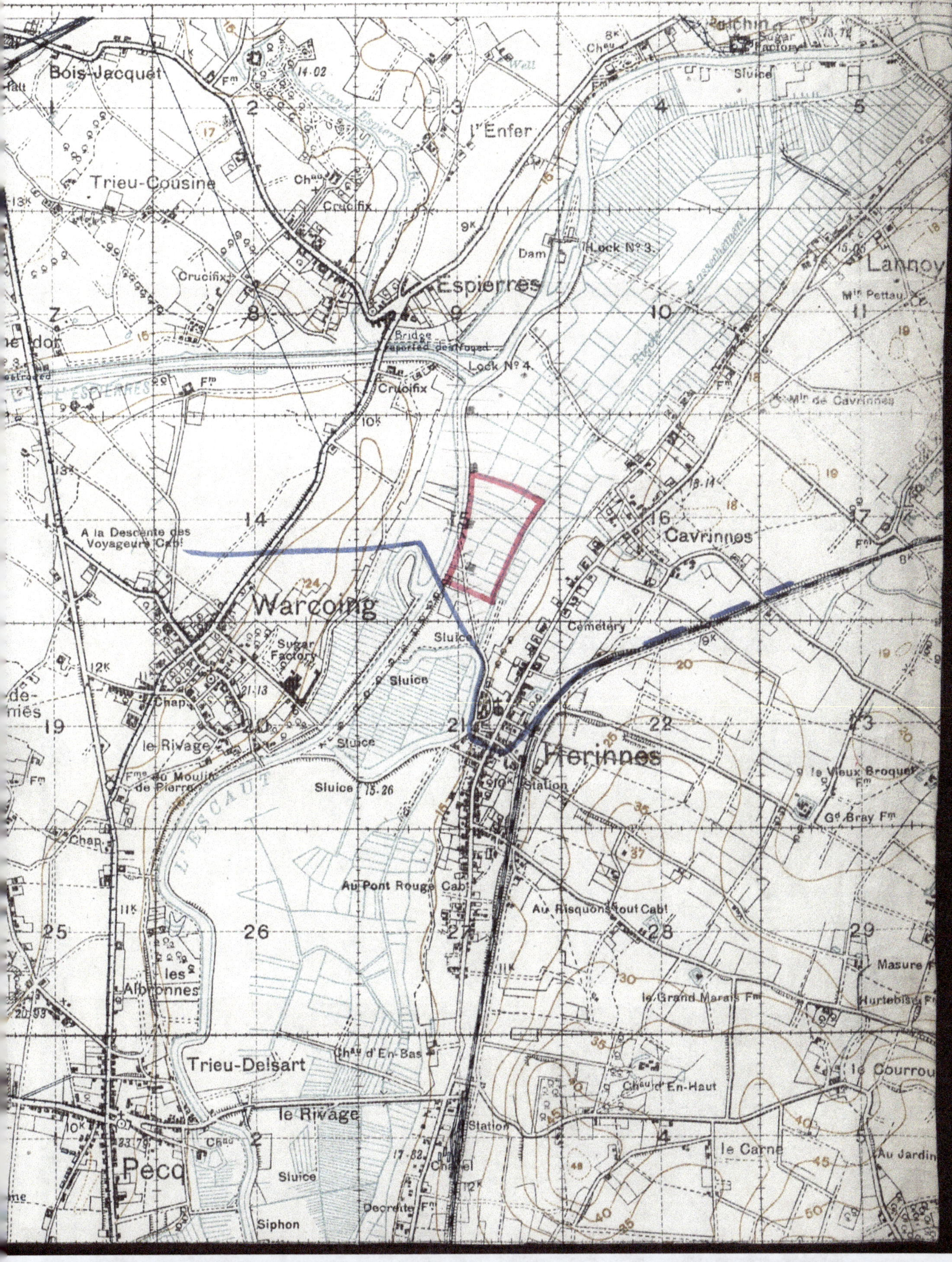

[illegible] Major

R

R A.P.O. 3 No. 223

D.A.G.

G.H.Q.

3rd. Echelon.

NL 1248

(6202) W 11186/M1151 350,000 12/16 McA. & W., Ltd. (Est. 781) Forms/W 3091/3. Army Form W. 3091.

Appendix E

Cover for Documents.

14th Division - General Staff

Nature of Enclosures.

War Diary - November 1918 -

VOLUME Appendix

8.

Orders and Instructions for forcing passage of River ESCAUT

Notes, or Letters written.

S E C R E T.

XV Corps No. 549/1 G,
dated 7/11/1918.

PROCEEDINGS OF CONFERENCE HELD BY CORPS COMMANDER AT SECOND ARMY HEADQUARTERS AT 1000 ON 7th NOVEMBER, 1918.

PRESENT :-

G.Os.C. C.R.As. G.S.Os. 1.	14th and 40th Divisions.
B.G.G.S. G.O.C. R.A. D.A. & Q.M.G. C.E. B.G., C.H.A.	XV Corps.

GENERAL STAFF. 14TH DIVISION. No. Date 8-11-18 File O.O.

1. The Corps Commander read and discussed with Divisional Commanders the proposals which they have submitted for the forthcoming operations.

2. Attention was drawn to the following points :-

(a) Machine guns to be used for enfilading roads to prevent reinforcements reaching enemy's front posts.

(b) The use of six-inch Trench Mortars.

(c) It was inadvisable to use signal lights for communication with Artillery. Lifts should be by time.

(d) Light Trench Mortars are invaluable for mopping up purposes and for dealing with Machine guns, and they should be got across the river by hand with the least possible delay.

(e) Liaison detachments, strength about two Machine guns and a half-company, working on the flanks of Divisions in rear of the leading waves, are invaluable.

(f) Wire cutters should be carried by leading troops.

(g) Company Commanders should be thoroughly instructed as to the action they are to take.

(h) Important tactical points are to be consolidated, but in the event of the advance progressing rapidly the changed situation may reduce the importance of these points, in which case further consolidation will be unnecessary.

(i) Wire may be required and should be made available.

3. The Corps Commander impressed on Divisional Commanders the importance of pushing on at one point if held up at another, and should the troops fail to cross the river at any one point, the attack is to be renewed by fresh troops with Artillery preparation as soon as possible.

4. The draft of the Corps Operation Orders was discussed and the various details arranged are included in those Orders.

H. Knox
Brigadier-General,
General Staff.

XV Corps,
7/11/1918.

P.T.O.

Issued to :- 14th Division.
40th Division.
D.A. & Q.M.G.
G.O.C. R.A.
C.E.
A.D.A.S.
"I".

Copy CRA (G.0.83)

SECRET.

Copy No. 2

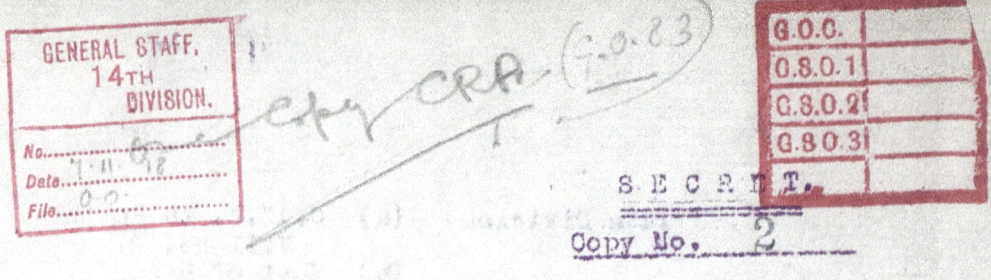

XV CORPS ORDER No. 281.

7th November, 1918.

Reference 1/40,000 map attached.

1. (1) The Second Army is to force the passage of the River ESCAUT on "J" day. The attack to be carried out by three Corps - XV, Xth (29th Division on right) and XIX. Objective:- J.11. - East of CELLES - AMOUGIES.

(2) The right of the Fifth Army is operating on "J" day South of TOURNAI, and on the same day the 59th Division (Left Division, XI Corps, Fifth Army) is to enlarge the bridgehead of CABT. LIETARD, connecting with the right of the XV Corps at the South-East corner of the Copse in I.11.a.3.5.

2. The XV Corps will cover the right flank of the Second Army, and will attack at "H" hour on "J" day.
The Corps will cross the inundations on the right bank of the ESCAUT between PECQ and HELCHIN (both inclusive).

Objective ("RED Line") :-

Copses in I.11.a. and b. - I.6.central - Farm in J.1.a. - Farm in D.25.d. - D.28.b.2.8. - Cross Roads in D.20.d.5.9.

3. (1) The 40th Division (Battle Headquarters, H.8.a.) will attack on the right, and the 14th Division (Battle Headquarters, DOTTIGNIES) on the left of the Corps.

(2) Boundary between Divisions :-

C.21.b.2.7. to C.22.central to J.1.central.

(3) Boundary between 14th and 29th Divisions :-

U.30.c.central to Cross Roads D.20.d.5.9. (inclusive to XV Corps).

(4) Each Division will attack with one Brigade in front. Support Brigades to cross the ESCAUT and to be used if required to push the attack home or to exploit success in the direction of Gd. REJET and Gd. CLAIRIEUX Farms respectively.

(5) To ensure liaison with the flanking Divisions, attacking Divisions will arrange inter-Divisional detachments on the flanks of their advance.

4. At "H" hour on "J" day the assaulting Infantry will advance from the right bank of the ESCAUT under a creeping barrage, and will cross the inundations by the following routes :-

40th Division: (a) LE RIVAGE.
(b) WARCOING - HERINNES Road.

14th Division: (a) C.15.c. to North of HERINNES Village.
(b) East of HELCHIN.

They will establish themselves on the line ("BLUE Line") I.4.c.1.1. - C.28.d.2.8. - C.23.c.2.2. - C.17.d.3.7. and thence along QUESNOY Road.

The barrage will lift from in front of the "BLUE Line" at "H" plus 51 on the left of the 14th Division front and at "H" plus 90 on remainder of the Corps front. The advance will then be continued to the "RED Line".

5. (1) The following Artillery will be at the disposal of Divisional Commanders :-

<u>40th Division.</u>

40th Divisional Artillery.
64th (Army) Brigade, R.F.A.
118th (Army) Brigade, R.F.A.

<u>14th Division.</u>

14th Divisional Artillery.
96th (Army) Brigade, R.F.A.

(2) In detailing Artillery to cross the ESCAUT, Divisional Commanders will select batteries from Army Brigades, not from Divisional Artillery.

(3) The XV Corps Heavy Artillery, consisting of 1st, 2nd, 33rd, 38th, 45th, 54th Brigades, R.G.A., will take part in the attack under the orders of the G.O.C., R.A., XV Corps.

(4) The creeping barrage will open at "H" hour, and will advance at the rate of 100 yards in three minutes. Approximately every 1,000 yards there will be a pause of ten additional minutes.
Detailed instructions will be issued.

(5) Vigorous Counter-Battery work in the form of neutralisation of all known hostile positions will commence at "H" minus "X" hours, and will continue as long as required after the capture of the "RED Line".
Heavy Artillery, not specially detailed for Counter-Battery work, will be available for bombardment purposes as required by Divisional Commanders on their respective fronts from "H" hour, and for thickening the creeping barrage as it advances from the "BLUE Line" to the "RED Line".

(6) A proportion of Field and Heavy Artillery will be detailed to answer "LL" and "GF" Calls during the creeping barrage.
Detailed instructions will be issued later.

(7) G.O.C., 40th Division will detail certain batteries under instructions to be issued later, to fire smoke to screen MONT DE LA TRINITÉ.

6. After the passage of the ESCAUT inundations has been forced, main bridges over the ESCAUT will be constructed :-

(a) At PECQ, under the orders of the Chief Engineer, XV Corps -

Wooden trestle, to carry all Military loads.

P.T.O.

(b) At HELCHIN, under C.R.E., 14th Division -

Steel girder bridge, to take Heavy Artillery except six-inch, Mark XIX.

All other bridging operations will be carried out under the orders of Divisions.

7. After the capture of the "RED Line", the Xth Corps is to advance Eastwards, and the XV Corps will be in reserve behind the right flank of the Army.

8. ACKNOWLEDGE.

Ack. 4H6

H. Knox

Brigadier-General,
General Staff.

Issued at 1630.

Copy No.	1	A.D.C. to Corps Commander.
	2 - 3	14th Division.
	4 - 5	40th Division.
	6 - 8	G.O.C.,R.A.
	9	D.A. & Q.M.G.
	10	"Q".
	11	C.E.
	12	A.D.A.S.
	13	D.D.M.S.
	14	4th Squadron, R.A.F.
	15	O.C. 2nd Wing, R.A.F.
	16	XV Corps Cyclist Battalion.
	17	No. 6 Balloon Company.
	18	Xth Corps.
	19	XI Corps.
	20-21	Second Army.
	22-29	G.S. and File.
	30	War Diary.

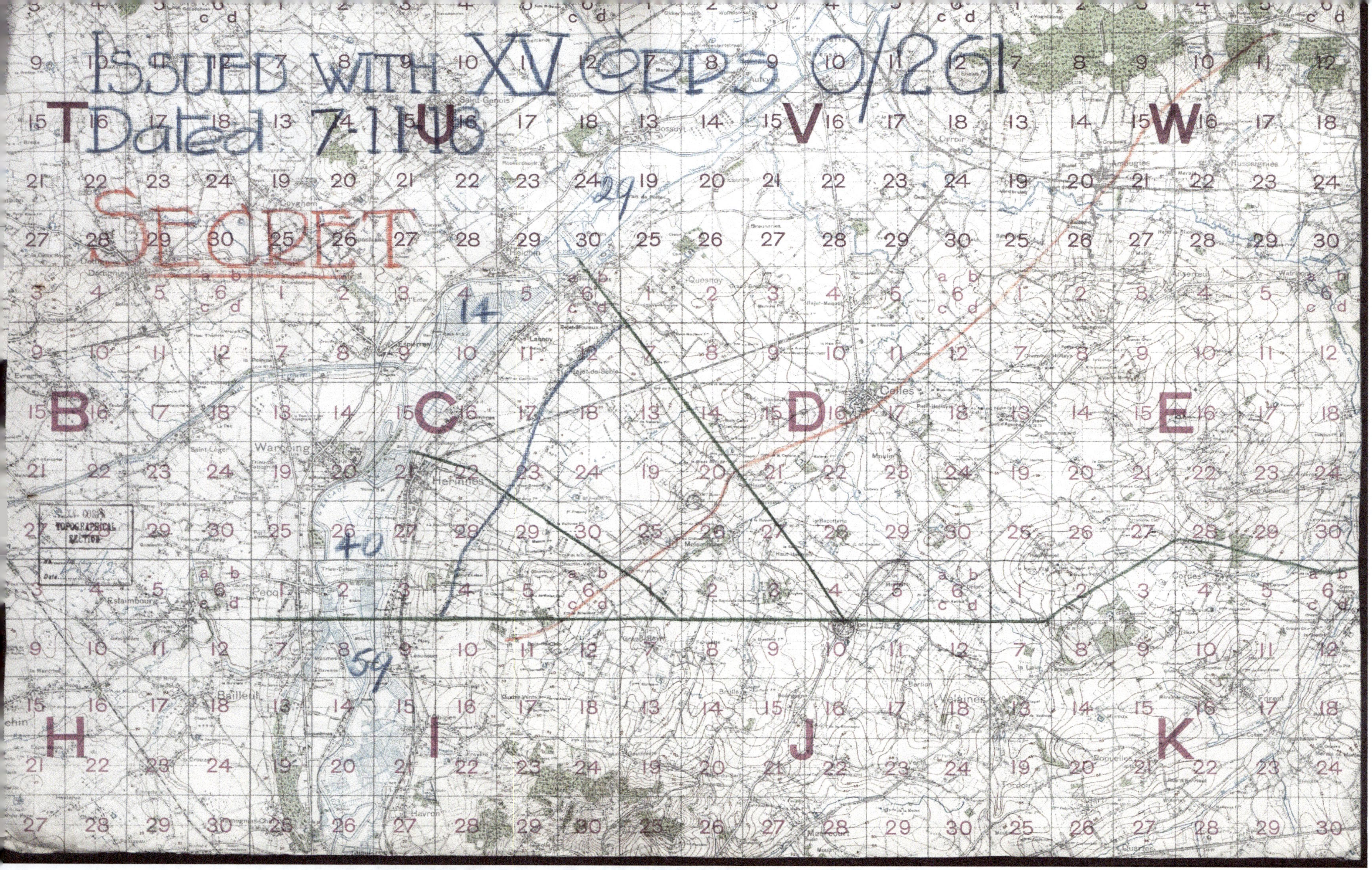
ISSUED WITH XV CORPS O/261
Dated 7.1.16
SECRET
Warcoing
Celles
Hérinnes
Estaimbourg
Pecq
Bailleul
Quesnoy
Saint Léger
Havron
Valaines
Cordes
Moulin
T
U
V
W
B
C
D
E
H
I
J
K
14
40
59
29

G.O.C.	
G.S.O.1	
G.S.O.2	
G.S.O.3	

S E C R E T.

XV Corps No. G.S. 2/158.
7th November, 1918.

ADDENDUM No. 1 to XV CORPS ORDER No. 261.

Reference to XV Corps Order No. 261, dated 7th November.

In para. 1 (1) for "Objective D.11." substitute "Objective I.11.".

for Brigadier-General,
General Staff.

XV Corps.
7/11/1918.

Issued to all recipients of XV Corps Order No. 261.

Copy to C.R.A.

GENERAL STAFF.
14TH
DIVISION
No.
Date. 8.11.18
File.

SECRET

G.O.C.	
G.S.O.1	[handwritten initials]
G.S.O.2	
G.S.O.3	

14 Division
S.G. 1486
Copy No. 19

14th DIVISION INSTRUCTIONS No. 1.

7 November 1918

Reference
Sheets 29 SW. 1/20,000
37 NW. 1/20,000
29 & 37. 1/40,000

1. The Second Army is to force the passage of the River ESCAUT on "J" Day. The attack to be carried out by the XV, X, and XIX Corps.

2. The right of the Fifth Army is operating on "J" Day south of TOURNAI, and its left Division (59th) is to enlarge the Bridgehead already existing at CABT.LIETARD.

3. The XV Corps is to cover the right flank of the Second Army, and attacks at "H" hour on "J" day, crossing the inundations on the right bank of the ESCAUT between PECQ and HELCHIN both inclusive.

4. The first objective of the XV Corps (Blue line) is the line -
I 4 c 1.1 - C 28 d 2.8 - C 23 c 2.2 - C 23 central - C 17 d 3.7, and thence along the road to REJET-MOULEUX.

The final objective (Red line) is the line - Copses in I 11 a and b - I 6 central - Farm in J 1 a - Farm in D 25 d - D 26 b 2.8 - Cross roads in D 20 d 5.9.

5. Boundary between 14th Division and 40th Division on its right is -
C 21 b 2.7 - C 22 central - J 1 central.

Boundary between 14th Division and 29th Division of X Corps on its left is -
Bridge at U 30 c central - Cross roads D 20 d 5.9, both inclusive to 14th Division.

6. The 14th Division will attack with -
43rd Infantry Brigade in front line;
42nd Infantry Brigade in Support;
41st Infantry Brigade in Reserve.

7. The artillery at the disposal of the Division consists of -

Field Artillery - 14th Divisional Artillery, 96th Army Brigade, R.F.A.

Heavy Artillery - Five heavy batteries for bombardments, exclusive of batteries detailed for counter-battery work.

8. The Field artillery creeping barrage will open at "H" hour, will lift at "H" plus 15, and advance at the rate of 100 yards in three minutes, with a pause of ten additional minutes at approximately every 1000 yards.
It will lift off the first objective in front of the Left Battalion at "H" plus 51, and in front of the right battalion at "H" plus 90.

/Heavy artillery

Heavy artillery will bombard selected points and will thicken the creeping barrage as it advances towards the final objective.

40th Division will screen MONT DE LA TRINITÉ with smoke.

9. The passage of the inundations by 43rd Infantry Brigade will be effected in two columns as follows :-

(a). Left Battalion.
Forming up area between Bridge at U 30 c central and SLUICE in C 5 b on right bank of L'ESCAUT.
First objective line of REJET-DE-SEBLE - REJET-HOULEUX Road.
Final objective - High ground in D 20 c and D 20 b, Cross roads D 20 d 5.9.
The advance of this battalion will be generally along the road GUERMIGNIES to cross roads D 20 d 5.9.

(b). Right battalion.
Forming up area in C 15 d, west of the RIGOLE D'ASSECHE-MENT.
First objective - High ground in C 23 central - Railway embankment about C 17 d 3.7, thence along road to REJET DE SEBLE.

(c). Reserve Battalion.
This battalion, less two companies, will cross in rear of Left Battalion S.E. of HELCHIN, and will attack and mop up LANNOY.
Two companies will cross in rear of the Left Battalion, will mop up CAVRINNES, and move on LANNOY establishing touch with the remainder of the Battalion.
The Reserve Battalion will then move on REJET DE SEBLE.

10. Machine guns.

Two sections will accompany each front line battalion, the guns being carried by hand.
Pack animals will follow by the bridge at Lock 3, so soon as possible after the Infantry.
Three companies will thicken the artillery barrage, enfilade roads, and fire in the intervals between the artillery barrage.
Of these Companies, one will be prepared to cross the ESCAUT so soon as the Infantry are beyond range at which the guns can render assistance.

11. Light Trench Mortars.

One Stokes Mortar will accompany each Infantry Battalion, the guns and ammunition being carried by hand.
One Stokes Mortar and ammunition per Battalion will be prepared to follow on pack mules.

12. By "H" hour on J Day, the 42nd Infantry Brigade will be on the line ST.LEGER - BOIS JACQUET - COYGHEM.
Brigade H.Q. at DOTTIGNIES.

41st Infantry Brigade will be on the line ESTAMPUIS - EVREGNIES - QUEVAUCAMP.
Brigade H.Q. EVREGNIES.

Divisional H.Q. will be at the normal H.Q. of the Brigade in the line at DOTTIGNIES

13. 42nd Infantry Brigade will advance to the River ESCAUT so as to begin the passage by the same crossings as used by the 43rd Infantry Brigade, at "H" plus two hours.
This Brigade will be prepared to support the attack or to exploit success towards GRAND CLAIRIEUX Farm (J 9 a)

43rd Infantry Bde. will advance S.E. of the REJET DE STBLE - QUESNOY Road, so as to clear the area between this road and the inundations for the 42nd Brigade.

14. To ensure liaison with the flanking Divisions, 43rd Infantry Brigade will detail a detachment of one half Company and two machine guns to operate in rear of the outer flanks of the leading companies of the front line battalions.

15. After the passage of the inundations has been forced, Main bridges over the ESCAUT are being constructed as follows:

(a). At PECQ, under the orders of the C.E. XV Corps. Wooden trestle to carry all military loads.

(b). At HELCHIN, under C.R.E., 14th Division, Steel girder bridge to take Heavy Artillery, except 6" Mark XIX.

16. Two additional bridges for Infantry are being placed across the ESCAUT, one at J 15 b 0.5, and one at U 30 c 1.5. The Bridge at Lock 3 is capable of taking Pack transport.

17. Four Bridges for Infantry will be thrown across the RIGOLE D'ASSECHEMENT at "H" hour, for the right column, and 18 "Infantry" bridges are required for the passage of the left column.
C.R.E. will ensure that the necessary material and R.E. assistance are available.

A track across the inundations, with the necessary [illegible] bridges, to take Pack transport is to be completed so soon after "H" hour as possible.

18. Artillery barrage tables, Instructions as to the action of Medium Trench Mortars, Heavy Artillery, and Machine guns (and Signal arrangements) will be issued separately

19. P.of W. cage will be at BOIS JACQUET (U 25 c 8.0)
Straggler Posts will be at Road Junction U 29 a 9580
Road Junction U 22 b 7080
Cross roads U 15 d 2.2
COYGHEM U 10 c 9090
Cottage U 14 b 8070
Cross roads U 13 a 9590
Bridge B 18 a 50
DOTTIGNIES.

20. Acknowledge.

T.E.Stanhope Chilcott [signature]
Lieut.Colonel
General Staff

14th Division
7/11/1918

Distribution overleaf.

Distribution of 14th Division Instructions No.1. (S.G.1486).

No. 1 - 41st Infantry Brigade.
2 - 42nd Infantry Brigade.
3 - 43rd Infantry Brigade.
4 - C.R.A.
5 - C.R.E.
6 - 14th Machine Gun Battalion.
7 - 15th Bn. L.N. Lancs.Regt. (Pioneers).
8 - A. & Q.
9 - D.A.P.M.
10 - A.D.M.S.
11 - 14th Div. Signal Coy.
12 - 14th Div. Train.
13 - D.G.O.
14 - 40th Division.
15 - 39th Division.
16 - XV Corps.
17 - XV Corps H.A.
18 - War Diary.
19 - File.

S E C R E T

14th Division S.G.1497

Amendment to 14th Division Instructions No 1 (S.G.1486).

para 9 c line 5 should read :-

2 Coys will cross in rear of Right Battalion, and will mop up CAVRINNES etc.

para 19 should read :-

P of W. cage will be at BOIS JACQUET (U 25 c 2.0)

P of W. directing posts will be at,

(1)	Road junction	U 29 a 95.30
	do	U 22 b 70.80
	X roads	U 15 d 2.2
	COYGHEM	U 19 c 90.20
	Cottage	C 14 b 80.70
	X roads	C 13 a 95.90
	Bridge	B 18 a 50.00

These posts will each consist of 2 O.R. from the 41st Infy. Brigade and will be in position at H plus 1 hr.

[signature]

Lieut-Colonel.
General Staff.
14th Division.

8/11/18.

Copies to all recipients of S.G.1486.

S E C R E T.

14th Division, S.G. 1186.
Appendix "A".
8th Novr.1918.

SIGNAL COMMUNICATIONS.

(Issued in conjunction with 14th Div. Instructions No.1).

LINES.

Before ZERO the following Headquarters will be in telegraphic and telephonic communication with Divisional H.Q. :-

(1) 43rd Inf.Bde.	Buried line to COYGHEM and from that point by cable.
(2) 42nd " "	Cable line.
(3) 41st " "	Air line.
(4) 29th Division.	Direct cable line.
(5) 40th "	Through Rear H.Q.
(6) XV Corps.	Direct line buried to MOUSCRON, Air line beyond.

In addition to the above, there will be direct lines from Divisional Artillery Headquarters to each group Headquarters under their command.

Lines will also be run from 43rd Inf. Bde. H.Q. to LA POINTE d'OR and HELCHIN, at which points advanced Report Centres will be formed.

As 43rd Inf. Bde. Headquarters advance, a line will be laid to connect up their Headquarters to the Divisional H.Q..

WIRELESS.

At ZERO, Trench Set at 43rd Inf. Bde. H.Q. will be in communication with Divisional H.Q. and also the Brigades on either flank.

Divisional H.Q. will be in communication with Corps and also the flank Divisions.

After ZERO. A Trench Set, with personnel, will move off with the advance party of the 43rd Inf. Bde. H.Q. and as soon as their new H.Q. are decided on, it will be erected and communication will be obtained with Divisional H.Q. and 43rd Bde. Rear H.Q. As it is thought traffic over the Bridges will be heavy and difficulty may be experienced in getting the telephone line quickly to the Advanced Report Centre, this means of communication should be fully utilised.

D.R.L.S.

Motor Cyclist D.Rs. will be distributed as follows :-

3 with 43rd Bde., 1 with 42nd Bde., 1 with 41st Bde., and 5 at Divisional Headquarters.

Horse D.Rs. will also be posted at 43rd Bde. H.Q. (2) and Divisional H.Q. (3).

VISUAL.

A Central Visual Station will be formed at a spot to be notified later, which will be in communication by wire to Division and Brigades. The duty of this Station will be to pick up any Station on the Eastern side of the SCHELDT, and transmit its message to its proper destination.

Battalion or Brigade H.Q. as soon as they arrive at their

/Advanced

Advanced H.Q. should at once get into communication (if weather conditions are favourable) with above station and exchange signals.
The Signallers should be fully instructed to set up their Station on some prominent point which can be clearly seen from the Central Station and at the same time under cover from the enemy.

After ZERO. There will be an Advanced Corps Signal Station at MONT de la TRINITÉ.
At this station the following methods of communication will be available:-

(1) Wireless.
(2) Visual.
(3) D.Rs.
(4) Lines.

If Brigades experience any difficulty in communicating with Divisional Headquarters direct messages should be transmitted through this Station.

SECRET

Identification Trace for use with Artillery Maps.

…e intended to facilitate the communication of information as to the position of targets, which have been located on a squared map. … this trace are 500 yards in length on the 1/10,000 scale, 1,000 yards in length on the 1/20,000 scale, and 2,000 yards in length …

…he trace are fitted to the squares of the map showing the targets, which are then drawn on the trace. Sufficient … also be added to enable the recipient to place the trace in the correct position on his own map. A little detail …his is not essential. The name and scale of the map to which the trace refers must be always given. The trace … 1/20,000, or 1/40,000 scale.

Tracing taken from Sheets 29 & 37

of the 1/20,000 *map of* ……

Signature …… *Date* ……

Copy No. 2

S E C R E T.

XV Corps No. G.S.2/159.
8th November 1918.

ADDENDUM NO. 2 TO XV CORPS ORDER NO. 261.

ARTILLERY.

1. (1) Reference para.5 (5) H minus X hours = H minus 2½ hours.

(2) The Heavy Artillery bombardment will open at H minus 20 minutes.

(3) The 40th Division creeping barrage will open at H minus 9 minutes.
The 14th Division creeping barrage will open at H minus 10 minutes ~~on the left~~.
~~The 14th Division creeping barrage will open at H on the right~~.
The assaulting infantry will advance under the barrage (para.4 of XV Corps Order 261 to be modified).

(4) The creeping barrage will lift from in front of the Blue Line at H plus 51 on the left of the 14th Division front, and at H plus 75 on remainder of the Corps front. (In second last line of para.4 of XV Corps Order for "plus 90" read "plus 75").

2. L.L. and G.F. Calls.

(1) L.L.Calls will be answered by one section of all Batteries of Heavy Artillery that can bear.

(2) G.F. will be answered by one section of all Batteries of Heavy Artillery in whose zone the call is.

3. Artillery, XI Corps, have arranged to carry out Counter-Battery work, and to fire a smoke barrage on the Northern and Western slopes of MT. de la TRINITE.

4. A Barrage Map will be issued later.

H. Knox
Brigadier-General,
General Staff.

Issued at 1830

Issued to all recipients of XV Corps Order No.261, dated 7th November 1918.

Copy to ~~Adv~~ CRA
For retention
8/11/18

G.O.C.	
G.S.O.1	✓
G.S.O.2	
G.S.O.3	

SECRET.

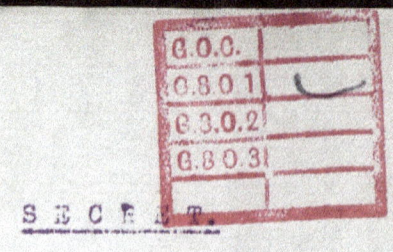

XV Corps No. G.S. 2/160.

Copy No. 2

ADDENDUM No. 3 to XV CORPS ORDER No. 261.
dated 7th NOVEMBER, 1918.

8th November, 1918.

INSTRUCTIONS FOR AEROPLANE CO-OPERATION.

1. (1) During the operations to be carried out on "J" day, contact aeroplanes will call for flares at "H" plus 45 minutes and at "H" plus four hours.

(2) Flares are to be lit by all advanced infantry when called for.

(3) Distinguishing marks of Contact Patrol Machines will be as laid down in paragraph 3 of Appendix "B", S.S. 135.

2. Messages from Contact Aeroplanes will be dropped at Divisional Advanced and XV Corps Headquarters.

Dropping Stations will be located :-
14th Division Advanced Headquarters DOTTIGNIES.
40th Division Advanced Headquarters. H.11.c.

H.P. Buckley Major
for Brigadier-General,
General Staff.

Issued at 1830

Issued to all recipients of XV Corps Order No. 261, dated 7th November, 1918.

1 Copy to 43 Bde
Pass to 42 to see

G.O.C.	
G.S.O.1	
G.S.O.2	
G.S.O.3	

S E C R E T.

XV Corps No. G.S.2/161.

Copy No. 2

ADDENDUM No. 4 to XV CORPS ORDER No. 261,
dated 7th NOVEMBER, 1918.

8th November, 1918.

INSTRUCTION FOR COMMUNICATIONS AND SYNCHRONISATION
OF WATCHES.

1. Owing to the limited advance to be made by the XV Corps during the forthcoming operations, the instructions contained * in XV Corps No. 57/173 G. dated 1st November, are modified as follows :-

(1) The organisation of a Corps Communication Centre will not be carried out.

(2) The Central Visual Station, ordered in para. 2 of the above letter, will be established on "J" day.as soon after "H" hour as the progress of the operations allows.

2. Watches will be synchronised with Divisions and Corps Heavy Artillery at 1000 on "J" - 1 day from the Corps Signal Office.

3. ACKNOWLEDGE.

GB 4418

[signature] Major
for Brigadier-General,
General Staff.

Issued at 1830

Issued to all recipients of XV Corps Order No. 261, dated 7th November, 1918.

* Only issued to those concerned.

GENERAL STAFF,
14TH
DIVISION.
No. SG 1503.
Date 8. 11. 18
File 00/09

Copy to O.C. Sigs.
8/11/18

For information
(Sd) [signature]
Lieut Col G.S.
14 Div.

XV Corps No. 57/173 G,
dated 1.11/1918.

14th Division. ✓
29th Division.
40th Division.
G.O.C. R.A.
Corps Observers.

G.O.C. | G.S.O.1 | G.S.O.2 | G.S.O.3

---

1. In the event of an advance East of the ESCAUT, there will be considerable difficulty in establishing satisfactory forward communications. To tide over the period which may elapse before normal communications are provided, XV Corps Signals will establish at the earliest possible moment a Communication Centre East of the river. This Communication Centre will receive messages from Corps Observers, Heavy Artillery Observers and any Divisional units which may desire to make use of it.

The position of the Communication Centre can only be decided as the advance progresses. It will be in the neighbourhood of a main road and, approximately, in the centre of the Corps area. When its exact position is decided all concerned will be informed.

2. To supplement and, primarily, to provide for the breakdown of other methods of communication, XV Corps Signals will arrange for a Central Visual Station to be available for all formations and units in the Corps.

3. The attached paper shows the organisation of the Corps Communication Centre and the arrangements for the Central Visual Station.

H. Knox
Brigadier-General,
General Staff.

XV Corps,
1/11/1918.

Copies to :- A.D.A.S. (12 copies).
"I".
"Q".
C.E.
Second Army.
XI Corps.

GENERAL STAFF,
14TH DIVISION.
No.
Date. 1-11-18
File. S.14-

~~[illegible]~~ O.C. Sigs has seen this – no further action MB

SIGNAL COMMUNICATION.

1. ORGANISATION OF A CORPS COMMUNICATION CENTRE.

(a) "Wilson" Wireless Spark Set ... Communicating to Army, Corps, Divisions and Infantry Brigades.

(b) Continuous Wave Wireless Set ... Communicating to Army, Corps, Heavy Artillery Headquarters, Heavy Artillery Brigades and Corps Observers.

(c) Mobile Exchange and Signal Service.

(d) Detachment of Motor-cycle Despatch Riders, Mounted and Cyclist Orderlies.

(e) Visual Signal Detachment.

(f) Cable Section.

TRANSPORT :-

Box Car and horsed wagons.

2. A Staff Officer will accompany the Mobile Communication Centre for the purpose of :-

(a) Enciphering and deciphering telegraph messages.

(b) Classifying messages in order of importance and urgency.

(c) Co-ordination and circulation of Intelligence information.

3. D.R.L.S. AND MOUNTED ORDERLIES SERVICE.

Despatch Riders will run between Corps Headquarters and the Communication Centre, and between the Communication Centre and Divisions. Mounted Orderlies will be used in case the roads prevent the use of motor-cycles.

4. WIRELESS.

The Communication Centre will place itself in immediate communication with all the Stations shewn in paragraph 1 (a). Wireless Sections of moving formations will exchange Signals with Communication Centre immediately they establish their Stations.

5. VISUAL SIGNALLING.

A Central Visual Station will be established by Corps Signals in the Convent Tower at I.30.a.8.6. as soon as possible after the line is advanced across the SCHELDT. The Station will be manned and equipped to send and receive by Lucas Lamps, heliograph and Morse flags, and will be maintained until satisfactory wire communication is established to points in advance of the Visual Range from the Station.

Messages will be accepted from any formation and unit and will be transmitted to the addressees by the quickest means.

A Visual Station will also be established in the tower of the Town Hall, TOURCOING, for night signalling.

It must be borne in mind that visual signalling by day will only be effective over short distances under Winter conditions and, therefore, messages must, in most cases, be relayed. If, therefore, the situation compels recourse to visual communication, traffic must be restricted to messages of tactical importance and abbreviated to the utmost.

XV Corps,
1/11/1918.

G.O.C.	
G.S.O. 1	[illegible]
G.S.O. 2	
G.S.O. 3	

SECRET.

XV Corps No. 819/73 G,
dated 8/11/1918.

14th Division.
40th Division.

In event of enemy withdrawal on the XV Corps front, the forward tactical boundaries between Divisions and with flanking Corps will be as in XV Corps Order No. 261, dated 7th November, 1918.

H. Knox
Brigadier-General,
General Staff.

XV Corps,
8/11/1918.

Copies to :- Second Army.
Xth Corps.
XI Corps.
G.O.C. R.A.
C.E.
"A".
"Q".

GENERAL STAFF,
14TH DIVISION.
No.
Date. 8. 11. 18
File. 00.

S E C R E T

14th Division
S.G. 1491

G.O.C.	
G.S.O. 1	[illegible]
G.S.O. 2	
G.S.O. 3	

41 Inf.Bde.
42 Inf.Bde.
43 Inf.Bde.
C.R.A.
C.R.E.
14th M.G.Bn.
15th L.N.Lancs.(Pioneers)
A & Q.
14th Div.Signal Coy.
14th Div.Train.
A.D.M.S.
D.A.P.M.
D.G.O.

~~XV Corps~~
~~XV Corps H.A.~~
~~29th Division~~
~~40th Division~~

Reference 14th Division S.G.1486 of 7/11/1918.

1. In the event of the enemy retiring before "J" Day, the XV Corps is to cross the ESCAUT and keep touch with the enemy as far as the RED Line only, as given in para. 4 of S.G.1486.
East of that line, the X Corps will carry on, and the XV Corps will come into Army Reserve.

2. The Advanced Guard, consisting of -
The Infantry Bde. in the Line,
1 Battery R.F.A. (18-prs.)
1 Section Hows.
2 Coys. M.G.Bn. (with pack mules)
1 Section R.E.,
will cross the ESCAUT and advance to the final objective given in para. 4 within the boundaries given in para. 5.

3. The Support and Reserve Brigades and Divisional Troops will be ready to move at Four Hours' notice

4. The C.R.E. will arrange for any additional bridges for the infantry to be thrown over the river, and for a bridge for light transport and field guns S.E. of HELCHIN.

5. Acknowledge.

14th Division
8/11/1918

J.S. Beaumont Capt.
for Lieut.Colonel
General Staff

G.O.C.	
G.S.O.1	
G.S.O.2	
G.S.O.3	

S E C R E T.

XV Corps No. G.S. 2/162.

Copy No. 2

ADDENDUM No. 5 to XV CORPS ORDER No. 261, dated 7th NOVEMBER, 1918.

8th November, 1918.

1. "J" day has been fixed for 11th November.

2. "H" hour has been fixed for 0630.

3. ACKNOWLEDGE BY WIRE.

Brigadier-General,
General Staff.

Issued at 2230.

To all recipients of XV Corps Order No. 261, dated 7th November, 1918.

Cancelled

GENERAL STAFF,
14TH
DIVISION
No.
Date 9.11.18
File 00

Army Form C. 2123.
(In books of 100.)

"C" FORM.

MESSAGES AND SIGNALS. No. of Message 52

Prefix Sm Code 1115 Words 27		Sent, or sent out.	Office Stamp.
Received from Pco	By Green	At YN m.	9. XI. 18
Service Instructions		To	SIGNALS
		By	

Handed in at Pco Office 1115 m. Received 1122 m.

TO 14 Dvn

*Sender's Number.	Day of Month.	In reply to Number.	AAA
G258	9th		
Addendum	no	5	to
15	Corps	order	no
261	of	7th	nov
is	cancelled		

G.O.C. ✓
G.S.O 1
G.S.O.2
G.S.O.3

FROM 15 Corps
PLACE & TIME 1100

* This line, except AAA, should be erased, if not required.

(3687) Wt. W54/P738 691,000 Pads. 2/18. A.P.Ltd. (E3013)

35807. W16879/M1879 500,000 3/17 R.T. (1074) Forms/W3091/3 Army Form W.3091.

Cover for Documents.

Appendix F.

Nature of Enclosures.

14th Division - General Staff.

War Diary - November 1918 -

VOLUME

Pursuit of Enemy from L'ESCAUT River
9 Nov. 1918

Notes, or Letters written.

SECRET

14th Division
S.G. 1491

41 Inf.Bde.
42 Inf.Bde.
43 Inf.Bde.
C.R.A.
C.R.E.
14th M.G.Bn.
15th L.N.Lancs.(Pioneers)
A & Q.
14th Div.Signal Coy.
14th Div.Train.
A.D.M.S.
D.A.P.M.
D.G.O.

~~XV Corps~~
~~XV Corps H.A.~~
~~29th Division~~
~~40th Division.~~

Reference 14th Division S.G.1486 of 7/11/1918.

1. In the event of the enemy retiring before "J" Day, the XV Corps is to cross the ESCAUT and keep touch with the enemy as far as the RED Line only, as given in para. 4 of S.G.1486.
East of that line, the X Corps will carry on, and the XV Corps will come into Army Reserve.

2. The Advanced Guard, consisting of -
The Infantry Bde. in the Line,
1 Battery R.F.A. (18-prs.)
1 Section Hows.
2 Coys. M.G.Bn. (with pack mules)
1 Section R.E.,
will cross the ESCAUT and advance to the final objective given in para. 4 within the boundaries given in para. 5.

3. The Support and Reserve Brigades and Divisional Troops will be ready to move at Four Hours' notice

4. The C.R.E. will arrange for any additional bridges for the infantry to be thrown over the river, and for a bridge for light transport and field guns S.E. of HELCHIN.

5. Acknowledge.

J.S. Beaumont Capt.
for Lieut.Colonel
General Staff

14th Division
8/11/1918

Army Form C. 2123.
(In books of 100.)

"C" FORM.

MESSAGES AND SIGNALS. No. of Message..........

Prefix SB Code 0501 Words 53

Received from P.O. By ...

Service Instructions Pty

Sent, or sent out At ....m. To .... By ....

Office Stamp. 9. XI. 18

Handed in at YDZ Office 0501 m. Received 0511 m.

TO 14 Divn

* Sender's Number.	Day of Month.	In reply to Number.	AAA
SC 819	9		

morning report aaa Right Battn reported advanced to Hill 48 and ridge aaa Left Battn to C22D45 to C28D aaa no opposition aaa all now quiet aaa Inundation diminishing canal fallen about three inches addsd 15 Corps repted 14 and 59 Divns 15 Corps HA 40 Divn Artly

FROM 40 Divn

PLACE & TIME 0530

* This line, except **AAA**, should be erased, if not required.

(3287) Wt. W54/P738. 691,000 Pads. 3/18 A.P. Ltd (E3013)

"C" FORM.
MESSAGES AND SIGNALS.

Army Form C. 2123.
(In books of 100.)

No. of Message............

Prefix Sm Code 0605 Words 72	Sent, or sent out. At .... m. To .... By ....
Received from PCO By WW	Office Stamp.
Service Instructions	

Handed in at P CO Office 0605 m. Received 0621 m.

TO 14 DIVN

* Sender's Number.	Day of Month.	In reply to Number.	AAA
G 573	9		

Morning report aaa Right Divn crossed ESCAUT and have reached Hill 48 (J 4 C) C 28 D and C 22 D 4.5 Left Divn have one Coy along road HERINNES-CAVRINNES C 16 C and patrols are crossing at HELCHIN aaa No opposition aaa Hostile Arty quiet since early evening aaa Our Arty carried out 6 gas concentrations and harrassing fire on hostile batteries aaa Inundations diminishing addsd 2nd Army repts all concerned

FROM
PLACE & TIME 15 Corps 0600

* This line, except AAA, should be erased, if not required.

(3287) Wt.W54/P738. 691,000 Pads. 3/18. A.P.Ltd. (E.3013)

Army Form C. 2123.
(In books of 100.)

"C" FORM.
MESSAGES AND SIGNALS.

No. of Message ....

Prefix SB Code 0502 Words 38	Sent, or sent out. At ....m. To .... By ....
Received from RCO By wu	Office Stamp.
Service Instructions Pty	

Handed in at YBJ Office 0502 m. Received 0515 m.

TO 14 Divn

*Sender's Number.	Day of Month.	In reply to Number.	AAA
JS864	9		

Morning report aaa Situation very quiet on front aaa Patrols being sent across the GRAND COURANT no reports yet received as to progress aaa addsd 10 Corps reptd flanking Divns

0530

FROM 29 Divn
PLACE & TIME 0500

* This line, except AAA, should be erased, if not required.

(3287) Wt. W54/P738 691,000 Pads 3/18 A P Ltd (E.3024)

"A" Form.
Army Form C. 2121.
(In pads of 100.)

MESSAGES AND SIGNALS.

No. of Message............

Prefix..........Code..........m.	Words.	Charge.	This message is on a/c of:	Recd. at......m.
Office of Origin and Service Instructions.	Sent		G.O.C.	Date
	At..........m.		G.S.O 1 Service.	From
	To		G.S.O.2	By
	By		G.S.O.3 (Signature of "Franking Officer.")	

TO C.R.A., C.R.E.

Sender's Number.	Day of Month.	In reply to Number.	AAA
G.O.100	9		

Following from XV Corps I aaa Todays photos show traffic bridge destroyed and foot bridges erected at C.21 b 22.73 aaa ends.

From
Place 14th Div.
Time

The above may be forwarded as now corrected. (Z)

Censor. Signature of Addressor or person authorised to telegraph in his name.

* This line, except AAA, should be erased if not required.

Wt. W 3253/P511. 500,000 Pads. 1/18. B. & S. Ltd. (E2389.)

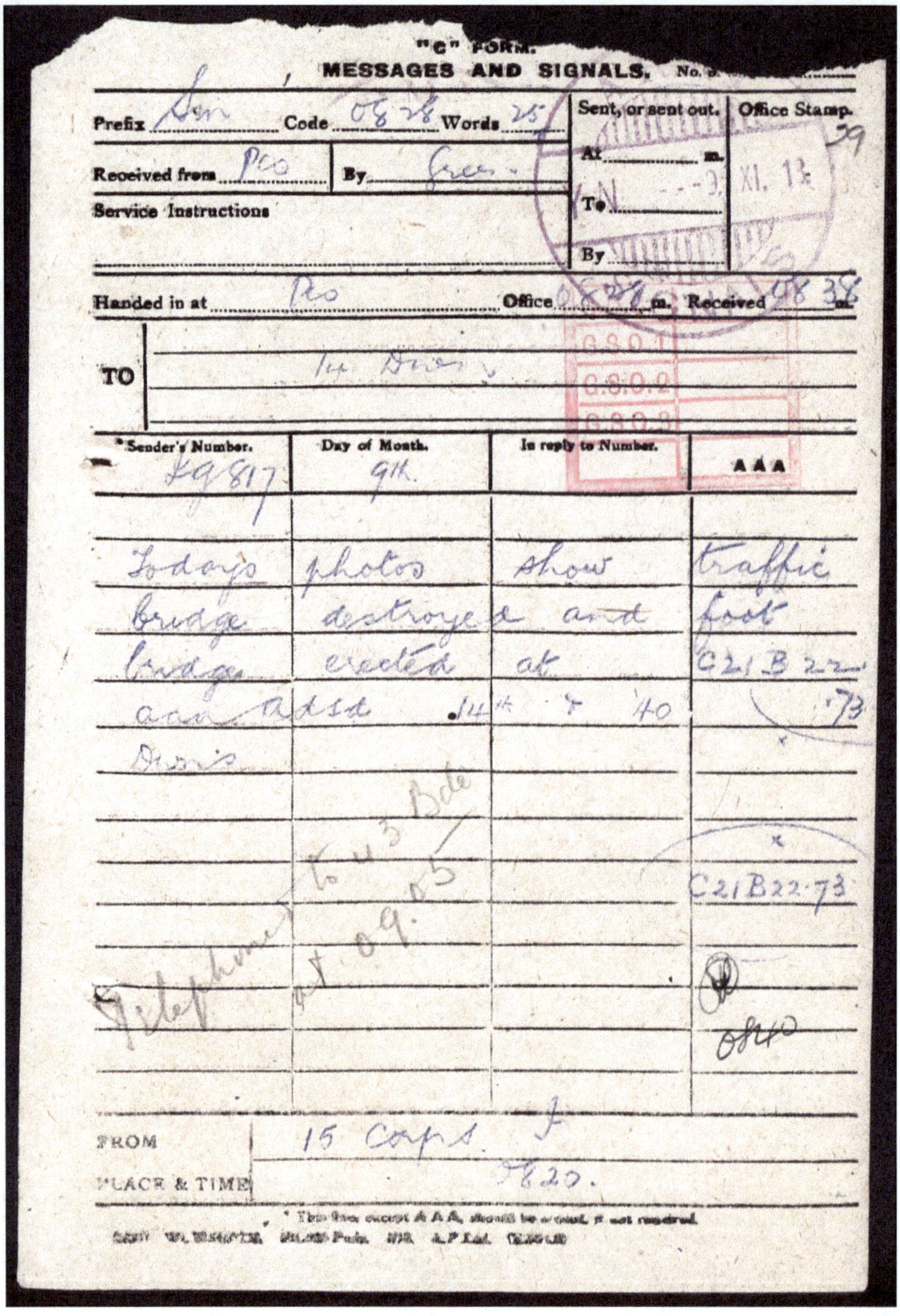

"C" FORM.
MESSAGES AND SIGNALS. No. ...

Prefix Sm	Code 08 28	Words 25	Sent, or sent out. At ... m. To ... By ...
Received from PCO	By Gree		Office Stamp. XI. 13
Service Instructions			

Handed in at Pco Office 08 2.. m. Received 08 38 m.

TO 1st Divn

G.S.O.1
G.S.O.2
G.S.O.3

*Sender's Number.	Day of Month.	In reply to Number.	AAA
Kq 817	9th		
Todays	photos	show	traffic
bridge	destroyed	and	foot
bridge	erected	at	C21B22.
aaa	addsd	14th	& 40	.73
Divns			

Telephoned to 43 Bde at 09.05

C21B22.73

0840

FROM 15 Corps

PLACE & TIME 0820.

* This line, except A A A, should be erased, if not required.

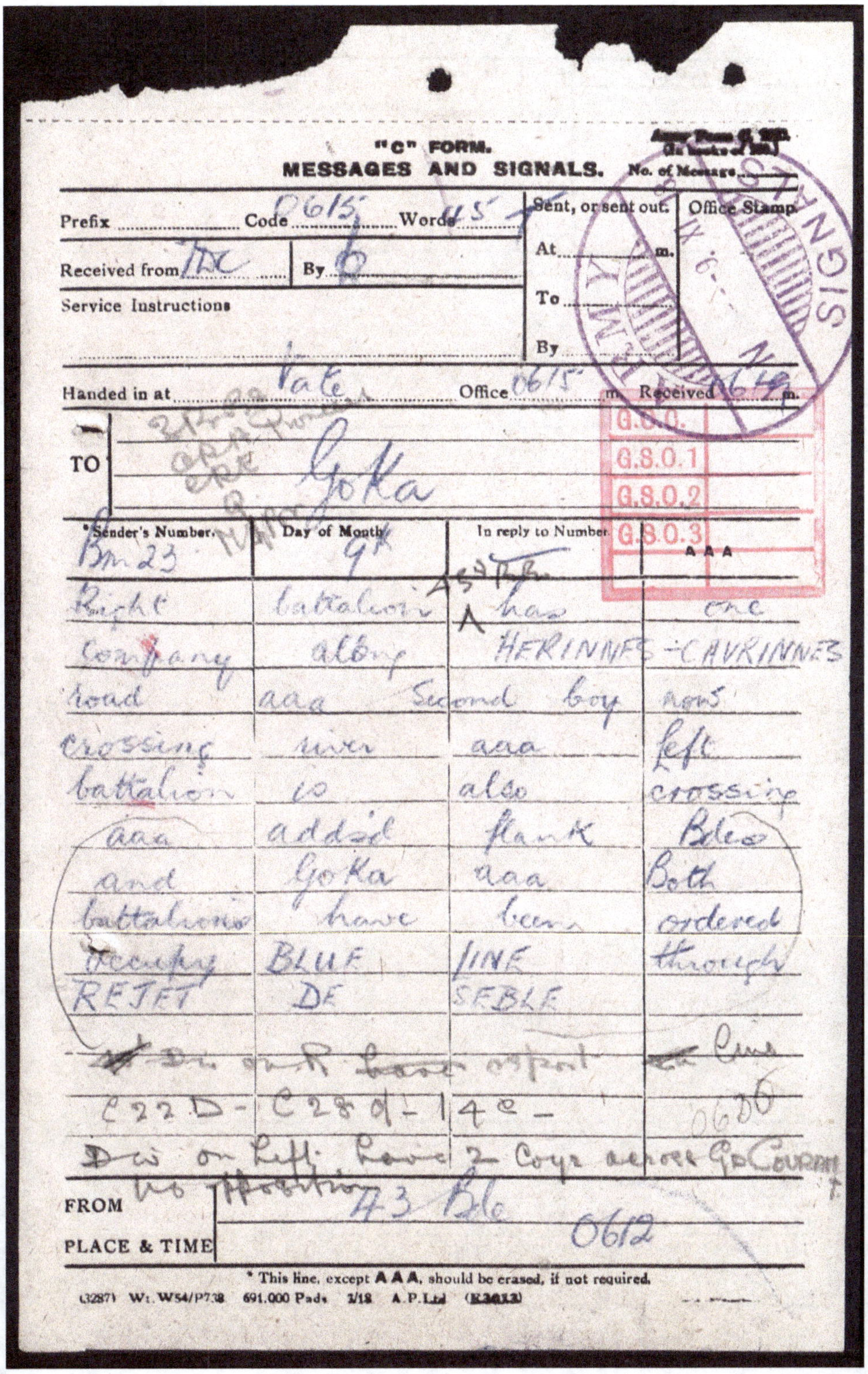

"C" FORM.
MESSAGES AND SIGNALS.

No. of Message

Prefix ______ Code 0615 Words 45

Received from TDC By G

Service Instructions

Sent, or sent out. At ___m. To ___ By ___

Office Stamp

Handed in at Vale Office 0615 m. Received 0649 m.

TO Goka

G.S.O.
G.S.O. 1
G.S.O. 2
G.S.O. 3

Sender's Number.	Day of Month	In reply to Number	AAA
BM 23	9th		
Right	battalion	has	one
company	along	HERINNES	-CAVRINNES
road	aaa	Second	boy
crossing	river	aaa	left
battalion	is	also	crossing
aaa	addsd	flank	Bdes
and	Goka	aaa	Both
battalions	have	been	ordered
occupy	BLUE	LINE	through
REJET	DE	SEBLE	

~~Div on R have~~ outpost ~~on~~ line

C22D- C28d- 14c- 0620

~~Div~~ on left have 2 Coys across G.d COURANT

FROM ~~no position~~ 43 Bde

PLACE & TIME 0612

* This line, except AAA, should be erased, if not required.

(3287) Wt. W54/P738 691,000 Pads 2/18 A.P.Ltd (E3613)

"A" Form.

Army Form C. 2121.
(In pads of 100.)

MESSAGES AND SIGNALS.

No. of Message ....

Prefix .... Code .... m. | Words. | Charge.

Office of Origin and Service Instructions.

Sent
At .... m.
To ....
By ....

This message is on a/c of:
.... *Service.*
(Signature of "Franking Officer.")

Recd. at .... m.
Date ....
From ....
By ....

G.O.C.
G.S.O 1
G.S.O 2
G.S.O 3

TO 15 CORPS
40 DIV
29 DIV

Sender's Number.	Day of Month.	In reply to Number.	
* G 346	9		AAA

Advanced Bde should be
on BLUE LINE 0930 AAA
Will not move forward
of this line before 0930
~~Acknowledge [illegible]~~

From 14 DIV
Place
Time 0823

The above may be forwarded as now corrected.
(Z)
.... *Censor.*
[illegible signature] Capt
Signature of Addressor or person authorised to telegraph in his name.

* This line, except **A A A**, should be erased if not required.

Wt. W 3253/P511. 500,000 Pads. 1/18. B. & S. Ltd. (E2389.)

TELEPHONE MESSAGE.

Date. 9. 11. 18 Time. 8.20

Office ringing ~~or rang~~ up. BGC 43 Bde

Officer spoken to. GSO3

MESSAGE

BGC reported that he hoped to have 2 battalions on BLUE LINE by 9.30 at which time he would move on to REDLINE.

He was moving 2 Coys of Reserve Battalion to HELCHIN at 0915

Action taken. Wire sent Corps & Flank Divs giving this information

[illegible] Signature
Capt

"A" Form. Army Form C. 2121, (In pads of 100.)

MESSAGES AND SIGNALS. No. of Message.........

Prefix.........Code.........m.	Words.	Charge.	This message is on a/c of:		Recd. at.........m.
Office of Origin and Service Instructions.			GOC		Date
~~URGENT~~	Sent		G.S.O.1	Service.	From
~~PRIORITY~~	At.........m.		G.S.O.2		By
~~OPERATIONS~~	To		G.S.O.3		
	By		(Signature of "Franking Officer.")		

TO 41/42/43 Inf. Bdes. CRA CRE 14 M.G.Bn Q ADMS

Sender's Number.	Day of Month.	In reply to Number.	
* G.O.99	9		AAA

Move to line EVREGNIES - DOTTIGNIES - COYGHEM aaa Be on the move by 12.00 aaa Bde. H.Q. will remain EVREGNIES aaa Addsd 42nd Bde reptd all concerned

From 14th Divn.
Place
Time 0825

The above may be forwarded as now corrected. (Z) [signature] Capt

Censor. Signature of Addressor or person authorised to telegraph in his name.

* This line, except **AAA**, should be erased if not required.

Wt. W 3253/P511. 500,000 Pads. 1/18. B. & S. Ltd. (E2389.)

Army Form C. 2121.
(In pads of 100.)

MESSAGES AND SIGNALS.

No. of Message..........

Prefix......... Code............m. | Words. | Charge.

Office of Origin and Service Instructions.

Sent
At..........m.
To
By

This message is on a/c of:
.... *Service.*
(Signature of "Franking Officer.")

Recd. at.......m.
Date
From
By

G.O.C.
G.S.O.1
G.S.O.2
G.S.O.3

TO 43 Inf Bde
CRA

Sender's Number.	Day of Month.	In reply to Number.	AAA
* G.O. 102	9		

40	DW	wire	begins
AAA	Patrols	nearing	CHEMIN
VERT	0600	AAA	Ends
AAA	Added	VATE	and
LOLA			

From 4 DW.
Place
Time 1015

The above may be forwarded as now corrected.
(Z)
.... *Censor.*
Signature of Addressor or person authorised to telegraph in his name. J Beaumont Capt

* This line, except **A A A**, should be erased if not required.

Wt. W 3253/P511. 500,000 Pads. 1/18. B. & S. Ltd. (E2389.)

TELEPHONE MESSAGE.

Date. 9 11. 18   Time. 11 20

Office ringing ~~or rang~~ up. G S O 3

Officer spoken to. B G C 43 Bde

M E S S A G E

B G C informed that 30th Div (X Corps) on left of 29th Div are on line of railway V 24 – D 4 d road D 5 a.

B G C reported 10th H L I (left Bn) on BLUE LINE 09 30, should be on RED LINE now. On reaching RED LINE he will order Bde to secure line CELLES – CLIPET to conform with 30th Div. This line will be handed over to 29th Div when they come up.

Action taken.

.........Signature [illegible] Capt

"C" FORM. Army Form C. 2123.
(In books of 100.)

MESSAGES AND SIGNALS. No. of Message

Prefix Sm Code 1147 Words 40
Received from PCO By Green
Service Instructions

Sent, or sent out. At m. To By
Office Stamp. SIGNALS
G.S.O.1 G.S.O.2 G.S.O.3

Handed in at PCO Office 1147 m. Received 1153 m.

TO 14 Divn

G.O.C. G.S.O.1 G.S.O.2 G.S.O.3

*Sender's Number.	Day of Month.	In reply to Number.	AAA
G259	9		
96	RUFF	is	transferred
forthwith	from	BADGER	to
HARRIET	and	will	be
attached	to	MIDGET	under
arrangements	to	be	made
by	TENCH	aaa	addsd
14	divn	rpd	10
Corps	GOCRA	and	Q15
Corps			

12.0

FROM
PLACE & TIME 15 Corps. 1145.

* This line, except AAA, should be erased, if not required.

(2827) Wt. W54/P730. 691,000 Pads. 3/18. A.P.Ltd. (E3013)

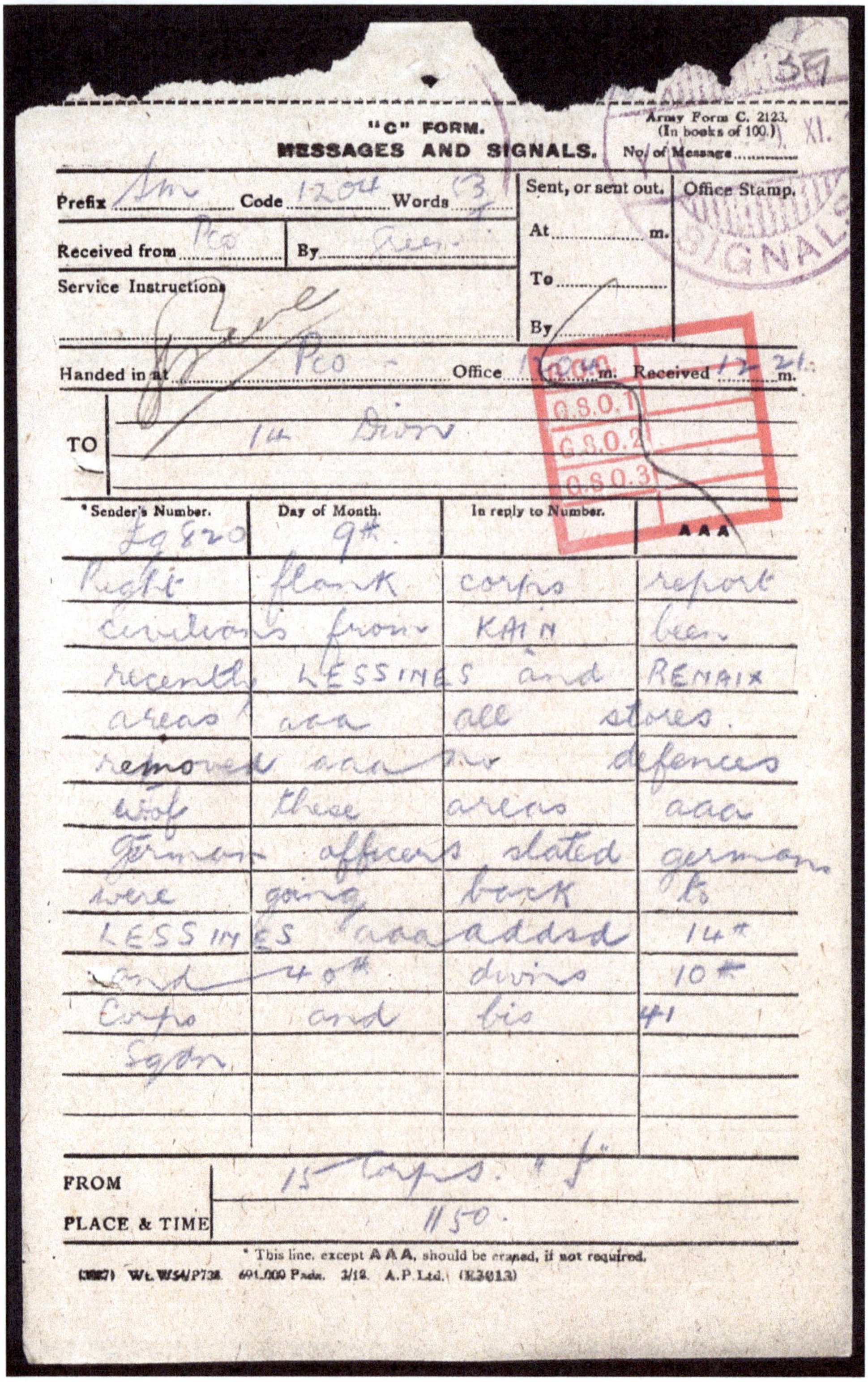

Army Form C. 2123.
(In books of 100.)

"C" FORM.

MESSAGES AND SIGNALS.

No. of Message ....

Prefix Am Code 1204 Words 13	Sent, or sent out.	Office Stamp.
Received from Pco By Green	At ....m.	SIGNALS XI.
Service Instructions	To	
	By	

Handed in at Pco Office 12.00 m. Received 12.21 m.

G.S.O.1 G.S.O.2 G.S.O.3

TO 14 Divn

* Sender's Number.	Day of Month.	In reply to Number.	AAA
Lg820	9th		
Right	flank	corps	report
civilians	from	KAIN	been
recently	LESSINES	and	RENAIX
areas	aaa	all	stores
removed	aaa	no	defences
W of	these	areas	aaa
German	officers	stated	germans
were	going	back	to
LESSINES	aaa	addsd	14th
and	40th	divns	10th
Corps	and	his	41
Sqdn			

FROM 15 Corps. "I"

PLACE & TIME 1150.

* This line, except AAA, should be erased, if not required.

(3827) Wt. W54/P738. 691,000 Pads. 3/18. A.P.Ltd. (E3013)

A.F. C. 2123.
(In ... of 100.)

"C" FORM.

MESSAGES AND SIGNALS.

No. of Message ...

Prefix: HQ | Code: 11.44 | Words: 100

Received from: PCO | By: Gun

Sent, or sent out. At ... m. To ... By ...

Office Stamp: YN -9. XI. 18 SIGNALS

Service Instructions: pty urgent Ops

Handed in at: ZBJ | Office: 11.40 m. | Received: 11.58 m.

G.O.C. / G.S.O.1 / G.S.O.2 / G.S.O.3

TO: 14 Div

*Sender's Number.	Day of Month.	In reply to Number.	AAA
G.S. 866	9th		

88 Bde will cross the river ESCAUT at once aaa Following moves will take place at once aaa 87 Bde to area vacated by 88 bde aaa 86th bde group to area vacated by 87 bde aaa 29th bn m g corps will detail one co to join 87 bde at once aaa 17th bde rfa will move to ST GENOIS and be ready to cross river at HELCHIN as soon as bridge is completed aaa addsd CRA 86 87 88 bdes 29 bn mg corps and Q and X corps 14 + 30th divs

FROM: 29 Div

PLACE & TIME: 12.05 (20)

* This line, except AAA, should be erased, if not required.

(3867) Wt. W54/P739. 691,000 Pads. 3/18. A.P.Ltd. (E3813)

57

GOC

Urgent Opns

Priority

TELEPHONE MESSAGE.

Date. 9. 11. 18 Time. 11.48

Office ringing ~~or rang~~ up. 29th Div G.

Officer spoken to. GSO3

MESSAGE

Asked when bridge at HELCHIN would be ready. Replied about 1630 but would not guarantee this. They report their troops on line of railway ~~16~~ 8, 9, & 10 at 10.30

Action taken. 43 Bde informed

[illegible] Signature
Capt

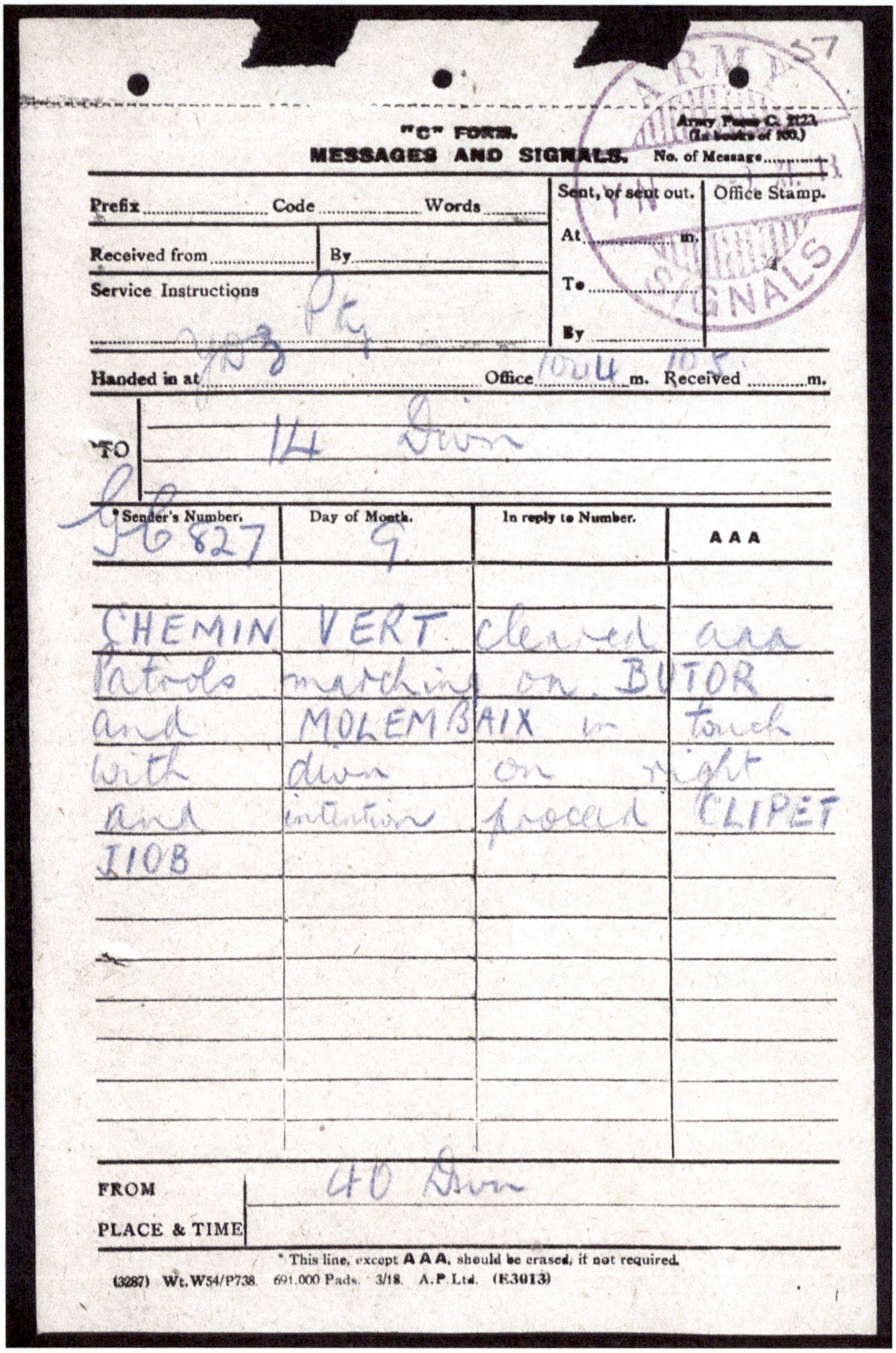

"C" FORM.
MESSAGES AND SIGNALS.

Army Form C. 2123.
(In books of 100.)
No. of Message.............

Prefix .... Code .... Words	Sent, or sent out. At ....m. To .... By ....
Received from .... By	Office Stamp. ARMY ... SIGNALS
Service Instructions	

Handed in at .... Office 1004 m. 10.5 Received ....m.

TO 14 Div

*Sender's Number.	Day of Month.	In reply to Number.	AAA
G 827	9		

CHEMIN	VERT	cleared	aaa
Ptys	marching	on	BUTOR
and	MOLEMBAIX	in	touch
with	divn	on	right
and	intention	proceed	CLIPET
I10B			

FROM 40 Div
PLACE & TIME

* This line, except AAA, should be erased, if not required.

(3287) Wt.W54/P738. 691,000 Pads. 3/18. A.P.Ltd. (E3013)

Army Form C. 2123.
(In books of 100.)

"C" FORM.

MESSAGES AND SIGNALS.

No. of Message ....

Prefix Am	Code 1147	Words 33	Sent, or sent out. At ....m. To .... By .... / Office Stamp. 14 DIV ... 9.XI.18 SIGNALS
Received from PCO	By [illegible]		
Service Instructions			

Handed in at 4153 Office 11.47 m. Received 12.40 m.

TO ~~14 Div~~ G ~~[illegible]~~

*Sender's Number.	Day of Month.	In reply to Number.	AAA
G5870	9.		
88	bde	report	trained
1040	aaa	are	advancing
to	line	of	railway F
in	D.8	9	and
10	aaa	Bde	hq
11.88D48	aaa	adsd	corps
flank	divs		
U18D4.8			

FROM
PLACE & TIME 29 Div G 1145

* This line, except AAA, should be erased, if not required.

(1887) Wt. W54/P738 691,000 Pads. 2/18. A.P.Ltd. (E3813)

Army Form C. 2123
(In books of 100.)

"C" FORM.

MESSAGES AND SIGNALS. No. of Message

Prefix Vm Code 1200 Words 12

Received from PCO By Green

Service Instructions

Sent, or sent out. At m. To By

Office Stamp. YN ... SIGNALS

Handed in at 3HH Office 1200 m. Received 1324 m.

TO ~~Bde~~ G.1 (for information)

G.O.C.
G.S.O. 1
G.S.O. 2
G.S.O. 3

* Sender's Number.	Day of Month.	In reply to Number.	AAA
Bm5	9th		

CELLES clear of enemy

FROM
PLACE & TIME 88 Bde 1200.

* This line, except AAA, should be erased, if not required.

W.... G.S.O. Pads. A.F.I.M. (E3013)

"C" FORM.

MESSAGES AND SIGNALS. No. of Message..........

Prefix SO Code 1144 Words 100

Received from PCO By Green

Service Instructions

pty. Urgent Operations

Sent, or sent out. At ......m. To ...... By ......

Office Stamp. YN SIGNALS

G.O.C. G.S.O. I G.S.O. II G.S.O. III

Handed in at YB 9 Office 1144 m. Received 1208 m.

TO 14 Divn

*Sender's Number.	Day of Month.	In reply to Number.	AAA
GS 868	9th.		

88 Bde will cross the river ESCAUT at once aaa Following moves will take place at once aaa 87 Bde to area vacated by 88 bde aaa 86th bde group to area vacated by 87 bde aaa 29th bn mg corps will detail one co to join 87 bde at once aaa 17th bde rfa will move to STGENOIS and be ready to cross river at HELCHIN as soon as bridge is completed aaa addsd CRA 86 87 88 bdes 29 bn mg corps and Q and X corps 14 & 30th divns

FROM 29 Divn

PLACE & TIME 12.05

* This line, except AAA, should be erased, if not required.

(2867) Wt. W54/P738. 691,000 Pads. 3/18. A.P.Ltd. (E3013)

G. 57

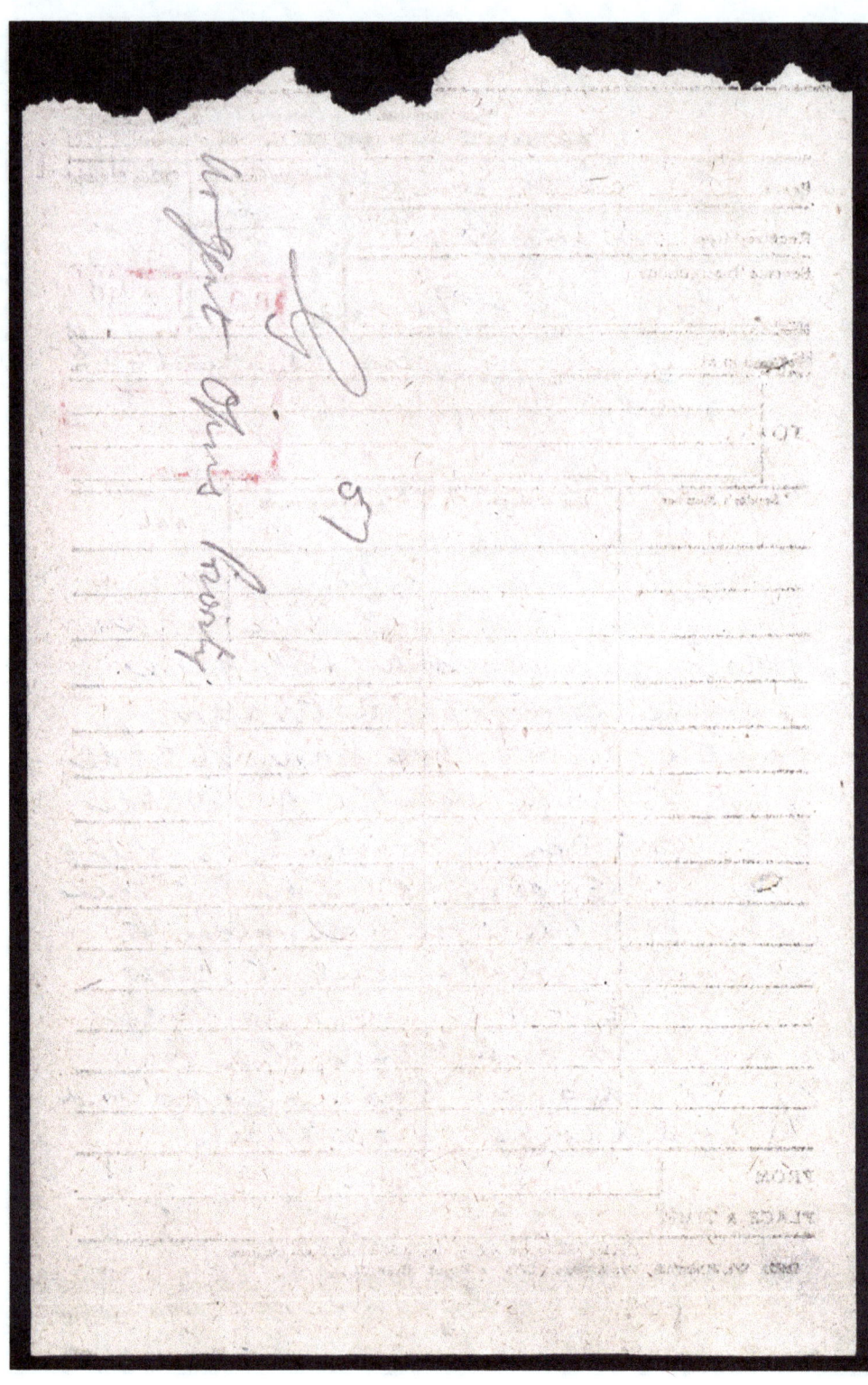

Urgent Ops Priority

Army Form C. 2123.
(In books of 100.)

"C" FORM.

MESSAGES AND SIGNALS. No. of Message 68

Prefix SM Code 1320 Words 60	Sent, or sent out. At .... m. To .... By ....
Received from PCo By Raf.	Office Stamp: YN SIGN
Service Instructions Pty – Ypz	
Handed in at .... Office 1320 m. Received 1323 m.	

TO 14th Devon

* Sender's Number.	Day of Month.	In reply to Number.	AAA
GC833	9		
outposts	have	been	established
on	line	CLIPET	J10B
to	MENHART	J5A	to
E	of	LA	BACOTTERIE
D28B	aaa	brigade	Hqrs
CHEMIN VERT		aaa	forward
roads	recommended	LA RIVAGE	to
Cross	roads	I4B	thence T Road
junction	C28D	Chemin	vert aaa
Support	Bde	Hdqs	and warcoing
Hqrs	Recq	aaa	addsd 15 Corps
&	flank	Divs	

FROM / PLACE & TIME 40 Devon 1300

* This line, except A A A, should be erased, if not required.

(2) Wt. W54/P738. 691,000 Pads. 3/18. A.P.Ltd. (E.3013)

Army Form C. 2123.
(In books of 100.)

"C" FORM.

MESSAGES AND SIGNALS. No. of Message..........

Prefix SM Code 1418 Words 84

Received from Pc By Rose

Service Instructions
Pco

Sent, or sent out. At.........m. To......... By.........

Office Stamp
YN ... SIGN

Handed in at .... Office 1418 m. Received ......m.

TO 14th Div

*Sender's Number.	Day of Month.	In reply to Number.	AAA
Yg821	9		

air observers report aaa 12.25 large explosion
bridge over railway at BIEST S of RENAIX
aaa 12.30 RENAIX deserted no civilians seen
aaa 12.35 aa & mg fire from ELLEZELLES
FLOBECQ QUESNAU BOIS DELENZE aaa aa
fire from Houtaing Chapelle a Wattines
(W of Ath) 12.40 aaa all railway junctions
in Renaix demolished aaa railway lines to
Renaix systematically destroyed aaa line past
Renaix to Flobecq destroyed aaa addsd
14th & 40th Divs repeated 10th Corps
"G"

FROM
PLACE & TIME 15 Corps "G" 13.45

* This line, except A A A, should be erased, if not required.

(C887) Wt. W54/P738. 691,000 Pads. 3/18. A.P.Ltd. (E3013)

"A" Form

Army Form C. 2121
(In pads of 100.)

MESSAGES AND SIGNALS.

No. of Message..............

Prefix.......... Code..........m	Words. Charge.	This message is on a/c of:	Recd. at..........m.
Office of Origin and Service Instructions	Sent	.... Service.	Date..............
	At..........m.		From ....
	To..............		
	By..............	(Signature of "Franking Officer.")	By ....

TO { 48th Inf BB.
29th Divn
40th Divne

Sender's Number.	Day of Month.	In reply to Number.	AAA
* G 104	9th		

48th	Inf	BB	will
secure	the	line	CELLES
CLIPET	to	conform	with
30th	and	40th	Divns
AAA	48th	BB	will
hand	over	this	line
to	29th	Divn	as
they	come	up.	

G.O.C.
G.S.O 1
G.S.O 2
G.S.O 3

12.10

From 14th Divn
Place
Time

[illegible]
Capt

The above may be forwarded as now corrected. (Z)

Censor. Signature of Addressor or person authorised to telegraph in his name.

* This line should be erased if not required.

(902) Wt. W2020/P911 200,000 Bks. 2/18 C. & Co. (E802)

"A" Form
MESSAGES AND SIGNALS.

Army Form C. 2121
(In pads of 100.)

No. of Message..............

Prefix.............. Code..............m | Words. | Charge.
Office of Origin and Service Instructions

Sent
At..................m.
To..................
By..................

This message is on a/c of:
..................Service.
(Signature of "Franking Officer.")

G.O.C.
G.S.O.1
G.S.O.2
G.S.O.3

Recd. at..........m.
Date..................
From..................
By..................

TO 43 Inf Bde

Sender's Number.	Day of Month.	In reply to Number.	AAA
GO 106	7		

Corps	message	reads	AAA
Right	flank	corps	report
civilians	from	RAIN	been
recently	LESSINES	and	RENAIX
areas	AAA	all	stores
removed	AAA	No	defences
W of	these	areas	AAA
German	officers	stated	Germans
were	going	back	to
LESSINES	AAA	message	ends

From 14 Div
Place
Time 12 30

The above may be forwarded as now corrected. (Z)
....
Censor.

Signature of Addressor or person authorised to telegraph in his name.

* This line should be erased if not required.

(4715) Wt. W3253/P511 1,113,336 Shts. 2/18 C. & Co. (.634)

"A" Form
MESSAGES AND SIGNALS.

Army Form C. 2121
(In pads of 100.)

No. of Message..........

Prefix.......... Code .... m. | Words | Charge.

Office of Origin and Service Instructions

Sent
At..........m.
To..........
By..........

This message is on a/c of:
G.O.C. .... Service.
G.S.O.1
G.S.O.2
G.S.O.3
(Signature of "Franking Officer.")

Recd. at........m.
Date..........
From..........
By..........

TO { C.R.A.

Sender's Number.	Day of Month.	In reply to Number.	AAA
G.O. 105	9		

~~The following~~ Message from XV Corps reads 96th A.F.A. Bde is transferred forthwith from XV Corps to X Corps and will be attached to 29 Div under arrangements to be made by 14 Div AAA message ends AAA for your information and necessary action

From 14 Div
Place
Time 1210

The above may be forwarded as now corrected. (Z) [signature] Capt G.S.

.... Censor. Signature of Addresser or person authorised to telegraph in his name.

* This line should be erased if not required.

(1806.) Wt. W12952/M1294. 187,500 Pads. 1/17 H.P.Ltd.,S. (E. 818).

62

Army Form C. 2123.
(In books of 100.)

"C" FORM.
MESSAGES AND SIGNALS.
No. of Message........

Prefix	Code	Words	Sent, or sent out.	Office Stamp
Received from 82C	By LKB		At YN m.	9. XI. 18 SIGNALS
Service Instructions.			To	
			By	

Handed in at Vate Office 1235 m. Received 1244 m.

G.O.C. / G.S.O.1 / G.S.O.2 / G.S.O.3

TO 14 Div.
~~88 Inf Bde~~
~~119 Inf Bde~~

*Sender's Number.	Day of Month.	In reply to Number.	AAA
BM27	9		
Am	moving	HQ	now
to	29/U29	A23	HELCHIN aaa
Addsd	Div	all	Bns
and	Flank	Bdes	

Sigs informed by phone 1250

FROM
PLACE & TIME Vate 1235

* This line, except AAA, should be erased, if not required.

(8827) Wt. W54/P738. 691,000 Pads. 3/18. A.P.Ltd. (E.3013)

D. D. & L., London, E.C.
(6561). Wt. W8419/M92) 50,000 Pads. 11/16 E 800.

Army Form C 2122

"B" Form.

MESSAGES AND SIGNALS.

No. of Message.................

Prefix XM Code 1300 m.

Office of Origin and Service Instructions. BG 314

Words. 20

Received At 1332 m. From PCo By Rafter

Sent At.........m. To......... By.........

Office Stamp.

G.O.C.
G.S.O.1
G.S.O.2
G.S.O.3

TO 43 Bde

Sender's Number J 101 | Day of Month 9 | In reply to Number | AAA

our troops now approaching
1st objective aaa CELLES reports
clear of enemy

From 88 Bde 1240
Place
Time

* This line should be erased if not required.

(1390) Wt. W 9044-1194. 12/14. 40,000 Pads. S. B. Ltd.

"B" Form.

Army Form C. 2122.

MESSAGES AND SIGNALS.

No. of Message

Prefix Xhr Code 1245 m.	Received	Sent	Office Stamp.
Office of Origin and Service Instructions. Yoba — Words. 37	At 1322 m. From 3DC By Gbb.	At m. To By	G.O.C. / G.S.O 1 / G.S.O 2 / G.S.O 3

TO { Sage

Sender's Number	Day of Month	In reply to Number	AAA
* ZF123	9		

One	section	across	now	in
U30	mules	swum	across	advancing
SE	AAA	One	section	less
pack	transport	across	at	LANWOY
two	remaining	section	at	TROIS
FARM	waiting	pontoon	bridge	at
C5A				

D Coy MG Batt

From Warren

Place

Time 1245

* This line should be erased if not required.

G.O.C.	
G.S.O.1	
G.S.O.2	
G.S.O.3	

ADDRESSED and REPEATED

41 Inf.Bde.	XV Corps
42 Inf.Bde.	[illegible] Divn.
43 Inf.Bde.	43 Divn.
[illegible]	4.
[illegible]	
14th [illegible] Bn.	

G. 347 9 AAA

Divisional Report Centre will open at [illegible] B5a4.8 at 1800 AAA Added. [illegible] [illegible] [illegible] [illegible] [illegible] [illegible] Corps flank Divisions and 4.

14 Division

[illegible]

D. D. & L., London, E.C.
(6561). Wt. W8419/M920 50,000 Pads. 11/16 E 500.

Army Form C 2122.

"B" Form.

MESSAGES AND SIGNALS.

No. of Message..................

Prefix XB Code 1412 m.		Received	Sent	Office Stamp.
Office of Origin and Service Instructions.	Words.	At 1502 m.	At ....m.	G.O.C.
3 HH		From PCO	To....	G.S.O.1 / G.S.O.2
PCy	22	By Ray	By....	G.S.O.3

TO 43rd Bde

Sender's Number	Day of Month	In reply to Number	AAA
BMS	9		

leinsters	and	worcesters	on	line
of	road	D13D 29	aaa	Concentration
in	D16			

From	88 Bde	1450	
Place			
Time			

* This line should be erased if not required.

"A" Form

Army Form C. 2121
(In pads of 100.)

MESSAGES AND SIGNALS.

No. of Message..............

Prefix............ Code..............m | Words. | Charge.

Office of Origin and Service Instructions

Sent
At......................m.
To.........................
By.........................

This message is on a/c of:

.... Service.

G.O.C.

....
(Signature of "Franking Officer.")

Recd. at..........m.
Date..................
From..................
By....................

TO 43 Bde

Sender's Number.	Day of Month.	In reply to Number.	AAA
*G0107	9		

message	from	40 Div	reads AAA
Outposts	have	been	established
on line	CLIPET	J10B	to
MENHART	J5a	to	E of
LA	BACOTTERIE	Road	AAA
brigade	Hqrs	CHEMIN	VERT
AAA	forward	roads	recommended
LA RIVAGE	to	CROSS	roads
I4b	hence	T Road	Junction
C28d	CHEMIN	VERT	AAA
Support	Bde	PECQ	and
WARCOING	Hqrs	PECQ	AAA
ends	AAA.		

From 14 Div.
Place
Time

The above may be forwarded as now corrected. (Z)

....
Censor.

[illegible] Capt. G.S.
Signature of Addressor or person authorised to telegraph in his name.

* This line should be erased if not required.

(4715) Wt. W3253/P511 1,113,336 Shts. 9/18 C. & Co. (.634)

"A" Form
MESSAGES AND SIGNALS.

Army Form C. 2121
(In pads of 100.)

No. of Message............

Prefix.............. Code..............m	Words. Charge.	This message is on a/c of:	G.O.C. / G.S.O. 1 / G.S.O. 2 / G.S.O. 3	Recd. at............m.
Office of Origin and Service Instructions	Sent	..................Service.		Date..............
	At..................m.			From ....
	To..................			
	By..................	(Signature of "Franking Officer.")		By..........

TO — 43 Inf Bde

Sender's Number.	Day of Month.	In reply to Number.	AAA
* G.O. 108	9		

~~ag~~	~~Bw~~	~~www~~	
88th	Bde	reported	at
1300	on	line	of
road	E 14 a 06	D24	central
J 5 c	08	aaa	Bde
HQ	U 26 c	35	

From 14 Division
Place
Time

The above may be forwarded as now corrected. (Z) [signature] Lt Col.

Censor. — Signature of Addressor or person authorised to telegraph in his name.

* This line should be erased if not required.

(4715) Wt. W3253/P511 1,113,336 Shts. 2/18 C. & Co. (..634)

"A" Form

Army Form C. 2121
(In pads of 100.)

MESSAGES AND SIGNALS.

No. of Message..............

Prefix.............. Code..............m | Words. | Charge.

Office of Origin and Service Instructions

Sent
At..................m.
To..................
By..................

This message is on a/c of:

.... *Service.*

(Signature of "Franking Officer.")

Recd. at..........m.
Date..............
From..............
By..............

G.O.C.
G.S.O.1
G.S.O.2
G.S.O.3

TO 15 Corps

Sender's Number.	Day of Month.	In reply to Number.	AAA
* G.O. 109	9		

Locations of HQ AAA
43 Inf Bde HELCHIN AAA
~~??~~ otherwise unchanged

From 14 Div.
Place
Time

The above may be forwarded as now corrected. (Z)

Censor.

Signature of Addressor or person authorised to telegraph in his name.
J. H. ... Johnston Lt Col. G.S.

* This line should be erased if not required.

(4715) Wt. W3253/P511 1,113,336 Sbts. 2/18 C. & Co. (..684)

Army Form C. 2121.
(In pads of 100.)

"A" Form.
MESSAGES AND SIGNALS.

No. of Message..........

Prefix......... Code............m. Office of Origin and Service Instructions. [illegible]	Words. Charge. Sent At.........m. To By	This message is on a/c of: .... Service. (Signature of "Franking Officer.") [stamp: G.O.C. / G.S.O.1 / G.S.O.2 / G.S.O.3]	Recd. at.......m. Date From By

TO: 43 BDE

Sender's Number.	Day of Month.	In reply to Number.	AAA
G 306	9	satisfied that	

As	soon	as	29
DIV	have	covered	your
front	reorganise	and	billet
in	MOLENBAIX	area	

From	14 DIV
Place	
Time	14 28

The above may be forwarded as now corrected. (Z) [illegible signature]

Censor. Signature of Addressor or person authorised to telegraph in his name.

* This line, except **A A A**, should be erased if not required.

Wt. W 3253/P511. 500,000 **Pads.** 1/18. B. & S. Ltd. (E2386.)

"A" Form

MESSAGES AND SIGNALS.

Army Form C. 2121
(In pads of 100.)

No. of Message..............

Prefix............ Code............m	Words.	Charge.	This message is on a/c of:	G.O.C. / G.S.O.1 / G.S.O.2 / G.S.O.3	Recd. at.........m.
Office of Origin and Service Instructions	Sent		........................Service.		Date..............
Urgent Ops	At..............m.				From ....
	To..............				
	By..............		(Signature of "Franking Officer.")		By..............

TO 43 Inf Bde

Sender's Number.	Day of Month.	In reply to Number.	AAA
* G.347	9		

Troops	must	not	be
quartered	in	MOLEMBAIX	
owing	to	gas	shelling
aaa	Billeting	areas	to
be	selected	by	BGC
further	West		

From 14 Dw
Place
Time 1530

The above may be forwarded as now corrected. (Z) (sd) [illegible]

....
Censor. Signature of Addressor or person authorised to telegraph in his name.

* This line should be erased if not required.

(4715) Wt. W3253/P511 1,113,336 Shts. 2/18 C. & Co. (.634)

86

Army Form C. 2123.
(In books of 100.)

"C" FORM.
MESSAGES AND SIGNALS. No. of Message

Prefix Sm Code 1550 Words 22

Received from Pca By Nay

Service Instructions
Pca

Sent, or sent out.
At ... m.
To
By

Office Stamp
YN ... XI. 18.
SIGNALS

G.O.O.
G.S.O.1
G.S.O.2
G.S.O.3 C

Handed in at ... Office ... m. Received ... 20 m.

TO 14th Divn

*Sender's Number.	Day of Month.	In reply to Number.	AAA
G265	9		
troops	must	avoid	MOLEMBAIX
and	vicinity	owing	to
gas	shelling	aaa	addsd
14	+	HQ	Divns

FROM
PLACE & TIME 15 Corps 1545

* This line, except A A A, should be erased, if not required.

(C287) Wt. W54/P738. 691,000 Pads. 3/18. A.P.Ltd. (E3013)

Army Form C. 2123.
(In books of 100.)

" FORM.

MESSAGES AND SIGNALS.

No. of Message 90

Prefix Sm	Code 1634	Words 60	Sent, or sent out.	Office Stamp.
Received from PCO	By Ref		At ... m.	YN
Service Instructions PCO			To ...	SIGNA
			By ...	

Handed in at ... Office 1632m. Received ... m.

TO 14th Div

*Sender's Number.	Day of Month.	In reply to Number.	AAA
G265	9th		
Sitn	1530	aaa	40th
Divn	report	touch	with
59th	Divn	in	J10
&	14th	Divn	in
D29	aaa	party	of
enemy	Cavalry	reported	in

VELAINES at 12.00 aaa air observers report 2 Germans in RENAIX 1345 otherwise place deserted aaa mg fire from BERGNEAU F13 at 1350 aaa addsd Second Army repeated all concerned

G.O.C.
G.S.O. 1
G.S.O. 2
G.S.O. 3

FROM
PLACE & TIME 15 Corps 1610

* This line, except A A A, should be erased, if not required.

(3887) Wt. W54/P738. 691,000 Pads. 3/18. A.P. Ltd. (E3913)

MESSAGES A

Prefix .... Code............m. | Words. | Charge.

Office of Origin and Service Instructions.

Sent
At ....m.
To
By

This message is on a/c of: ....*Service.*

(Signature of "Franking Officer.")

Recd. at ....m.
Date
From
By

G.O.C.
C.S.O 1
C.S.O 2
C.S.O.3

TO XV Corps
29' Div.

Sender's Number.	Day of Month.	In reply to Number.	
*G 348	9		AAA

Pontoon bridge at HELCHIN
C.S.B now through

From 14' Div
Place
Time 1730

The above may be forwarded as now corrected. (Z)

Censor.

Signature of Addressor or person authorised to telegraph in his name. [illegible]

* This line, except AAA, should be erased if not required.

Wt. W 3253/P511. 500,000 Pads. 1/18. B. & S. Ltd. (E2389.)

"C" FORM.
MESSAGES AND SIGNALS.

Army Form C. 2123.
(In books of 100.)
No. of Message.........

Prefix [illegible] Code 1830 Words 92

Received from PO By [illegible]

Service Instructions

Sent, or sent out.
At .... m.
To ....
By ....

Office Stamp.

Handed in at PO Office 1830 m. Received 1836 m.

TO 14 Divn

* Sender's Number.	Day of Month.	In reply to Number.	AAA
G456	9		

Evening report aaa 40
Divn outposts established on
line LECLIPPET J10 b MENHART
J5a LABACOTTERYE J28 a aaa
In touch with Div on
flanks aaa Cyclists
ordered forward but no
report yet received aaa
124 Bde on objective
and troops being disposed
in depth aaa Pontoon
bridges at HECA and
HELCHIN and foot bridge
WARCOING expected completed

FROM
PLACE & TIME

* This line, except A A A, should be erased, if not required.

Army Form C. 2123.
(In books of 100.)

"C" FORM.

MESSAGES AND SIGNALS. No. of Message............

Prefix .... Code .... Words ....

Received from .... By ....

Service Instructions

Sent, or sent out. At ......m. To ...... By 1831

Office Stamp.

Handed in at 14 D Office ......m. Received ......m.

TO

*Sender's Number.	Day of Month.	In reply to Number.	AAA

this evening but causeway impassable to transport for many hours that area under 2nd Army reports all [illegible]

FROM 15th Corps

PLACE & TIME 1755

* This line, except AAA, should be erased, if not required.

(6627) Wt. W30/P130. 500,000 Pads. 2/18. A.P. Ltd. (E.2682)

Army Form C. 2121
(In books of 100.)

"C" FORM.
MESSAGES AND SIGNALS. No. of Message.........

Prefix Sm Code .... Words ....

Received from APAR By [illegible]

Service Instructions

Sent, or sent out. At .... m. To .... By ....

Office Stamp. SIGNALS

Handed in at VATE Office 1900 m. Received 2059 m.

TO GOKA

*Sender's Number.	Day of Month.	In reply to Number.	AAA
BM28	9		

Information received from GOKA that 40TH and 29th Divns are in touch across our front aaa You will therefore concentrate in billets W of MOLEMBAIX aaa No troops to be billetted in MOLEMBAIX owing to gas aaa Rations will be delivered to FRESNOY FARM C24c61 aaa Company areas to be reported to this office aaa acknowledge

G.O.C.
G.S.O.1
G.S.O.2
G.S.O.3

FROM
PLACE & TIME VATE 1705

* This line, except A A A, should be erased, if not required.

to 4

Army Form C. 2123.
(In books of 100.)

"C" FORM.

MESSAGES AND SIGNALS. No. of Message..........

Prefix .... Code .... Words	Sent, or sent out. At .... m. To .... By	Office Stamp.
Received from .... By		
Service Instructions		
Handed in at PCO Office 1850 m.		Received 1956 m.

G.O.C. / G.S.O. 1 / G.S.O. 2 / G.S.O. 3

ARMY SIGNALS

TO 14 Divn

*Sender's Number.	Day of Month.	In reply to Number.	AAA
G 248	8		
Cyclist	battn	will	place
one	Company	at	disposal
of	each	Divn	forthwith
aaa	One	officer	to
report	to	each	Divl
Comdr	for	Orders	at
once	aaa	Cyclist	Battn
less	Two	Coys	will
be	in	Corps	Reserve
aaa	added	Cyclist	Bn
Reptd	14	4	40
Divns	and	15	Corps
& "Q"			

FROM 15th Corps

PLACE & TIME 1845

* This line, except A A A, should be erased, if not required.

Fixed with O.C. Coy
G.S.O. 1

Army Form C. 2123.
(In books of 100.)

"C" FORM.
MESSAGES AND SIGNALS.

No. of Message ...

Prefix ... Code ... Words ...

Sent, or sent out. At ... m. To ... By ...

Office Stamp.

Received from ... By ...

Service Instructions

Handed in at ... Office ... m. Received ... m.

TO 14th Divn

*Sender's Number.	Day of Month.	In reply to Number.	AAA
G 152	1		

Corps moves east tomorrow aaa 40 Divn to billet in depth LANNOY to CHEMIN-VERT aaa 14th Div in depth HERSEAUX DOTTIGNIES WARCOING RUJET DE SEBLE aaa area north of GD ESPIERRES river to be cleared as far as possible for 10 Corps aaa bridging and road repairs to continue under divs as already ordered aaa 18th

FROM

PLACE & TIME

* This line, except AAA, should be erased, if not required.

(2827) Wt. W3007/38. 600,000 Pads. 2/16. A.P. Ltd. (E.2083)

"C" FORM.
MESSAGES AND SIGNALS.

Army Form C. 2123.
(In books of 100.)
No. of Message

Prefix ___ Code ___ Words ___

Received from ___ By ___

Service Instructions

Sent, or sent out.
At ___ m.
To ___
By ___

Office Stamp.
1836

Handed in at ___ Office ___ m. Received ___ m.

TO

*Sender's Number.	Day of Month.	In reply to Number.	AAA
Corps	to	have	priority
on	BELCHIN	Bridge	and
11th	Div	to	have
priority	over	40th	Div
for	traffic	on	WARCOING
Bridge	aaa	Not	more
than	one	Bde	each
Div	east	of	River
aaa	Divs	to	keep
touch	with	situation	by
cyclist	patrols	aaa	ACKNOWLEDGE
aaa	added	11th	40
Div	and	10th	Corps
rep	Second	Army	11th

FROM Corps GOCRA "Q" ADMS
PLACE & TIME and CE

* This line, except AAA, should be erased, if not required.

15 Corps
1820

Ack GR452

"C" FORM.
MESSAGES AND SIGNALS.

Army Form C. 2123 (In books of 100.)

No. of Message 108

Prefix ... Code ... Words	Sent, or sent out. At ... m. To ... By ...	Office Stamp.
Received from ... By ...		
Service Instructions Priority		

Handed in at Y53 Office ... m. Received 2019 m.

G.O.C.
G.S.O.1
G.S.O.2
G.S.O.3

TO 1st Divn

*Sender's Number.	Day of Month.	In reply to Number.	AAA
JC 845	9		

our troops entered VELAINES
1300 and in touch
with Divn on right
aaa asking Corps
right flank driving

10.25

FROM 1st Div
PLACE & TIME

* This line, except A A A, should be erased, if not required.

(8827) Wt. W3009/T.M. 600,000 Pads. 3/16. A.P. Ltd. (E.3003/0)

137

"C" FORM.
MESSAGES AND SIGNALS.

Army Form C. 2121 (In books of 100.)

No. of Message

Prefix	Code	Words	Sent, or sent out.	Office Stamp.
Received from	By		At m.	
Service Instructions 2 of six adds			To	
			By	

Handed in at VATE Office 22.15 m. Received 22.25 m.

TO Goka

G.O.C. / G.S.O.1 / G.S.O.2 / G.S.O.3

* Sender's Number.	Day of Month.	In reply to Number.	AAA
BM30	9		

Unexploded mine reported at Cross Roads C12B77 aaa Addsd Goka repeated Brigade Units

Acquaint CRE

22.30

FROM VATE

PLACE & TIME 22.15

* This line, except A A A, should be erased, if not required.

W. & S. 200,000 Pads. 1918. A.P.Ltd. (E.3613)

"A" Form

Army Form C. 2121
(In pads of 100.)

MESSAGES AND SIGNALS.

No. of Message..............

Prefix.............. Code..............m | Words. | Charge.

Office of Origin and Service Instructions

Sent

At..................m.

To..................

By..................

This message is on a/c of:

..................*Service.*

(Signature of "Franking Officer.")

Recd. at..........m.

Date..............

From..............

By..............

G.O.C.
G.S.O. 1
G.S.O. 2
G.S.O. 3

TO C.R.E.

Sender's Number.	Day of Month.	In reply to Number.	AAA
* GO 110	9		

Following from ~~VIII E~~ 43rd Bde aaa unexploded mines reported at Cross Roads C12 b 77

From 14 Div.

Place

Time 22.45

The above may be forwarded as now corrected. (Z)

....

Censor.

Signature of Addressor or person authorised to telegraph in his name.

[signature] Capt

* This line should be erased if not required.

(4715) Wt. W3253/P911 1,113,336 Shts. 2/18 C. & Co. (..684)

SECRET.

Copy No. 20.

OPERATION ORDER No. 21 by Colonel J. Hay Campbell, D.S.O., A.M.S., Commanding R.A.M.Corps, 14th Division ... ...

---------------------------- oOo ----------------------------

G.O.C.	
G.S.O.1	
G.S.O.2	
G.S.O.3	

Reference Maps:- Sheets, 29 and 37, 1/40,000.

1. O.C., 44th Field Ambulance will move the Advanced Dressing Station to ESPIERRES Chateau, 37/C.2 d 8.5. by 1250 on November 9th.

2. The Main Dressing Station will remain for the present at WATTRELOS.

Field Ambulances to acknowledge.

A.D.M.S. 9/11/18. Date 14th DIVISION

A. R. Saint
Major
for Colonel, A.D.M.S.,
14th Division.

Distribution:-

1-3. Field Ambulances.
4-18. R.M.Os.
19. 14 M.A.C.
20. 14th Div: "G".
21. " " "A".
22. C.R.A., 14th Divn:
23. C.R.E., " "
24. 14th Signal Coy, R.E.
25. D.G.O., 14th Divn:
26. H.Q., 41st Inf: Bde.
27. " " 42nd " "
28. " " 43rd " "
29. 14th Div: Train.
30. D.D.M.S., XV Corps.
31. A.D.M.S., 29th Divn:
32. " " " " 40th "
33-34. War Diary.
35. File.

GENERAL STAFF, 14TH DIVISION.
No.......
Date.......
File.......

G.O.C.
G.S.O.1
G.S.O.2
G.S.O.3

S E C R E T

Copy No. 17

14th DIVISION ORDER No. 241.

Ref. Sheets
29 and 37, 1/40,000

9 November 1918

1. 14th Division will billet tomorrow S. of ESPIERRES River: 43rd Infantry Brigade Group, REJET DE SEBLES area and WARCOING (one Battn. to be West of R. ESCAUT), Brigade H.Q. to be selected and location reported to this office ;
42nd Infantry Brigade Group in EVREGNIES, DOTTIGNIES, Brigade H.Q. DOTTIGNIES.
41st Infantry Brigade Group remain in present billets.

2. 43rd Infantry Brigade will keep touch with the situation by sending Cyclist patrols to :-
POPUELLE, K 21,
CORDES, K 4 b,
ARC AINIERES, E 23 c,
BAUREUX, E 22 a.

3. 43rd Infantry Brigade will supply working parties under Brigade arrangements to ensure the passage round all existing craters and clearing roads East of L'ESCAUT.
(List of some mines and craters attached to 43rd Infantry Brigade only).

4. 42nd Infantry Brigade will be responsible for clearing the ESPIERRES - HELCHIN Road, both villages inclusive work to commence early on November 10th.

5. X Corps have priority over HELCHIN Bridge, and 14th Division have priority over 40th Division for traffic on WARCOING Bridge.

6. Acknowledge.

J. F. Beaumont Capt
for Lieut. Colonel
General Staff
14 Division

Issued at 2100

Copies to - No. 1 - 41 Infantry Bde.
2 - 42 Infantry Bde.
3 - 43 Infantry Bde.
4 - CRA.
5 - CRE
6 - 15th L.N.Lancs. (Pioneers)
7 - 14th M.G.Bn.
8 - 14th Div. Signal Coy.
9 - 14th Div. Train.
10 - S.S.O.
11 - A & Q.
12 - D.A.P.M.
13 - A.D.M.S.
14 - 40th Division.
15 - 29 Division
16 - XV Corps.

43rd Infantry Bde.

List of some mines and craters East of R. ESCAUT in order of importance :-

C 6 a central,
C 12 b 88
C 10 d 60
C 17 d 39
C 12 c 23
C 24 c 84
D 13 a 99
D 25 a 83
D 25 d 29
D 26 a 29
D 20 d 59

2 Tunnellers attached to 61st Field Coy. are working through the area E. of R. ESCAUT, removing unexploded mines,

No unexploded mines will be tampered with by the Infantry.

J.H.[illegible] Capt

for Lieut.Colonel G.S.
14 Div.

9/11/1918

Secret.

43rd Infantry Brigade Order No.53.   Copy No.....

11

Ref Sheet. COURTRAI. 1/40,000.   9th Nov, 1918.

1. The following moves will take place to-morrow, 10th inst :-

(a) 43rd Inf. Bde.H.Q. will move from HELCHIN to WARCOING closing at HELCHIN at 10.00. and opening at WARCOING at same hour.

(b) 20th Middx. Regt. will move from HELCHIN to WARCOING via ESPIERRES - head of column to pass HELCHIN Cross Roads at 10.00.

(c) 1st Line Transport will move to WARCOING to-morrow, 10th inst. under arrangements to be made by B.T.O. Transport to arrive in new area before 13.00. - not to clash with march of 20th Middx Regt.

(d) All other Brigade Units will remain in their present locations.

2. O.C. 20th Middx Regt. will detail billetting parties to report to Staff Captain at Cross Roads WARCOING C.30.a.4.7. at 09.15. Arrival in billets and location of H.Q. to be reported to Brigade H.Q.

3. 43rd Inf. Bde. are responsible for supplying working parties to ensure the passage round all existing craters and for clearing roads E. of L'ESCAUT.
This work will be begun to-morrow, 10th inst., under arrangements to be made by C.O's.
The following mines and craters which are of the greatest importance are allotted as under, these will be dealt with first.-

12th Suffolk Regt.	C.6.a.Central. C.12.b.8.3. C.12.a.2.3. D.13.a.9.9.
20th Middx Regt.	C.10.d.9.0. C.17.d.3.9. D.30.d.5.9.
10th H.L.I.	C.24.c.8.4. D.25.a.9.5. D.25.d.2.3. D.27.a.3.9.

On completion of these tasks, and until receipt of further instructions, attention will be paid to further mines and craters at the discretion of the C.O's.
No unexploded mines will be tampered with by the Infantry.

4. C.O's. will arrange to draw from Brigade H.Q., in addition to the tools ~~those~~ carried as mobile reserve by their own 1st Line Transport, the following tools from ~~Brigade H.Q. Transport~~ as Brigade Mobile Reserve :-

12th Suffolk Regt. 10th H.L.I.	09.00. at HELCHIN.	Up to 100 shovels and 50 picks per Battalion.
20th Middx Regt.	on arrival at WARCOING.	

5. O.C. Cyclist Coy. will arrange to keep communication between 43rd Inf. Bde.H.Q. and Division in the line by sending cyclist patrols to POPUEME K.21. CORDES. K.6.b. ARC AINIERES. E.23.c. SAUREUX E.28.a.

6. Brigade Units and O.C. Cyclist Coy. to acknowledge.

A. N. Rucker Lt for
Captain,
Brigade Major,
43rd Infantry Brigade.

Issued to Signals at 23.59.

Copies to :-

1. B.G.C.
2. B.M.
3. S.C.
4. Signals.
5. 12th Suffolk Regt.
6. 20th Middx Regt.
7. 10th H.L.I.
8. Cyclist Coy.
9. B.A.O.
10. B.T.O.
11. 14th Division G.
12. 14th Division. Q.
13. 41st Inf. Bde.
14. 42nd Inf. Bde.
15. 36th Bde. R.G.A.
16. C.R.A.
17. 46th Bde.R.F.A.
18. 47th Bde.R.F.A.
19. 61st F.C.R.E.
20. C.R.E.
21. A.D.M.S.
22. 14th M.G.Bn.
23. "A" Coy. 14th M.G.Bn.
24. "D" Coy. do.
25. S.O.
26. No.4. Coy. Train.
27. W.D.
28. File.

G.O.C.	
G.S.O 1	✓
G.S.O.2	
G.S.O 3	

Copy No...23

SECRET.

40th DIVISION ORDER NO. 250. 9/11/18.

****

1. As a result of the forward movement of the XIth and Xth Corps in an Easterly and South-Easterly direction respectively, the XVth Corps will probably become 'squeezed out' to-morrow.

2. In this event, the 40th Division will billet in depth between LANNOY and CHEMIN VERT and the 14th Division between HERSEAUX and REJET DE SEBLE.

3. When therefore the 59th and 29th Divisions join hands N. of VELAINES, the 119th Infantry Brigade will concentrate and billet in the area CHEMIN VERT - GRAND REJET - BOIS-DE-CHIN, but will keep touch with the situation by means of cyclist patrols.

4. The 14th Division is to have priority over 40th Division for traffic on WARCOING Bridge.

5. The 120th Infantry Brigade and the 121st Infantry Brigade will remain where they are, i.e. in the PECQ and LANNOY areas respectively.

6. The Divisional Artillery and attached Artillery Brigades will stand fast until further orders.

7. ACKNOWLEDGE.

GR 452

C.H.F. Black Lieut. Col.

Issued at.. 23.30 General Staff, 40th Division.

****

Copy No.1 to G.O.C.
2 119th I.B.
3 120th I.B.
4 121st I.B.
5 C.R.E.
6 40th Div. Arty.
7 17th Worc. R(P).
8 Signals.
9 39th Bn:M.G.C.
10 S.A.A.Sect.
11 Div.Train.
12 S.S.O.
13 40th Div.M.T.Coy.
14 "Q".
15 A.D.M.S.
16 D.A.D.V.S.
17 D.A.D.O.S.
18 D.A.P.M.
19 Div. Gas Off.
20 Div.Claims Off.
21 Div. Recept. Camp.
22 Div. Empl. Coy.
23 ✓ 14th Div.
24 59th Div.
25 XV Corps G.
26 ,, Q.
27 ,, R.A.
28 ,, H.A.
29 War Diary
30 ,,
31 File
32 29th Div.

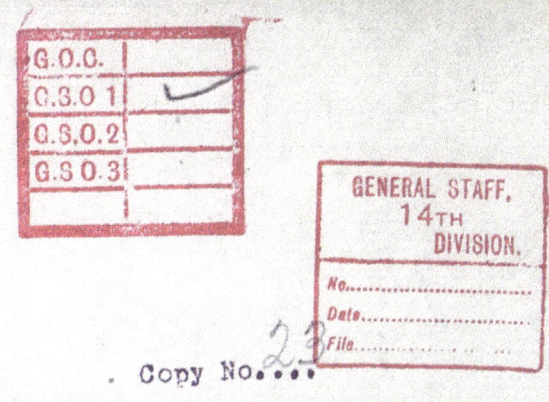

14 Division
S.G. 1486
Copy No. 18

SECRET

14th DIVISION INSTRUCTIONS No. 1.

7 November 1918

Reference
Sheets 29 SW. 1/20,000
37 NW. 1/20,000
29 & 37. 1/40,000

1. The Second Army is to force the passage of the River ESCAUT on "J" Day. The attack to be carried out by the XV, X, and XIX Corps.

2. The right of the Fifth Army is operating on "J" Day south of TOURNAI, and its left Division (59th) is to enlarge the Bridgehead already existing at CABT.LIETARD.

3. The XV Corps is to cover the right flank of the Second Army, and attacks at "H" hour on "J" day, crossing the inundations on the right bank of the ESCAUT between PECQ and HELCHIN both inclusive.

4. The first objective of the XV Corps (Blue line) is the line -
I 4 c 1.1 - C 28 d 2.8 - C 23 c 2.2 - C 23 central - C 17 d 3.7, and thence along the road to REJET-MOULEUX.

The final objective (Red line) is the line - Copses in I 11 a and b - I 6 central - Farm in J 1 a - Farm in D 25 d - D 26 b 2.8 - Cross roads in D 20 d 5.9.

5. Boundary between 14th Division and 40th Division on its right is -
C 21 b 2.7 - C 22 central - J 1 central.

Boundary between 14th Division and 29th Division of X Corps on its left is -
Bridge at U 30 c central - Cross roads D 20 d 5.9, both inclusive to 14th Division.

6. The 14th Division will attack with -
43rd Infantry Brigade in front line;
42nd Infantry Brigade in Support;
41st Infantry Brigade in Reserve.

7. The artillery at the disposal of the Division consists of -

Field Artillery - 14th Divisional Artillery, 96th Army Brigade, R.F.A.

Heavy Artillery - Five heavy batteries for bombardments, exclusive of batteries detailed for counter-battery work.

8. The Field artillery oreeping barrage will open at "H" hour, will lift at "H" plus 15, and advance at the rate of 100 yards in three minutes, with a pause of ten additional minutes at approximately every 1000 yards.

It will lift off the first objective in front of the Left Battalion at "H" plus 51, and in front of the right battalion at "H" plus 90.

/Heavy artillery

Heavy artillery will bombard selected points and will thicken the creeping barrage as it advances towards the final objective.

40th Division will screen MONT DE LA TRINITÉ with smoke.

9. The passage of the inundations by 43rd Infantry Brigade will be effected in two columns as follows :-

(a). Left Battalion.
Forming up area between Bridge at U 30 c central and SLUICE in C 5 b on right bank of L'ESCAUT.
First objective line of REJET-DE-SEBLE - REJET-HOULEUX Road.
Final objective - High ground in D 20 c and D 20 b, Cross roads D 20 d 5.9.
The advance of this battalion will be generally along the road GUERMIGNIES to cross roads D 20 d 5.9.

(b). Right battalion.
Forming up area in C 15 d, west of the RIGOLE D'ASSECHEMENT.
First objective - High ground in C 23 central - Railway embankment about C 17 d 3.7, thence along road to REJET DE SEBLE.

(c). Reserve Battalion.
This battalion, less two companies, will cross in rear of Left Battalion S.E. of HELCHIN, and will attack and mop up LANNOY.
Two companies will cross in rear of the Left Battalion, will mop up CAVRINNES, and move on LANNOY establishing touch with the remainder of the Battalion.
The Reserve Battalion will then move on REJET DE SEBLE.

10. Machine guns.

Two sections will accompany each front line battalion, the guns being carried by hand.
Pack animals will follow by the bridge at Lock 3, so soon as possible after the Infantry.
Three companies will thicken the artillery barrage, enfilade roads, and fire in the intervals between the artillery barrage.
Of these Companies, one will be prepared to cross the ESCAUT so soon as the Infantry are beyond range at which the guns can render assistance.

11. Light Trench Mortars.

One Stokes Mortar will accompany each Infantry Battalion, the guns and ammunition being carried by hand.
One Stokes Mortar and ammunition per Battalion will be prepared to follow on pack mules.

12. By "H" hour on J Day, the 42nd Infantry Brigade will be on the line ST.LEGER - BOIS JACQUET - COYGHEM.
Brigade H.Q. at DOTTIGNIES.

41st Infantry Brigade will be on the line ESTAMPUIS - EVREGNIES - QUEVAUCAMP.
Brigade H.Q. EVREGNIES.

Divisional H.Q. will be at the normal H.Q. of the Brigade in the line at DOTTIGNIES

/13

13. 42nd Infantry Brigade will advance to the River ESCAUT so as to begin the passage by the same crossings as used by the 43rd Infantry Brigade, at "H" plus two hours.
This Brigade will be prepared to support the attack or to exploit success towards GRAND CLAIRIEUX Farm (J 9 a)

43rd Infantry Bde. will advance S.E. of the REJET DE SEBLE - QUESNOY Road, so as to clear the area between this road and the inundations for the 42nd Brigade.

14. To ensure liaison with the flanking Divisions, 43rd Infantry Brigade will detail a detachment of one half Company and two machine guns to operate in rear of the outer flanks of the leading companies of the front line battalions.

15. After the passage of the inundations has been forced, Main bridges over the ESCAUT are being constructed as follows:

(a). At PECQ, under the orders of the C.E. XV Corps. Wooden trestle to carry all military loads.

(b). At HELCHIN, under C.R.E., 14th Division, Steel girder bridge to take Heavy Artillery, except 6" Mark XIX.

16. Two additional bridges for Infantry are being placed across the ESCAUT, one at C 15 b 0.5, and one at U 30 c 1.5.
The Bridge at Lock 3 is capable of taking Pack transport.

17. Four Bridges for Infantry will be thrown across the RIGOLE D'ASSECHEMENT at "H" hour, for the right column, and 18 "Infantry" bridges are required for the passage of the left column.
C.R.E. will ensure that the necessary material and R.E. assistance are available.

A track across the inundations, with the necessary ... bridges, to take Pack transport is to be completed so soon after "H" hour as possible.

18. Artillery barrage tables, Instructions as to the action of Medium Trench Mortars, Heavy Artillery, and Machine guns (and Signal arrangements) will be issued separately

19. P.of W. cage will be at BOIS JACQUET (U 25 c 8.0)

Straggler Posts will be at	Road junction	U 29 a 9560
	Road junction	U 22 b 7080
	Cross roads	U 15 d 2.2
	COYGHEM	U 19 a 9020
	Cottage	U 14 b 8070
	Cross roads	U 13 a 9590
	Bridge	C 18 a 50
	DOTTIGNIES.	

20. Acknowledge.

14th Division
7/11/1918

J.E. Hutchinson (?)
Lieut.Colonel
General Staff

Distribution overleaf.

Distribution of 14th Division Instructions No.1. (S.G.1486).

No. 1 - 41st Infantry Brigade.
2 - 42nd Infantry Brigade.
3 - 43rd Infantry Brigade.
4 - C.R.A.
5 - C.R.E.
6 - 14th Machine Gun Battalion.
7 - 15th Bn. L.N. Lancs.Regt. (Pioneers).
8 - A. & Q.
9 - D.A.P.M.
10 - A.D.M.S.
11 - 14th Div. Signal Coy.
12 - 14th Div. Train.
13 - D.G.O.
14 - 40th Division.
15 - 59th Division.
16 - XV Corps.
17 - XV Corps R.A.
18 - War Diary.
19 - File.

S E C R E T

14th Division S.G.1497

Amendment to 14th Division Instructions No 1 (S.G.1486).

para 9 c line 5 should read :-

2 Coys will cross in rear of Right Battalion, and will mop up CAVRINNES etc.

para 19 should read :-

P of W. cage will be at BOIS JACQUET (U 25 c 2.0)

P of W. directing posts will be at,

(1)	Road junction	U 29 a 95.30
	do	U 22 b 70.80
	X roads	U 15 d 2.2
	COYGHEM	U 19 c 90.20
	Cottage	C 14 b 80.70
	X roads	C 13 a 95.90
	Bridge	B 18 a 50.00

These posts will each consist of 2 O.R. from the 41st Infy. Brigade and will be in position at H plus 1 hr.

[illegible]

Lieut-Colonel.
General Staff.
14th Division.

8/11/18.

Copies to all recipients of S.G.1486.

S E C R E T.

14th Division, S.G. 1183.
Appendix "A".
8th Novr.1918.

SIGNAL COMMUNICATIONS.
(Issued in conjunction with 14th Div. Instructions No.1).

LINES.

Before ZERO the following Headquarters will be in telegraphic and telephonic communication with Divisional H.Q. :-

(1) 43rd Inf.Bde.	Buried line to COYGHEM and from that point by cable.
(2) 42nd " "	Cable line.
(3) 41st " "	Air line.
(4) 29th Division.	Direct cable line.
(5) 40th "	Through Rear H.Q.
(6) XV Corps.	Direct line buried to MOUSCRON, Air line beyond.

In addition to the above, there will be direct lines from Divisional Artillery Headquarters to each group Headquarters under their command.

Lines will also be run from 43rd Inf. Bde. H.Q. to LA PORTE d'OR and HELCHIN, at which points advanced Report Centres will be formed.

As 43rd Inf. Bde. Headquarters advance, a line will be laid to connect up their Headquarters to the Divisional H.Q..

WIRELESS.

At ZERO, Trench Set at 43rd Inf. Bde. H.Q. will be in communication with Divisional H.Q. and also the Brigades on either flank.

Divisional H.Q. will be in communication with Corps and also the flank Divisions.

After ZERO. A Trench Set, with personnel, will move off with the advance party of the 43rd Inf. Bde. H.Q. and as soon as their new H.Q. are decided on, it will be erected and communication will be obtained with Divisional H.Q. and 43rd Bde. Rear H.Q. As it is thought traffic over the Bridges will be heavy and difficulty may be experienced in getting the telephone line quickly to the Advanced Report Centre, this means of communication should be fully utilised.

D.R.L.S.

Motor Cyclist D.Rs. will be distributed as follows :-

3 with 43rd Bde., 1 with 42nd Bde., 1 with 41st Bde., and 5 at Divisional Headquarters.

Horse D.Rs. will also be posted at 43rd Bde. H.Q. (2) and Divisional H.Q. (3).

VISUAL.

A Central Visual Station will be formed at a spot to be notified later, which will be in communication by wire to Division and Brigades. The duty of this Station will be to pick up any Station on the Eastern side of the SCHELDT, and transmit its message to its proper destination.

Battalion or Brigade H.Q. as soon as they arrive at their

/Advanced

Advanced H.Q. should at once get into communication (if weather conditions are favourable) with above station and exchange signals.

The Signallers should be fully instructed to set up their Station on some prominent point which can be clearly seen from the Central Station and at the same time under cover from the enemy.

After ZERO. There will be an Advanced Corps Signal Station at MONT de la TRINITÉ.

At this station the following methods of communication will be available:-

(1) Wireless.
(2) Visual.
(3) D.Rs.
(4) Lines.

If Brigades experience any difficulty in communicating with Divisional Headquarters direct messages should be transmitted through this Station.

Appendix G.

14th Division – General Staff.

War Diary – Nov. 1918.

VOL. XLV

Move orders – November 1918

SECRET.

Copy No. 23

13th Novr. 1918.

G.O.C.
G.S.O.1
G.S.O.2
G.S.O.3 ✓

14th Division Order No. 242.

Ref. Sheets 36 & 37 1/40,000.

1. (a) On November 14th the 41st Inf. Bde. Group consisting of 41st Inf. Bde. and No. 2 Coy. Train will move from HERSEAUX Area to the BONDUES Area.
To be clear of HERSEAUX by 11.00 hrs.

(b) Boundaries of BONDUES Area and billeting arrangements will be notified by 14th Division 'Q'.

2. (a) On November 14th 42nd Inf. Bde. Group consisting of 42nd Inf. Bde. and No. 3 Coy. Train will move from DOTTIGNIES Area to HERSEAUX Area. To be clear of DOTTIGNIES Area by 12.00 hours. Not to enter HERSEAUX Area before 11.00 hours.

(b) Billets in HERSEAUX Area will be taken over from 41st Inf Bde.

3. ACKNOWLEDGE.

J.S. Beaumont Capt
Lieut-Colonel,
General Staff,
14th Division.

Issued at 14.00.

Copies to :-

No. 1 - 41st Inf.Bde.
2 - 42nd Inf.Bde.
3 - 43rd Inf.Bde.
4 - C.R.A.
5 - C.R.E.
6 - 14th M.G.Bn.
7 - 15th L.F.Lancs.(Pnrs.)
8 - 14th Div.Sig.Coy.
9 - 14th Div. Train.
10 - S.S.O.
11 - 14th Div. M.T.Coy.

No.12) = A. & Q.
13)
14 - A.D.M.S.
15 - D.A.D.V.S.
16 - D.A.D.O.S.
17 - D.A.P.M.
18 - D.G.O.
19 - D.R.C.
20 - XV Corps G
21 - XV Corps Q
22 - War Diary.
23 - File.

G.O.C.	
G.S.O.1	✓
G.S.O.2	
G.S.O.3	✓

To all recipients of 14th Divisional Order No. 242.

Addendum to 14th Division Order 242. 43rd Field Ambulance will move under orders of 41st Inf. Bde on November 14th.

J F Beaumont Capt
for Lieut-Colonel,
General Staff,
14th Division.

Issued at 1600 hours
13th November, 1918.

"A" Form
MESSAGES AND SIGNALS.

Army Form C. 2121
(In pads of 100.)

No. of Message..............

Prefix............ Code..............m | Words | Charge

Office of Origin and Service Instructions

Sent
At.................m.
To.................
By.................

This message is on a/c of: .... Service.
(Signature of "Franking Officer.")

G.O.C.
G.S.O.1
G.S.O.2
G.S.O.3

Recd. at..........m.
Date..........
From..........
By..........

TO CRE
Q.

Sender's Number.	Day of Month.	In reply to Number.	AAA
* G.Q. 135	14		

Move	62nd Field Coy		from
DOTTIGNIES	to	LA MADELEINE	
tomorrow	Nov 15th	AAA	Route
PETIT AUDENARDE -	ROUBAIX	- MOUVAUX	
AAA	To be	clear	of
Railway	Crossing	PETIT	AUDENARDE
by	0900	hrs	AAA
Billets	from	area	Commt
MARCQ	AAA	On	arrival
at	LA MADELEINE		62nd Coy RE
will	come	under	orders
CE	XV Corps	for	work
AAA	Acknowledge	AAA	addsd
CRE	repeated	Q	

From 14th Division
Place
Time

The above may be forwarded as now corrected. (Z)

Censor.

J.W. Beaumont Capt

Signature of Addressor or person authorised to telegraph in his name.

* This line should be erased if not required.

Copy No. 23

S E C R E T

14th DIVISION ORDER No. 243

Ref. Sheets
36 and 37, 1/40,000

14 Nov. 1918

1. On 15th November 1918, 43rd Infantry Brigade Group, consisting of 43rd Infantry Brigade, No. 4 Coy. Train, and 44th Field Ambulance will move from WARCOING - ST.LEGER area to Western TOURCOING area. Billets from Area Commandant TOURCOING. No restrictions as to route or time of march.

2. (a). On 15th November, 62nd Field Coy. R.E. will move from DOTTIGNIES to neighbourhood of LA MADELEINE. Route - PETIT AUDENARDE - ROUBAIX - MOUVAUX. To be clear of railway crossing at PETIT AUDENARDE by 0900 hours. Billets from Area Commandant MARCQ.

(b). On arrival in LA MADELEINE area, 62nd Field Coy. R.E. will come under orders of C.E. XV Corps for work on railways.

3. ACKNOWLEDGE.

Issued at 2000.

J.F. Beaumont Capt.
for Lieut.Colonel
General Staff

Copies to :-
No. 1 - 41 Inf Bde.
2 - 42 Inf.Bde
3 - 43 Inf.Bde
4 - C.R.A.
5 - C.R.E.
6 - 14th M.G.Bn.
7 - 15th L.N.Lancs
8 - 14th Sig.Coy.
9 - 14th Train
10 - S.S.O.
11 - 14th M.T.Coy
12 & 13 - AQ.
14 - A.D.M.S.
15 - D.A.D.V.S.
16 - D.A.D.O.S.
17 - D.A.P.M.
18 - D.G.O.
19 - Div.Reception Camp.
20 - XV Corps G.
21 - XV Corps Q.
22 - War Diary.
23 - File.
24 - Area Comdt Tourcoing

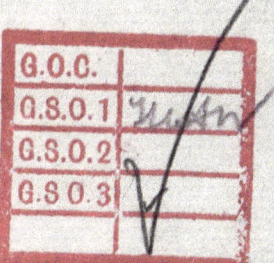

G.O.C.	
G.S.O.1	[illegible]
G.S.O.2	
G.S.O.3	

SECRET.

Copy No. 21

15th November, 1918.

14th DIVISIONAL ORDER NO. 244.

1. The following Units will move to TOURCOING on November 16th :-

61st Field Company, R.E.
89th " " "
15th Bn. L.N. Lancs. Regt. (Pnrs.).
14th Machine Gun Battalion.

2. Moves will be carried out in accordance with the attached March Table.

3. Units will apply to Area Commandant, TOURCOING for billets.

4. Locations of H.Q. will be reported to this Office.

5. ACKNOWLEDGE.

J.M. Beaumont Capt
for Lieut-Colonel,
General Staff,
14th Division.

Issued at 17-00 hours.

Distribution.

Copy No. 1 - 41st Infantry Brigade.
2 - 42nd Infantry Brigade.
3 - 43rd Infantry Brigade.
4 - C.R.A.
5 - C.R.E.
6 - 14th M.G. Battalion.
7 - 15th Bn. L.N.Lancs. Regt.
8 - 14th Div. Signals.
9 - 14th Div. Train, A.S.C.
10 - S.S.O.
11 - 14th Div. M.T. Coy.
12)
13)- A. & Q.
14 - A.D.M.S.
15 - D.A.D.V.S.
16 - D.A.D.O.S.
17 - D.A.P.M.
18 - D.G.O.
19 - D.R.C.
20 - War Diary.
21 - File.
22 - 61 Field Coy R E
23 - 89 Field Coy R.E
24 - Area Comdt TOURCOING.

MARCH TABLE - To accompany 14th D.O. No 244

Unit	From	To	Route	Remarks
14th M.G.Battn.	HERSEAU DOTTIGNIES	TOURCOING	PETIT AUDENARDE WATTRELOS	To be clear of Railway crossing PETIT AUDENARDE by 10-00 hrs.
15th L.N.Lancs.R.	ESTAIMPUIS & DOTTIGNIES	TOURCOING	PETIT AUDENARDE WATTRELOS	Not to pass railway crossing PETIT AUDENARDE before 10-30 and to be clear before 11-15.
89th Field Co.R.E.	T 30 a.	TOURCOING	PETIT AUDENARDE WATTRELOS	To march 500 yards in rear of Coys. 15th L.N.Lancs.R.
91st Field Co.R.E.	C 8 b.	TOURCOING	DOTTIGNIES PETIT AUDENARDE WATTRELOS	Not to enter DOTTIGNIES before 10-30.

Appendix H.

14th Division – General Staff.

War Diary – Nov. 1918

VOL. XLV.

Thanksgiving Service
ROUBAIX 17 Nov. 1918

WAR DIARY.

14th Division G.S. 1552

41/42/43 Infy.Bdes. A.D.M.S. C.R.A.
C.R.E. D.A.D.V.S. D.A.D.O.S.
14th M.G. Battn. D.A.P.M. 14th Div. Emp. Coy.
15th L.N. Lancs.Regt. Camp Cmmdt. 14th Div. Sig. Coy.
14th Div. Train. Q. 14th M.T. Coy.

THANKSGIVING SERVICE.

1. A thanksgiving Service will be held at the CASINO PALACE Theatre, GRANDE RUE, ROUBAIX on Sunday next 17th inst. at 10-00 hrs. for all denominations except Roman Catholic.

After the Service the troops will march past the (Acting) Army Commander (Lt.Gen. Sir C.W. JACOB, K.C.B.).

2. Attendance of Officers.

10 seats for the service are allotted to the Division as follows :-

Divisional H.Q. (inc. CRA & CRE)	... ...	5
41st Inf. Bde.	... ...	2
42nd Inf. Bde.	... ...	2
43rd Inf. Bde.	... ...	1

3. The Divl. Detachment will be formed as a composite battalion with H.Q. as follows :-

Commanding Officer	Lt.Col. L. LLOYD, DSO.
Second in Command	41st Inf. Bde. (Major MILLAR, D.L.I.)
Adjutant	42nd Inf. Bde. (Capt. W.L.SIMON A&SH)
R. S. M.	42nd Inf. Bde.

Detachments from Units will be formed into Platoons each 25 strong, commanded by a subaltern.

Detachments will be detailed as follows and will march past in the order shown :-

			Markers.
Divisional Artillery	... ...	100)	2
R.E. (including Div. Signals)	... ...	50)	2
41st Infantry Brigade	... ...	150	2
42nd Infantry Brigade	... ...	150	2
43rd Infantry Brigade	... ...	150	2
15th L.N.Lancs. Regt	... ...	25)	2
14th M.G. Battalion	... ...	50)	2
Composite Platoons made up as follows :-		)	
A.S.C.(to include 5 M.T.Co. 1 A.O.C.)	15)	)	
R.A.M.C. " 1 A.V.C. 1 D.E.C.)	10)	25)	2

Column will be constituted in 7 Coys., each of 4 Platoons.

Coy. Commanders will be sent as follows :-

C.R.A.	1	Battery Commander.
M.G. Battn.	1	Company "
41st Inf. Bde.	1	" "
42nd " "	2	" "
43rd " "	2	" "

Preference will be given to Officers & O.R. who have medals or wound stripes.

4. With the exception of the 43rd Inf.Bde and the composite platoon all troops taking part in the Parade will billot during the night 16/17th in TOURCING & will report to the Adjutant at "Q" Office at 14 hours.

The Adjutant will report at "Q" Office 14th Division at 1200 hours for billets.

/Rations will

Rations will be carried for Novr. 17th. 41st and 42nd Infy. Bdes. will each detail one cooker. Camp Commandant 14th Division will provide a water cart.

5. The Divl. Detachment will parade at 16-00 hrs under Lt.Col. L. LLOYD DSO in the PLACE THIERS in the order laid down in para.3.

6. GUIDES

Each Corps will detail a Corps Sergeant Major to act as a guide to the Corps Group which will consist of the Corps troops and the Divisions in that Corps. The guides will meet their respective formations in BOULEVARD de GAMBETTA and conduct them to their markers in the PLACE de la LIBERTE. (at the forming up place)

7. MARKERS

Markers as detailed in para 3 will report to the R.S.M. to be detailed by 42nd Infy. Bde. in the PLACE de la LIBERTE at 07-30 hrs

The R.S.M. will then report with his markers to the Parade Adjutant Lieutenant DAVIES, Worcester Regt. 2nd Army H.Q. in the PLACE de la LIBERTE at 07-45 hrs., where they will receive their instructions and be in position by 08-15 hrs.

8. RENDEZVOUS

The rendezvous is the PLACE THIERS TOURCOING, at 07-30 on the 17th inst.

9. ASSEMBLY

The Divl. detachment will be formed up by 09-15 in the PLACE de la LIBERTE and will then be given orders to march into the Church by a Staff Officer A.H.Q.

10. (a) Rifles will not be taken into the Church but will be piled in the PLACE de la LIBERTE.

(b) 43rd Infy. Bde. will detail a guard of 1 N.C.O and 2 men (in addition to the 150) for the purpose of guarding the rifles of the Divl. detachment.
This guard will also be responsible for the rifles of the XV Corps troops detachment.

11. On conclusion of the service the troops will not be formed up outside the building but will proceed direct to the PLACE de la LIBERTE and form up there.

12. The order for the March Past to commence will be given by a Staff Officer A.H.Q., and the troops will then proceed and march pass in column of route in the following order, by the route indicated on the attached map:-
- Army troops.
- X Corps Group.
- XV Corps Group.
- 2nd Bde. R.A.F.

The order of march of XV Corps Group will be as follows:-
- XV Corps troops detachment.
- 14th Divn. detachment.
- 40th Divn. detachment.

Intervals of 50 paces between Corps and 10 paces between detachments of the Corps will be maintained.

13. SALUTING POINT. The saluting point will be opposite the entrance to the HOTEL de VILLE. On reaching the Red flag the command 'EYES RIGHT' will be given by Platoon Commanders.

14. AFTER MARCH PAST. Each unit when past the saluting point will continue along the route shown on the attached map and will proceed to its destination with as little delay as possible.

/ DRESS

15. DRESS.

The dress will be drill order. i.e., equipment less pack and haversack and box respirator.

Caps will be worn and rifles carried by units in possession of them.

Bayonets will not be fixed during the march past.

Officers on parade will not carry sticks or swords.

G.O.C. formations and their Staffs will not march past.

16. BAND

A band of the 40th Division has been detailed by XV Corps to play the march past.

17. MEDICAL

Arrangements have been made for a Medical Officer to be in attendance in the Office of the Commandant ROUBAIX, HOTEL de VILLE.

18. SANITATION

Latrine accommodation will be found in the PLACE de la LIBERTE.

J.S. Beaumont Capt
for Lieut-Colonel.
General Staff.
14th Division.

15/11/18.

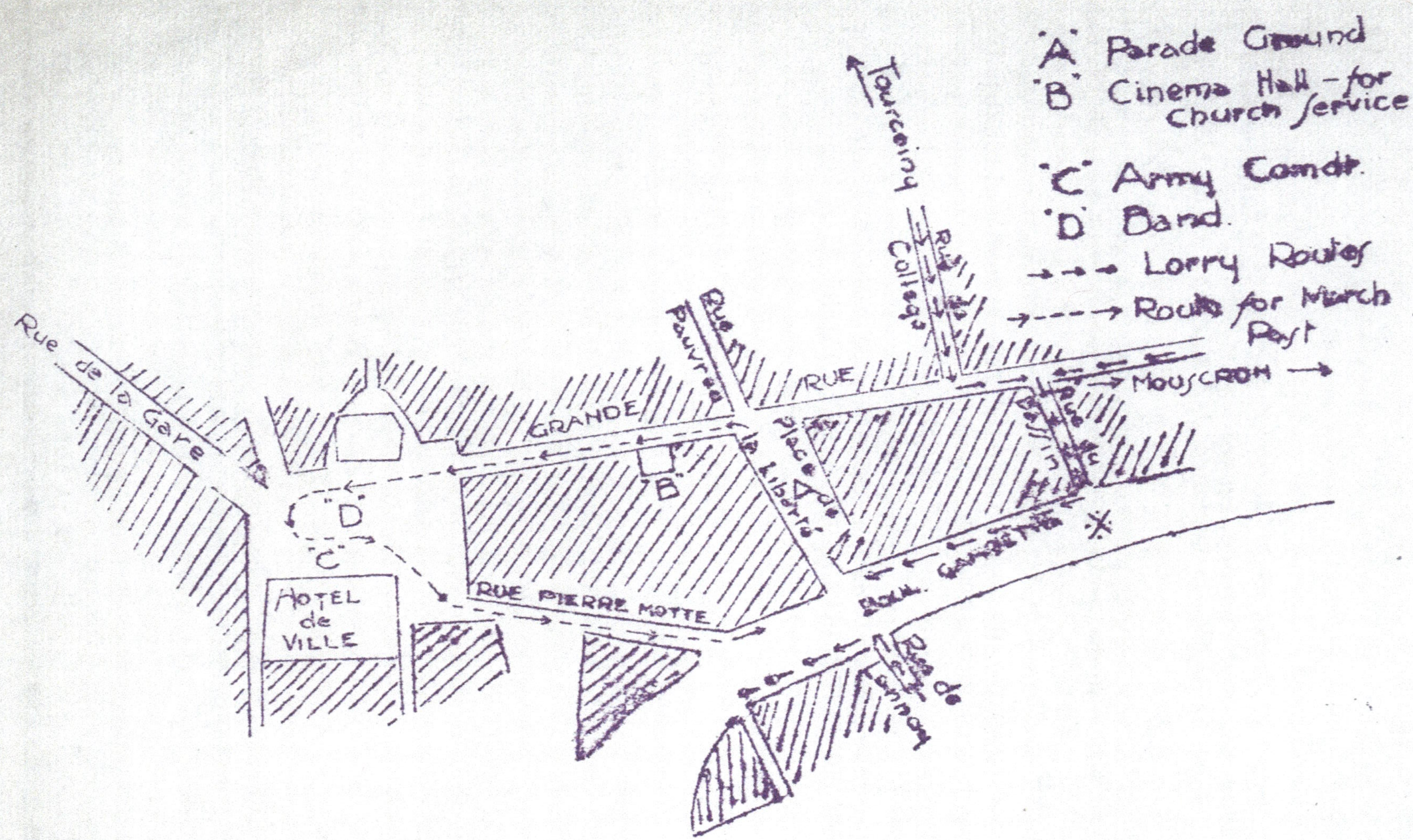
"A" Parade Ground
"B" Cinema Hall – for Church Service
"C" Army Comdr.
"D" Band.
Lorry Routes
Route for March Past
Tourcoing
Rue du College
Rue St Pauvree
GRANDE RUE
Place de la Liberté
MOUSCRON
Rue du Bassin
BOUL. GAMBETTA
Rue de Lannoy
RUE PIERRE MOTTE
HOTEL de VILLE
Rue de la Gare
"D"
"C"
"B"

14th Division.
G.S. 1556.

To all recipients of 14th Division, G.S.1552.

The following amandments will be made to 14th Division G.S.1552 of 15th inst.:-

Para. 3. In consequence of Orders received from XV Corps that Divisional troops will march at the head of the Composite battn., and companies and platoons will be made up having regard to the seniority in the Army of the Units of which they are composed, the order in which troops will march past is amended as follows :-

No. 1 Coy.	Divisional Arty.
2 "	(R.E.
	(L.N.Lancs.
	(Composite platoon.
3 "	Machine Gun Battalion.
	12th Suffolk Regt.
4 "	20th Middlesex Regt.
	6th Wiltshire Regt.
5 "	16th Manchester Regt.
	18th York & Lancs. Regt.
6 "	29th Durham L.I.
	10th Highland L.I.
7 "	14th Argyll & Sutherland Hrs.
	33rd London Regt. (R.B.).

2. In consequence, Company Commanders will be supplied as follows :-

No. 1 Coy.	R.A.	No. 5 Coy.	16th Manch.R.	42 Bde.
2 "	R.E.	6 "	29th D.L.I.	41 Bde.
3 "	12th Suffolks. (43 Bde.)	7 "	14th A.& S.H.	42 Bde.
4 Coy.	20th Mddx.Regt. 43rd Bde.			

3. Para. 4. Line 4, after '14 hours', add "16th instant."
Line 6, after 'hours' add "16th instant."
Para. 5. Line 1, after '16.00 hrs.' add "16th instant".

J. L. Beaumont Capt
for Lieut-Colonel,
General Staff,
14th Division.

15/11/18.

14th Division No. G.S.1560

All Recipients of 14th Division No. G.S.1552.

Amendment to G.S.1552 para. 15 of 15.11.1918.

Dress will be drill order, that is rifles, belts and bayonets only, no haversacks, water bottles or entrenching tools.

Puttees will be worn.

H. Beaumont Capt
for Lieut-Colonel.
General Staff.
14th Division.

16/11/1918.

35807. W16879/M1879 500,000 3/17 R.T. (1074) Forms/W3091/3 Army Form W.3091.

Cover for Documents.

Appendix I.

Nature of Enclosures.

14th Division - General Staff -
War Diary - Volume -
Intelligence Summaries
1 — 8 Nov. 1918

—

Notes, or Letters written.

CONFIDENTIAL.

14th Division No. I.S. 49.

NOT TO BE TAKEN BEYOND BATTALION HEADQUARTERS.

14th Division.
Summary of Operations & Intelligence
from 06.00 31st Oct. to 1st Nov. 1918.

PART I - INTELLIGENCE.

1. HOSTILE ARTILLERY - Between 05.30 and 06.45 enemy put down light barrage on a line running from S.W. to N.E. through 37C 3 a and 29U 27 d. Very few guns appeared to be firing but a rapid sweeping fire was kept up.

Between 05.45 and 09.00 Chateau in C 4 a was intermittently shelled from direction of REJET MOULEUX.

C 3 d, C 9 a, C 9 b were also lightly shelled during the day.

Between 11.30 and 12.15 about 80-15 cm. fell around our M.G. positions at U.29.a.85.10 apparently coming from due EAST.

During the night there was intermittent shelling. Medium H.E. and some Gas in vicinity of TRIEU COUSINE, CHATEAU in C 4 a, U 26 cent. ESPIERRES was heavily shelled between 17.00 and 17.45.

BOSSUYT-ESPIERRES Road was also shelled. Some of the guns appeared to be firing at very long range

2. ENEMY M.Gs. - Slight activity on left Battalion front.

C.5.b.32.40 M.G. active from vicinity of causeway in C.5.b. central, believed to be in house here.

3. ENEMY T.Ms. - A few light T.M. shells fell in HELCHIN.

4. MOVEMENT -

C.16.a.8.5. Civilians were seen here and smoke was observe rising from houses in the vicinity.

5. ENEMY PATROLS - At 20.45 a party of about 20 enemy approached our post at C.9.d.50.55 from direction of Causeway running through C.15.cent. They were driven off with L.G. and rifle fire.

6. INFORMATION GAINED BY OUR PATROLS - Patrol was held up at C.5.b.2.6. by heavy M.G. fire apparently coming from house at C.5.b.32.40.

Enemy snipers fired along the towpath and at house C.5.a. 9 4 where they evidently imagined our patrol to be.

Numerous Very lights were fired from behind house at C 5 b 32 40 and there were frequent bursts of M.G. fire along towpath and about sluice.

Patrol report that the water in the sluice appears to be about the same level as the water in the river.

The bank of the river is steep and about 6 ft. high on an average. Towpath appears to be in fairly good condition.

PART II - OUR OPERATIONS.

1. Our ARTILLERY - engaged M.G. at C.5.b.32.40.

Eric Smithers
Lieut
for Lieut-Colonel,
General Staff,
14th Division.

1st November, 1918.

CONFIDENTIAL. 14th Division No. I.S. 50.

NOT TO BE TAKEN BEYOND BATTALION HEADQUARTERS.

14th DIVISION
Summary of Operations and Intelligence
from 06.00 1st to 06.00 2nd Nov.1918.

PART I. INTELLIGENCE.

1. ENEMY ARTILLERY - Very active. Brigade front intermittenly shelled with H.E. and Gas during period with heavy bursts of fire from all calibres during the evening and night. At dawn, too, there was considerable activity.

15.00 - Concentration of all calibres on our forward area between ST. LEGER and POMME d'OR for ten minutes.

19.07 to 19.20 - concentration on C.9. C.9 was also intermittently shelled during the night.

19.10 to 19.20 - Northern Fork roads at ESPIERRES and area about C.8.b.8.4 were fairly heavily shelled.

Northern Fork Roads ESPIERRES were again heavily shelled from 19.30 to 19.40 and from 21.30 to 21.50.

Enemy artillery was also more than usually active this morning.

2. ENEMY M.Gs. - Intermittent activity. Frequent bursts of fire during the night and at daybreak into HELCHIN area. Active by day against our low flying planes. M.G. posts suspected at :-

CHAPEL	V.26.a.1.0.
CHATEAU & HOUSES	V.26.c.1.2.
GUERMIGNIES	C. 6.a.20.68.

3. ENEMY T.Ms. - L.T.Ms. active by day firing into HELCHIN and vicinity. Emplacements not yet located. Large percentage of the shells were gas shells (Phosgone).

4. MOVEMENT.

C.18.a. 8. 4.	-	At 1000 some civilians were observed here Observers report that one woman looked very much like a man in disguise.
C.12.a.85.05.	-	Four-horse wagon seen here at 15.10 going N.E.
C.18.b. 2. 8.	-	One German seen to enter house.

5. HOSTILE AIRCRAFT - Inactive. 1 E.A. over our lines at 15.15 was driven off by A.A.

PART II. OUR OPERATIONS.

1. OUR ARTILLERY - Engaged M.Gs. at C.21.b.05.70 and C.21.a.8.8.

2. OUR AIRCRAFT - Our aircraft were very active.

E.C. Smithers Lieut
for Lieut-Colonel,
General Staff,
14th Division.

2nd November, 1918.

THE NEWS.

18-00.

2/11/18.

VALENCIENNES FRONT - As result of yesterday's fighting S. of VALENCIENNES our line runs MARESCHES (incl) W. outskirts of PRESSEAU along PRESSEAU-AULNOY road to 500 yards E. of AULNOY thence due N. to railway S. of MARLY - along railway S. and W. of VALENCIENNES where Canadians have crossed the SCHELDT and are pushing through the town. Very severe fighting yesterday and large numbers of of the enemy killed. 21 battalions of 5 different German divisions were identified by 49th Divn and 4th Canadian Div. Prisoners between 2000 and 3000.

AMERICAN FRONT - The First American Army attacked West of the MEUSE and advanced about 2 miles on a front of 10 miles reaching the approx. line :- CLERY-le-GRAND - ANDEVANNE - BAYONVILLE - IMECOURT (all incl) BEFFU (excl) - 3,600 prisoners were captured.

FRENCH FRONT - The Fourth French Army attacked on the left of the Americans on a 20 km. front from S.E. of VOUZIERS to ATTIGNY. Crossing the AISNE they captured FALAISE - CHESTRES - high ground E. and N. of VANDY - part of VONCQ WOOD - SENVY. Several hundred prisoners and a certain amount of guns were captured.

BELGIAN FRONT - Enemy reported to be retreating opposite Belgian front. Belgians are advancing towards LAETHEM - ST. MARTIN - ST. DENIS - WESTREM and EECLOO.

ITALIAN FRONT - On the MONT GRAPPA front the enemy has entirely collapsed, and it is not possible to estimate the number of prisoners who are coming down the mountains in droves. All the enemy's artillery has been captured in this neighbourhood.

CAPTURES.-

BRITISH Captures in France 1st Aug.1918 to 31st Oct.1918
175,000 prisoners. 2,380 guns. 17,000.M.Gs. 2,750 T.Ms.

FRENCH Captures 14th July 1918 to 20th Oct.1918
112,500 prisoners. 1,575 guns. 8,000 M.Gs. 570 T.Ms.

British captures since commencement of the war (approx)
310,000 prisoners. Over 3,000 guns. 22,000 M.Gs. 3,700 T.Ms.

G.S.

14th Division.

CONFIDENTIAL. 14th Division No. I.S.51.

NOT TO BE TAKEN BEYOND BATTALION HEADQUARTERS.

14th DIVISION
Summary of Operations and Intelligence
from 06.00 2nd to 06.00 3rd Nov.1918.

PART I. INTELLIGENCE.

1. ENEMY ARTILLERY - Very active. Scattered shelling and heavy bursts of fire at intervals.
Most of the shelling was with 10.5 cm. & 77 mm. and much less gas shell was used than during the previous 24 hours.
ESPIERRES and HELCHIN were frequently shelled and CHATEAU in C.4.a.

2. ENEMY M.Gs. - Active during the day against our aircraft. During the night there were occasional bursts of fire.
C.6.a.20.65 M.G. reported firing from house here and vicinity until midnight.

3. ENEMY T.Ms. - Active throughout period, chiefly on HELCHIN. T.M. firing from outskirts of GUERMIGNIES.
C.10.d.75.80)
C.16.a.) Active T.Ms. reported.
For the most part light T.Ms. were firing, but a few heavy T.Ms. were reported.

4. MOVEMENT - Considerable enemy transport heard opposite U.24.b.

5. INFORMATION OBTAINED BY OUR PATROLS - Patrol which started out to reconnoitre ground between U.24.d.75.40 and U.24.b.5.5 report that on reaching point U.24.c.80.35 it was found impossible to proceed in any direction owing to deep dykes on all sides.
Very marshy ground was seen to the E. and N.E. which was clearly quite impassable, being flooded.
The LANDBEEK between U.30.a.2.6 and U.24.c.80.35 was reconnoitred by patrol. It contains 6 ft. to 10 ft. of standing water and is about 8 ft. wide - quite impassable without bridging material.
Road between U.24.a.5.0 and U.24.b. was shelled for about an hour by T.Ms. Very lights were frequently sent up by the enemy.

6. GENERAL - There is apparently an O.P. in the Chapel Tower at POTTES, as at 16.00 the observation hole was seen to be closed; also in main part of building there is a large slit which is possibly a M.G. Emplacement.

PART II. OUR OPERATIONS.

1. OUR ARTILLERY - Suspected hostile battery at D.8.a.9.3 was harassed.

2. OUR M.Gs. -
2000 to 0430 2 guns fired 5000 rounds at following targets :-
Track in C.11.a.
Cross Roads C.11.b.20.80
S. end of causeway C.6.a.00.00

2800 rounds were also fired during night on suspected M.G.E.

3. OUR T.Ms. - At 2030 and 0405 our 6" T.M.s fired on houses at C.5.b.4.5 and C.5.a.3.3. 135 rounds expended.

Eric Smithers
for Lieut-Col. G.S.
14th Division.

3/11/18.

CONFIDENTIAL. 14th Division No. I.S.

NOT TO BE TAKEN BEYOND BATTALION HEADQUARTERS.

14th DIVISION
SUMMARY of OPERATIONS AND INTELLIGENCE
from 06.00 3rd to 06.00 4th Nov.1918.

MINOR ENTERPRISE.- We established posts on the East bank of the ESCAUT at -

C.4.b. 6.4.
C.5.a. 2.4.
C.5.a.20.05.
C.5.b. 3.4.

PART I. INTELLIGENCE.

ENEMY ARTILLERY - Scattered shelling throughout the period. ESPIERRES was shelled during the afternoon with 15 cms. Other areas shelled C 2 d, C 8 b, U 29 c, U 23 a, BOIS JACQUET, U 22, U 16, ST. GENOIS, Railway through U 26 21 22 & 16, L'ENFER and U 29 c.

ENEMY M.Gs. - were active against our planes by day, also fired on areas U 22 c, 23 a and 23 c.

Between 1800 and 1900 one M.G. fired short bursts every 10 mins towards ESPIERRES from direction of HERINNES and between 0130 and 0330 2 M.Gs. from approx: C 11 fired occasional bursts traversing U area 28 and 29.

At intervals during the night Road in C 3 b was fired on from direction of CAVRINNES.

ENEMY T.Ms. Were again active firing for the most part into HELCHIN.

ENEMY AIRCRAFT. Slight activity. Six planes in all reported between 0910 and 1115.

MOVEMENT.
C 18 a & c. Considerable civilian movement. Some civilians were wheeling barrows.
CAVRINNES - LA ROY Road. Some civilian movement.

RECONNAISSANCE REPORT OF COUNTRY W. of CANAL in U 24 central by R.E. Officer.

I left Platoon H.Q. at 30/ U 24 a 0.4 at 1700 and proceeded along main road to U 24 b 3.9, passing wire entanglement running at right angles to the road at 24 b 1.7. There is a good track running from the road to the bank of the canal at 24 b 8.7 where section of canal is approx. as follows :-

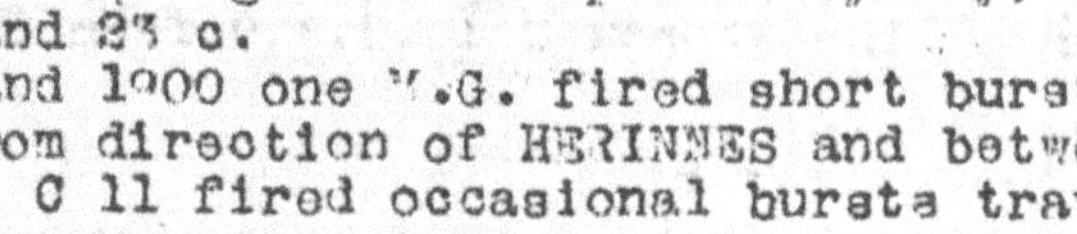

Track is only 200 yds. long, and is capable of taking horse transport it being the track used to connect the farm at 24 b 4.7 with the main road.

Walking due south from this farm I came across a footpath, running from the main road at 24 b 38 and following this I arrived at the sluice at 24 b 8.3 crossing two ditches on the way which were already bridged with planks. This would make a good path for Infantry. Section of canal where this path meets it similar to that previously given. Along this reach of the canal there is no definite bank on west side of [illegible] tow path, but the ground lies about 3 ft. from ditch 20 yds. W. of canal bank.

The sluice at U.24.b.6.6 consists of a brick arch culvert with an iron drop gate. A portion of the arch has been blown in thus damming the stream. Water level in the stream is about 1 foot higher than that of the canal, and section at sluice is as follows 

From here I tried to get on to mud track at U.24.c.9.7 but was stopped by a deep ditch running along the track. I followed this up to the main road where I was able to cross by a brick arch bridge (U 24.c.1.9). I went along the mud track until it got lost in the marshes about U 24.d.1.5, beyond which point it was impassable. Deep ditches are on either side of the road.

Section of LANDBEEK at U.24 c.9.5 as follows
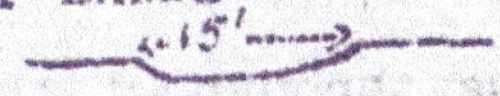

It is worthy of note that the ground north of grid line running through the figures of U.24 is not marshy but south of this the land very soon becomes impassable.

GENERAL. A light was seen signalling towards our lines at 22.20 and 00.20 on a line approx U 19.d.3.9 from C.4.a.3.4.

PART II OUR OPERATIONS.

1. OUR ARTILLERY. In conjunction with H.A. concentrations were fired during night on five Hostile Batteries in D.8.a and c and d. M.G. Posts at C.11 c.0.6., C.11.c.10.15., C.16.a.8.5., and cross roads at C.6.a.50.65 were harassed during the night.

2. OUR M.Gs. Active against enemy aircraft. 2,500 rounds were fired at Roads in C 12.c and d.

3. OUR AIRCRAFT Active all day over enemy lines. Heavily engaged by enemy A.A.

Eric Smithers
Lieut
for Lieut-Colonel.
General Staff.
11th Division.

4/11/1918.

CONFIDENTIAL. 14th Division No. 1.S.53.

NOT TO BE TAKEN BEYOND BATTALION HEADQUARTERS.

14th DIVISION.
Summary of Operations and Intelligence
from 06.00 4th to 06.00 5th November 1918.

MINOR OPERATION.

A Minor Operation was carried out at 23.30 on 4th Nov. by Left Bn. with the object of establishing Posts on East bank of L'ESCAUT between U.30.c.40.00 and U.24.b.60.50.

The operation was successfully accomplished and posts were established at the following points :-

U.30.c.55.10., U.30.c.40.30., U.30.d.10.70., U.30.b.05.15., U.30.b.15.25., U.30.b.35.70., U.24.d.85.20., U.24.d.85.50., U.24.b.90.05., U.24.b.95.90.

Bridges were also thrown across at

U.30.c.40.50., U.30.c.80.95., U.24.b.60.60.

21 Prisoners were taken belonging to 95th I.R. and 98th I.R. (38th Divn). also 3 light M.Gs.

15 Dead Germans were counted along E. bank of River.

PART I INTELLIGENCE.

1. ENEMY ARTILLERY. Active during the morning on ESPIERRES and CHATEAU in J.2.d. ESPIERRES Church was set on fire. HELCHIN, U.27.a and b, U.28, J.5.a and b, St. GENOIS and area South of it were shelled and there was also activity throughout the day over the Brigade front. In reply to our barrage at 23.00 there was scattered shelling of our front, U.22 and 28 being shelled all night.

2. ENEMY M.Gs. Engaged our Aircraft by day.

During the night HELCHIN and the roads in the vicinity were harassed chiefly from direction of GUERMIGNIES.

M.G. from HERINNES was also active firing onto ESPIERRES Square.

3. ENEMY T.Ms. Fired on our posts in J.4.b., J.5.a., U.29.b. and HELCHIN from direction of LANNOY and POTTES; they also co-operated with Artillery in shoots on our front line at 03. and 03.50.

4. ENEMY MOVEMENT.

C.18.a and c J.21.b J.11.a J.5.d	Considerable movement between 09.00 and 15.20 both men and women.
C.11.c.20.15.	Three enemy seen at Windmill going West, disappeared behind houses at C.10.d.5.2. This mill is a suspected O.P.

5. ENEMY AIRCRAFT. Between 07.15 and 15.00 15 E.A. in all were reported mostly flying high. They were engaged by our A.A.

Five Balloons were reported up during the day as follows :-

08.55 - 11.20	Grid bearing from	J.4.a.8.6		113	degrees.
08.00 - 10.00	"	"	-do-	147	"
08.15 - 10.35	"	"	-do-	86	"
09.00 - 10.11	"	"	-do-	151	"
08.30 - 10.25	"	"	-do-	154	"

6. GENERAL. During last night's operations enemy sent up various Red and white lights during shelling.

D.20.a.8.3. Clouds of smoke seen at 10.30

J.11.a.8.2 Ground fire seen 10.40.

2 ---

PART II OUR OPERATIONS.

1. OUR ARTILLERY. A barrage was fired at 23.30 in support of Infantry Operations. Two concentrations in conjunction with Heavy Artillery during the night.

2. OUR M.Gs., fired 22,800 rounds during the night.
(i) Sweeping approaches to new bridges.
(ii) Known Enemy M.G. Emplacements.
(iii) Preventing enemy using bridges across GRAND COURANT River.

From 00.01 till 05.40 Harassing fire was carried out on Road Junction in LANNOY and farm C.10.d.70.40.

3. OUR T.Ms. 6" and 3" Stokes active firing on targets during the night.

4. OUR AIRCRAFT were very active between 06.45 and 15.15. many of them flying very low.

Eric Smither
Lieut
for Lieut-Colonel,
General Staff.
14th Division.

6/11/1918.

LATEST NEWS.

Nov. 6th. Situation report received 08.05. VALENCIENNES Front Line reported yesterday evening as follows - North to South - VICQ - MARCHIPONT (both inclusive) ANGRE (exclusive) ANGREAU - MEARAIN (both inclusive) - ST. WAAST - LA VALLEE (exclusive) North East extremity FORET DE MORMAL - BERLAIMONT - PRISCHES (both inclusive). French line continues BERSY - ESQUEHERIES (both inclusive) - LA VAQUARESSE (exclusive) - MALZY - SAINS - RUHAUMONT - CHATILLON - MARLE - GOUDELANCOURT (all inclusive). Prisoners taken by British on 4th and 5th about 11,000.

ITALIAN FRONT. On the 3rd November, the 10th Army Commanded by Lord CAVAN reached the line of the TAGLIAMENTO from the neighbourhood of ST. VITO to the North of SPILIMBERGO. The river was crossed at several places. The number of prisoners captured by this Army on the 2nd and 3rd November exceeds 20,000, including 4 Divisional Commanders. Several hundred guns were also captured.

Total prisoners on Italian front 500,000.

CONFIDENTIAL. 14th Division No. I.S.54

NOT TO BE TAKEN BEYOND BATTALION HEADQUARTERS.

14th DIVISION
Summary of Operations & Intelligence
from 0900 5th to 0900 6th Nov. '18.

PART I. INTELLIGENCE.

ENEMY ARTILLERY - Much more active than usual. Gas was used 1335 to dusk on U.29 and C4 and 2300 to 2359 on U.25.b. and d.

Harassing fire was heavy and very scattered on whole front.

ENEMY M.Gs. - Intermittently active along our front from HERINNES to ESPIERRES (incl) in bursts of traversing fire about every 10 minutes from 1125 to 1230 and 1300 to 1800.

C.5.b.8.4	M.G. traversed banks of Canal at intervals throughout the night.
U.30.d.	M.G. reported active.
C.21.b.7.7.	M.G. firing into ESPIERRES.

ENEMY T.Ms. - Considerable T.M. fire on our front posts at intervals during the night - chiefly about C.5.b.

MOVEMENT - Usual civilian movement is reported between 0925 and 1430 in neighbourhood of JAVRINNES.

Between 0935 and 1510 five enemy were seen moving about behind HERINNES, 2 were apparently examining something.

SIGNALS - At 1513 three green lights followed by two more green lights were fired apparently from C.21.b.5.8. Two minutes later a salvo of 15 cm. was fired into ESPIERRES.

ENEMY AIRCRAFT - Inactive.

ENEMY RAID - The enemy raided one of our posts at C.5.b.4.5 under cover of a heavy T.M. barrage. A direct hit was obtained by the enemy on the post and after a stiff fight the garrison were forced to withdraw.

PART II. OUR OPERATIONS.

OUR ARTILLERY - POTTES Church was fired on at intervals with shrapnel.

M.Gs. at U.30.d.5.5 and U.30.d.9.0 were shelled and enemy tracks and M.Gs. were vigorously harassed at intervals during the whole 24 hrs

In conjunction with H.A. 60 rounds were fired in concentrations on hostile batteries.

OUR M.Gs. - Short bursts fired at intervals during the day at O.P. in Church Tower, POTTES.

1000 rounds fired on C.16.a.90.40.

500 rounds fired on C.10.d.70.40.

OUR AIRCRAFT - Active during the fine weather, flying low over the enemy lines.

Eric Smithers
Lieut for Lieut-Colonel,
General Staff,
14th Division.

6th November, 1918.

PRELIMINARY EXAMINATION
of Prisoners of No. 1 Coy. 95th I.R. and Nos. 1 & 2 Coys. 96th I.R. (38th Div.) captured night of 4th/5th November, 1918 between U.24.b. and U.30.c.

---

1. ENEMY ORDER OF BATTLE - North to South.

88 I.R. 56th Div.

95 I.R.)
96 I.R.) 38th Div.
94 I.R.)

18th Div.

2. Method of holding line - 95th and 96th I.R.

1 Bn. (three Coys) in line, and 1 Bn. in support.
2 light M.Gs. per Coy. in forward outpost line and 2 light M.Gs. in main line of resistance.
In addition to this there is a Sapper light M.G. post with the 95th I.R.
Main Line of Resistance MARAIS-de-POTTES - POTTES - GUERNIGNIES - LANNOY.
Support Line, CHATEAU in V.26 - REJET-a-MOUCHONS - REJET-de-SEBLE. GREUNERIES -
Heavy M.Gs. are scattered about in the houses and in GARDEN of CHATEAU at V.26.c.
One prisoner knew of 2 in MARAIS-de-POTTES but could not give their locations.

3. Composition of Regiments.

All three regiments of 38th Division have only 2 Bns. each of three Coys.

4. Company Strength.

35/40 fighting strength.

5. M.G. Coys.

Two per Regiment to conform with the number of Bns.
Prisoners were uncertain as to number of M.Gs. per Coy. but thought that Coys. were up to establishment - viz. 12 M.Gs.

6. DISPOSITIONS.

As regards 95th I.R. the Company Sectors along the SCHELDT were as follows from E. to W. :-

No. 3 Coy.	from	V.15.c.25.99	to	V.20.a.9.9.
2 "	"	V.20.a. 9. 9	"	V.13.c.91.13.
1 "	"	V.13.c.91.13	"	U.24.b.70.38.

No. 3 Coy. were originally in the Sector now held by No. 1 Coy., but the Coy. Commander of No. 3, who happened to be the senior Coy. Commander, objected to his Sector owing to the swampy ground to be crossed and changed Sectors with No. 1 Coy. on night 2/3 inst.
The posts shown on aeroplane photos were not all occupied.

7. ROUTES.

The route to the Right Coy. Outpost line, whose main line of resistance was in the houses between L'ESPINOIS and PONT-A-L'HAIE was free of flood. After crossing the fields in U.15.c. to GRAND
/COURANT

JOURANT the latter was crossed by a footbridge at about U.15.c.2.5. Prisoner said the GRAND JOURANT was quite narrow here, at the most 2 metres broad, so it is possible that the crossing was really a little further WEST.

The extreme Right post was close to house at V.13.a.35.02. which was then occupied by a post of 88 I.R.

To get to Left Coy. Outpost line, the track running through V.19.d. and b was used which crosses the GRAND COURANT at V.19.d.3.7.

Just short of the GRAND JOURANT, the Bridge over which was destroyed, it was necessary to leave the track and bear off to the Right for about 50 metres to a spot where a plank bridge had been thrown across. The Road was regained a little further on. In crossing the GRAND JOURANT they had to wade through water knee deep and the going was very bad owing to various shell holes under the water in the vicinity of the old bridge. The plank bridge was very hard to distinguish.

As regards No.2 Coy., Prisoner stated that the track running from L'ESPINOIS to River Bank at V.20.a.78.00 was used.

The Bridge here was also destroyed but he thought that there was a plank bridge similar to the one leading to No.1 Coy's outpost line.

8. RELIEFS.

I/95 relieved a Bn. of 63 I.R. 7 or 8 days ago.
I/96 relieved III/95 night of 2/3 November.

9. LOCATIONS.

38th Divisional H.Q. in RENAIX
H.Q. III/96 in CELLES.
H.Q. III/95 in vicinity of CELLES.
? Bn. H.Q. in CHATEAU in V.26.c.
O.P. in CHAPEL in V.26.c.

10. ENEMY INTENTIONS.

Several of the prisoners state that they have heard constant rumours of a withdrawal, but they thought that it had been postponed. One prisoner had heard that they were to withdraw as far as MONS.

The 2nd Line Transport had gone to BRUSSELS. Several prisoners stated this quite independently.

11. LOSSES.

Division suffered very heavy losses in October when in neighbourhood of SOLESMES.

12. MORAL.

Indifferent. All the prisoners seemed very glad to be taken. There seemed to be a general impression that it was only a matter of a few days before PEACE would be declared and one prisoner stated that none of them were anxious to be killed when Peace was so near.

13. REINFORCEMENTS. A draft of 40 O.R. - mainly returned wounded - joined the 38th Div. from the Field Recruit Depot on 27th Octr.

A number of men from the first line transport, specially employed men, have been brought up as reinforcements.

Eric Smithers
Lieut
for Lieut-Colonel.
General Staff.
14th Division.

6/11/18.

CONFIDENTIAL. 14th Division No. I.S. 55

NOT TO BE TAKEN BEYOND BATTALION HEADQUARTERS.

14th DIVISION.
Summary of Operations and Intelligence
from 06.00 6th to 06.00 7th November 1918

PART I INTELLIGENCE.

1. HOSTILE ARTILLERY. Very active on Forward areas. The following locations in particular were actively shelled :- [U 28 b and d, U 23 c] ST. GENOIS, HELCHIN, U.22a and c, C.9.a and b, C.4.a and b.
At 15.00 DOTTIGNIES was lightly shelled with H.E. and Gas. The shelling throughout was unusually scattered.

2. ENEMY M.Gs. Active with bursts of traversing fire along our front especially at dusk and during the early part of the night.
By day our Aircraft were fired on chiefly from GUERMIGNIES.
Our Patrols report M.Gs. active at -
U.30.d.6.6., U.30.c.9.2., U.30.c.9.5.
Forty flash bearings of Enemy M.Gs. are reported from O.P. at U.23.c.2.9 on a Grid Bearing of 148 degrees and 118 degrees.

3. ENEMY T.Ms. Usual activity. About 50 rounds fell in vicinity of Lock 3. C.10.a.

4. ENEMY MOVEMENT.
CAVRINNES. Civilian movement seen.
U.30.d. Four enemy stretcher bearers seen carrying wounded man into house near Church.

5. PRISONER'S STATEMENT. According to a reliable Sergt. of No. 1 Coy. 95 I.R. the 38th Divn. was brought to RONSE prior to coming into the line as "EINGRIFF DIVISION" or Counter Attack Division.
Prisoner confirmed statements made by other prisoners of 95 I.R. (see Summary of 6/11/18).
(a) Outpost Line. No. 1 Coy. had two Light M.G. posts and one Infantry Post in the outpost line along the canal.
The M.G. posts consisted of 1 N.C.O. and 4 men each and the Infantry post of 1 N.C.O. and 6 men.
In addition to this there was one Sapper light M.G. post, which was located in No. 1 Coy. sector.
(b) Coy. Sector about 800 yards.
(c) Locations. KTK (H.Q. of Commander of Front Line troops) in Farm at V.22.c.3.1.
Coy. Commander Right Coy. in one of the houses about V.15.c.50.25.
(d) Footbridge The footbridge leading to Right Coy. Outpost line was a Sluice Gate at approx. V.15 c.28.55 (No photo of this area).
(e) General. Prisoner stated that they had to "lie low" by day on account of low flying planes.

PART II OUR OPERATIONS.

1. OUR ARTILLERY. A few rounds fired at intervals at POTTES CHURCH. A concentration was fired on GUERMIGNIES and harassing fire directed on centres of activity, C.6.a.central and C.6.c.00.97.

2. OUR M.Gs. One gun harassed Tower of POTTES CHURCH all day.
Harassing fire was carried out during the night on following targets:- Road Junction C.6.d.25.20., V.26.c.10.20., CAVRINNES. Track U.30.d.50.50., C.6.a.central., C.6.b.10.35., C.10.d.70.40., 11,000 rounds were fired in all

Eric Smithers Lieut
for Lieut. Col. G.S.
14 DIVISION

7/11/18

CONFIDENTIAL. 14th Division No.I.5.56.

NOT TO BE TAKEN BEYOND BATTALION HEADQUARTERS.

14th DIVISION
Summary of Operations and Intelligence
from 06.00 7th to 06.00 8th Nov.1918.

PART I. INTELLIGENCE.

HOSTILE ARTILLERY - Active on forward area. Several concentrations of Gas and H.E. chiefly by heavy and medium calibres were fired on U.28.c., U.27 and 28, area round Chateau in C.2.d. ESPIERRES, ST.GENOIS HELCHIN and back areas.

ENEMY M.Gs. - Fired bursts at intervals throughout the period along the front, chiefly between the HELCHIN - ESPIERRES Road and front posts. Chief activity from vicinity of GUERMIGNIES on a G.B. of 96° from C.4.a.8.6 and between 0930 and 1445 on G.B. of 62° from C.9.a.7.3.
C.5.d.95.95 M.G. active from house here.
C.10.d.8.7.)
C.16.a.70.55) M.Gs. reported active by Patrols.

Flash bearings of M.Gs. from O.P. at C.4.b.4.7 were 73°, 63° 102° Grid.

SNIPERS - Enemy snipers were active during the day from various points on the GUERMIGNIES - LANNOY Road.

ENEMY T.Ms. - Light T.Ms. are reported firing at 15.30 at Island in C.10.a. and C.9.b. Two direct hits were obtained on houses on the Island.
At 0450 about 40 rounds light T.M. fell in vicinity of Bridge No. 1 at U.30.c.1050.
Some rounds also fell in U.29.d. from direction of U.16.a. A flash bearing taken from C.4.b.4.7 gave 102° Grid.

MOVEMENT - Civilian movement in C.16.a. & c., C.11.c. & C.21.b. between 1020 and 1450 - chiefly women walking along roads and in gardens. At 1340 three enemy seen to enter house at C.11.a.9.9 and at 1425 three more entered house at C.16.a.8.5.

ENEMY AIRCRAFT - Slight activity. 2 E.A. were over our lines in C.4.a. at 1110.

INFORMATION OBTAINED BY OUR PATROLS - The following information was obtained by patrol which was out last night :-

1) Track running S. from C.5.a.2.0 is indiscernable and inaccessible
The flood water in this area has risen considerably and the flooded area extended towards river. The strip of dry ground between R.SCHELDT and the flood water in squares C.4.b, C.5.a and C.5.b. has been reduced to about 70 to 100 yds. in width.
2) Track running E. from C.5.a.2.0 is submerged.
3) Enemy M.Gs. were definitely located at C.5.b.3.4 (in house) and at C.5.d.95.95 (in house).
These were both active all night and were still being fired at 0300 this morning.
The former M.G. is about 70 yds. away only from my nearest post and the movements of the enemy occupying post can be distinctly heard. This gun sweeps right down the towing path and the road to HELCHIN village continually throughout the night.
4) The area between C.5.b.4.2 and the causeway could not be closely approached owing to the hostile M.G., but it appears to be
/now

now submerged, and impracticable for movement of troops.

5) Enemy M.G. exists at C.6.a.2.6 still, and was active during the night.

6) Area between l'ESCAUT and GRAND COURANT between points C.6.a.1,7 and C.30.d.1,5 was reconnoitred and was found to be wet and full of shell holes, but it is passable by infantry: there are no marked approaches. The area further towards the N.E. had already been handed over and was not patrolled. The ground there, however, is known to be marshy with dry tufts of earth scattered about and is passable for infantry.

The Officer i/c patrols reports that he was unable to ascertain width of the GRAND COURANT owing to darkness.

The condition of ground between points C.5.b.4.5 - C.6.a.0.0 - C.6.a.5.1 - C.6.a.2.7 cannot be ascertained, this area being entirely cut off by enemy M.G. posts.

7) The river rose about 1ft. on night of 6th/7th after the heavy rain but fell slightly last night.

The river banks are steep, however, and the rise has not affected the Bridges at all beyond the fact that the current has slightly increased and is apt to weaken the structure of the bridge, rendering constant attention necessary.

Water at approx. C.15.b.80.15 was found by patrol to be 2 ft. deep. Patrol was unable to reach banks of RIGOLE d'ASSECHEMENT owing to deepening water and mud. The banks are under water and not visible.

Track from C.15.d.00.75 to C.21.b.20.75 was patrolled as far as C.15.d.15.20 but further progress was impossible owing to mud and water - about 6" mud and 1 ft. water. Enemy posts at C.15.d.15 was passed over by patrol on their way along the track and was evidently evacuated and awash.

M.G. fired on patrol from approx. C.21.b.20.30.

Enemy posts at C.21.a.50.75 was visited and found to be unoccupied.

There are M.Gs. at S.E. ends of tracks running from Lock 3 to C.10.d.8.8 and from C.9.d.7.8 to C.16.c.8.5. The area between the tracks is impassable as well as the tracks themselves.

The ground S.W. is also flooded 150 to 200 yds. from the river bank to C.15.d.8.8.

PART II. OUR OPERATIONS.

MACHINE GUNS - Harassing Fire on following targets :-

CROSS ROADS	U. 5.d.10.00
" "	U. 6.a.50.10
	C.10.d.70.40
	C.16.a.00.40.

OUR AIRCRAFT - Very active.

Eric Smithers
Lieut
for Lieut-Colonel,
General Staff,
14th Division.

8th November, 1918.

appendix J.

14th Division – General Staff

War Diary – Nov. 1918

VOL. XLV

Locations. Nov. 1918

14th Division L.R.30

SECRET.

14th DIVISION LOCATION TABLE
Forecast to 06.00 2nd November 1918.

1.	~~14th Divisional~~ H.Q.	MAERIE.	MOUSCRON.
2.	14th Divisional Arty.H.Q.	MAIRIE	MOUSCRON.
3.	46th Bde. R.F.A.	37/B 15.b.60.50.	
4.	47th Bde. R.F.A.	37/B.5.d.6.0.	28/X.23.c.2.6.
5.	D.A.C.		28/X.22.c.2.2.
6.	No. 3 Section S.A.A.		29/U.20.d.6.4.
7.	D.T.M.O.		
8.			37/B.5.a.4.8.
8.	41st Infantry Bde. H.Q.		29/U.26.c.9.7.
9.	18th Yorks. & Lancs. Regt.		37/B.5.a.3.7.
10.	29th Durham L.I.		29/U.22.c.1.8.
11.	33rd London Regt. (R.B.)		
12.	41st L. T. M. Battery.	Split up amongst Battalions.	
			37/A.5.d.25.45.
13.	42nd Infantry Bde. H.Q.		29/S.23.d.20.90
14.	6th Wilts Regt.		37/A.15.b.0.8.
15.	16th Manchester Regt.		37/A.5.d.2.2.
16.	14th A. & S. Hrs.		37/A.5.d.25.45.
17.	42nd L. T. M. Battery.		
			37/B.15.b.
18.	43rd Infantry Bde. H.Q.	EVREGNIES	H.Q. Church.
19	12th Suffolk Regt.	EVREGNIES.	
20	20th Middlesex Regt.	LUIGNE.	37/B.4.c.40.45.
21.	10th Highland L I	EVREGNIES.	
22.	43rd L. T. M. Battery.		
			37/B.20.a.1.8.
23.	15th L. N. Lancs. Regt. Pioneers H.Q.		29/T.29.a.3.2.
24.	"A" Company.		29/T.29.d.3.0.
25	"B" "		37/B.14.c.1.6.
26	"C" "		
			29/S.23.b.2.0.
27.	14th Machine Gun Bn. H.Q.		37/C.2.d.80.25.
28.	"A" Company.		37/B.15.a.99.70
29.	"B" "		29/T.29.d.40.30
30	"C" "		29/U.20.d.
31	"D" "	TROIS FARM	
		MAIRIE	MOUSCRON.
32.	C.R.E.		37/B.15.b.3.7.
33.	61st Field Company R.E.		37/B.13.d.5.5.
34.	62nd Field Coy. R.E.		29/T.30.a.3.6.
35	89th Field Coy. R.E.		
		MAIRIE	MOUSCRON.
36.	A.D.M.S.		37/A.18.b.9.3.
37	42nd Field Ambulance.		37/A.22.c.9.9.
38	43rd Field Ambulance.		-do-
39	44th Field Ambulance.		

[signature] Capt.
for Lieut-Colonel.
General Staff.
14th Division.

1/11/1918.

S E C R E T. 14th Division L.R. 31.

LOCATION TABLE.
(Forecast to 06.00 5th November,1918.)

Ser.No.	Unit.	Location.	
1.	14th Divisional H.Q.	TOURCOING	36/F.10.b.6.8.
2.	14th Divisional Arty. H.Q.	do.	do.
3.	46th Bde. R.F.A.		37/B. 5.b.10.90.
4.	47th Bde. R.F.A.		37/B. 5.d. 6. 0.
5.	D.A.C.		28/X.23.c.2. 6.
6.	No. 3 Section, S.A.A.		28/X.22.c. 2. 2.
7.	D.T.M.O.		29/U.20.d. 6. 4.
8.	41st Infantry Brigade H.Q.		37/B. 5.a. 4. 8.
9.	18th Y. & L. Regt.		29/U.26.c. 9. 7.
10.	29th Durham L.I.		37/B. 5.a. 1. 7.
11.	33rd London Regt. (R.B.)		29/U.22.c. 2. 8.
12.	43rd L.T.M. Battery		37/B. 5.a. 4. 8.
13.	42nd Infantry Brigade H.Q.		37/A. 5.d.25.45.
14.	6th Wilts. Regt.		37/A.22.a. 8. 7.
15.	16th Manch. Regt.		37/A.15.b. 0. 8.
16.	14th A. & S. Hrs.		37/A. 5.d. 2. 2.
17.	42nd L.T.M. Battery.		37/A. 5.d. 25.45.
18.	43rd Infantry Brigade H.Q.	EVREGNIES.	37/B.15.b.
19.	12th Suffolk Regt.	do.	H.Q. Church.
20.	20th Middx. Regt.		37/A.12.d.78.12.
21.	10th Highland L.I.		37/B. 4.c.40.45.
22.	43rd L.T.M. Battery.	EVREGNIES	
23.	15th L.N. Lancs. Regt.(Pnrs.)H.Q.		37/B.20.a. 1. 8.
24.	"A" Company.		29/T.29.a. 3. 2.
25.	"B" "		29/T.29.d. 3. 0.
26.	"C" "		37/B.14.c. 1. 6.
27.	14th Machine Gun Battalion H.Q.	HERSEAUX	37/A. 5.c.90.30.
28.	"A" Company.		37/C. 2.d.80.25.
29.	"B" "		37/B.11.a. 5. 8.
30.	"C" "		29/T.29.d.40.30.
31.	"D" "	TROIS FARM	29/U.20.d.
32.	C.R.E.	TOURCOING.	36/F.10.b. 6. 8.
33.	61st Field Company, R.E.		37/B.15.b. 3. 7.
34.	62nd " "		37/B.13.d. 5. 5.
35.	89th " "		29/T.30.a. 3. 6.
36.	A.D.M.S.	TOURCOING	36/F.10.b. 6. 8.
37.	42nd Field Ambulance.		37/A.18.b. 9. 3.
38.	43rd " "		37/A.22.c. 9. 9.
39.	44th " "		do.

3/11/18.

R.P. Fitzgerald Capt
for Lieut-Col. Gen. Staff G.S.
14th Division.

SECRET. 14th Division L.R.32

LOCATION TABLE.
(Forecast to 06-00 9th Novr.1918)

Ser.No.	Unit.	Location.	
1.	14th Divisional H.Q.	TOURCOING	36/F 10 b 6.8.
2.	14th Divisional Arty. H.Q.	do	do
3.	46th Bde. R.F.A.		37/B 5 b 10.90.
4.	47th Bde. R.F.A.		37/U 19 c 63.60.
5.	D. A. C.		37/A 24 b 90.10.
6.	No 3. Section S.A.A.		37/A 24 a 60.90.
7.	D. T. M. O.		29/U 20 d 6. 4.
8.	41st Infy. Brigade H.Q.		37/A 5 d 25.45.
9.	18th Y & L Regt.		37/A 22 a 8.7.
10.	29th Durham L.I.		37/A 5 d 2.2.
11.	33rd London Regt (R.B.)		37/A 15 b 0.8.
12.	41st L. T. M. Battery.		37/A 5 d 25.45.
13.	42nd Infy. Brigade H.Q.	EVREGNIES	37/B 15 b.
14.	6th Wilts Regt.		37/B 4 c 40.45.
15.	16th Manchester Regt.		37/A 12 d 78.12.
16.	14th A. & S. Hrs.	EVREGNIES	37/B 15
17.	43rd Infy. Brigade H.Q.		37/B 5 a 4.8.
18.	12th Suffolk Regt.		29/U 26 c 9.7.
19.	20th Middlesex Regt.		37/B 5 a 1.7.
20.	10th H. L. I.		29/U 22 c 2.8.
21.	15th L.N.Lancs R. (Pnrs) H.Q.		37/B 20 a 1.8.
22.	'A' Company.		29/T 29 a 3.2.
23.	'B' Company.		29/T 29 d 3.0.
24.	'C' Company.		37/B 20 a 1.8.
25.	14th Machine Gun Battn. H.Q.	HERSEAUX	37/A 5 c 90.30.
26.	'A' Company.		37/C 2 d 80.25.
27.	'B' Company.		37/B 11 a 5.8.
28.	'C' Company.		29/T 29 d 40.30.
29.	'D' Company.	TROIS FARM	29/U 30 d.
30.	C. R. E.	TOURCOING	36/F 10 b 6.8.
31.	61st Field Coy. R. E.		37/B 15 b 3.7.
32.	62nd Field Coy. R. E.	DOTTIGNIES	
33.	89th Field Coy. R. E.		29/ T 30 a 3.6.
34.	A. D. M. S.	TOURCOING	36/F 10 b 6.8.
35.	42nd Field Ambulance .		37/A 18 b 9.3.
36.	43rd Field Ambulance		37/A 22 c 9.9.
37.	44th Field Ambulance		do

[illegible signature]
for Lieut-Colonel. Capt
General Staff.
14th Division.

8/11/18.

SECRET. 14th Division L.R.33

LOCATION TABLE (Forecast to 0600 11th Novr.1918).

Ser.No.	UNIT.	LOCATION.	
1	14th Divisional H.Q.	TOURCOING	36/F.10.b. 6. 8.
2	14th Divisional Arty. H.Q.	"	do.
3	46th Bde. R.F.A.		37/B. 5.b.10.90.
4	47th Bde. R.F.A.		29/U.19.c.63.60.
5	D.A.C.		37/A.24.b.90.10.
6	No. 3 Section S.A.A.		37/A.24.a.60.90.
7	D. T. M. O.		29/U.20.d. 6. 4.
8	41st Infy. Bde. H.Q.	HERSEAUX	37/A. 5.d.25.15.
9	18th Y. & L. Regt.	WATTRELOS	37/A.28.a. 8. 7.
10	29th Durham L.I.	HERSEAUX	37/A. 5.d. 2. 2.
11	33rd Lond.Regt. (R.B.)	LE PETIT TOURNAI	37/A.15.b.0.8.
12	41st L.T.M. Battery.	HERSEAUX	37/A. 5.d.25.15.
13	42nd Infy.Bde. H.Q.	DOTTIGNIES.	29/T.29 c 4·2
14	6th Wilts Regt.	DOTTIGNIES	37/B. 5.c. 8. 7.
15	16th Manch.Regt.		37/B. 5.a.18.80.
16	14th A. & S. Hrs.	EVREGNIES	37/B.15.b. 8. 9.
17	43rd Infy. Bde. H.Q.	WARCOING	37/C.20.b. 0. 6.
18	12th Suffolk Regt.		29/U.28.c. 9. 7.
19	20th Middlesex Regt.	WARCOING	37/C.20.a.70.45.
20	10th H.L.I.		29/U.22.c. 2. 8.
21	15th L.N. Lancs. R.(Pnrs)		37/B.20.a. 1. 8.
22	'A' Company		29/T.29.a. 3. 2.
23	'B' "		29/T.29.d. 3. 0.
24	'C' "	29/U 29 c 5·2	
25	14th Machine Gun Bn. H.Q.	HERSEAUX	37/A. 5.c.90.30.
26	'A' Company 29/B 5 a 95 75	DOTTIGNIES	
27	'B' "		37/B.11.a. 5. 8.
28	'C' "		29/T.29.d.40.30.
29	'D' "	LANNOY Fm.	37/D 20 c
30	C. R. E.	TOURCOING	36/F.10.b. 6. 8.
31	61st Field Coy.R.E.	37/C 8 b 3·7	
32	62nd " " "	DOTTIGNIES	(6 Rue du PONT BLEU)
33	89th " " "		29/T.30.a. 3. 6.
34	A. D. M. S.	TOURCOING	36/F.10.b. 6. 8.
35	42nd Field Ambulance		37/A.18.b. 9. 3.
36	43rd " "		37/A.22.c. 9. 9.
37	44th " "		do.

for Lieut-Col. G.S.
14th Division.

10/11/18.

SECRET. 14th Division LR 34.

LOCATION TABLE
forecast to 08-00 18/11/18.

Ser.No.	Unit.	Location.	
1.	14th Divisional H.Q.	TOURCOING	36/F 10 b 6.8
2.	14th Divisional Arty.H.Q.	do	do
3.	46th Bde. R.F.A.		37/A 26 b 2.8
4.	47th Bde. R.F.A.	34 Rue de PARIS TOURCOING	36/F 3. d 8.8
5.	D.A.C.		37/A 24 b 90.10
6.	No 3 Section S.A.A.		37/A 24 a 60.90
7.	D. T. M. O.		
8.	41st Infy. Bde. H.Q.		36/E 17 b 7.2
9.	18th Y & L Regt.		36/E 23 b 6.8
10.	29th Durham L.I.		36/F 13 b 0.9
11.	33rd L. R. B.		36/E 16 b 2.3
12.	41st L. T. M. Batty.		36/E 17 b 7.2
13.	42nd Infy. Bde. H.Q.	HERSEAUX	37/A 5 d 25.15
14.	6th Wilts Regt.		37/A 22 a 8.6
15.	16th Manch. Regt.		37/A 15 b 2.8
16.	14th A & S.Hrs.	HERSEAUX	37/A 5 d 2.2
17.	43rd Infy. Bde. H.Q.		36/F 4 central
18.	12th Suffolk Regt.		36/F 4 d 7.4
19.	20th Middlesex Regt.		36/F 11 b 2.5
20.	10th H.L.I.		36/F 5 d 0.3
21.	15th L.N.Lancs.R. (Pnrs)		36/F 4 b 3.9
22.	A,B & C Companies.		do
23.	14th M.Gun Battn. H.Q.	35 Rue de WAILLY	36/F 4 d 3.4
24.	'A' Company	14 Rue de SENTIER	TOURCOING
25.	'B' "	21 Rue de la BLANCHE PONT	"
26.	'C' "	Factory Rue de PARIS	"
27.	'D' "	1 Bis Rue GAMBETTA	"
28.	C.R.E.	TOURCOING	36/F 10 b 6.8
29.	61st. Field Co. R.E.		36/F 4 b 7.5
30.	62nd Field Coy. R.E.		36/K 21 d 5.7
31.	89th Field Coy. R.E.	18 Rue de BUS TOURCOING	36/F 4 b 9.9
32.	A.D.M.S.	TOURCOING	36/F 10 b 6.8
33.	42nd Field Ambulance		37/A 18 b 9.3.
34.	43rd Field Ambulance		36/E 22 b 9.3.
35.	44th Field Ambulance		36/F 4 b central

[illegible signature]
for Lieut-Colonel. Capt
General Staff

Appendix K

14th Division - General Staff

War Diary - VOL. XLV - Nov. 1918

Corps Commanders Inspections

XV Corps No. A.C.75/3.

14th Division.
40th Division.

The Corps Commander would like to inspect the troops under your command at an early date. Please arrange dates and places most convenient to the troops.

It is suggested that Infantry Brigades, or Brigade Groups, should parade separately and the R.A. and M.G.Battalion combined.

1 The Troops, formed up in line of Quarter Column at close order will present arms when the Corps Commander reaches the Saluting point, the Union Jack being "broken" at the same time.

2. During the Inspection the Massed Marching Bands (Divisional Band in case of R.A.) will play a TROOP.

3. The Troops will march past by Companies (or Batteries) reforming on the Parade Field. The Massed Bands will follow the last unit playing until it reaches its position.

4. The Troops will advance in Review Order and give a General Salute.

5. The Troops will march to quarters in column of route, Bands at the head of each Battalion.

As each Battalion reaches the Corps Commander the Band will wheel off the route and play its Battalion past following in rear of the last unit and playing it away.

Battalion Commanders will fall out beside the Corps Commander and each Platoon will salute when passing.

6. A suggested programme of Inspections giving date - place - time will be forwarded to XV Corps 'A' as soon as possible.

Major,
D.A.A.G., XV Corps.

XV Corps H.Q.
12/11/18.
FB.

Confidential

14th Division - General Staff

WAR DIARY - December (1-31) 1918

VOLUME XLVI

Appendices

A - Army Commander's Inspection

B - Recreations

Instructions regarding War Diaries and Intelligence Summaries are contained in F. S. Regs., Part II. and the Staff Manual respectively. Title pages will be prepared in manuscript.

WAR DIARY
or
INTELLIGENCE SUMMARY.
(Erase heading not required.)

Army Form C. 2118.

Place	Date	Hour	Summary of Events and Information	Remarks and references to Appendices
TOURCOING	Dec 1st		Usual Church Parades. Sacred Concert held at TOURCOING.	WB
	2nd		Lecture by Col. SWAYNE RE on SIBERIA held in the CIRQUE Cinema Hall TOURCOING.	WB
	3rd		Torchlight Tattoo given by mixed troops & massed bands of the Division in the GRANDE PLACE ROUBAIX at 6-0 p.m. Weather showery	App. B. WB
	4th		Normal Routine - Divisional Boxing Competition in the CIRQUE Cinema Hall TOURCOING in the afternoon.	WB
	5		Lecture by ~~Col~~ Major Manners on Reconstruction Divisional Boxing Competition ~~continued~~ continued	WB
	6		Divisional Boxing Competition concluded. The Divisional Commander held a practice ceremonial parade of the Division (less 42nd Inf Bde and 61st & 62nd Coy RE) at MOUVAUX. at 11 0 a.m.	App B WB
	7th		Lecture by Col BOURNE on "Settlement of soldiers on the land" at TOURCOING at 10-30 a.m. in the CIRQUE Cinema Hall TOURCOING and to the 41st & 42nd Inf Bde during the afternoon.	WB
	8th		Church parades. Sacred Concert in Municipal Theatre.	WB

Army Form C. 2118.

Instructions regarding War Diaries and Intelligence Summaries are contained in F. S. Regs., Part II. and the Staff Manual respectively. Title pages will be prepared in manuscript.

WAR DIARY
or
INTELLIGENCE SUMMARY.
(Erase heading not required.)

Place	Date	Hour	Summary of Events and Information	Remarks and references to Appendices
TOURCOING	9th		Normal Routine – Divisional Cross Country Run at MOUVEAUX won by team of 14th M.G. Battn.	App B.
			Torchlight Tattoo in Place de la Republique TOURCOING at 6.0 pm.	MB
	10th		Corps Commander inspected the Division (less 61st & 62nd Coys R.E.) at MOUVEAUX at 11.0 a.m. Corps Commander dismissed parade after March Past owing to the weather.	App A. MB
	11th		Lectures at 10.30 am & 2.30pm in TOURCOING by [illegible] on "Dickens"	MB
	12th		Lectures to 41st & 42nd Inf. Bdes by Rev. G. STUDDART KENNEDY MC on "Demobilization"	MB
	13th		Lecture to 43rd Inf. Bde and Divisional Troops by Rev. G. STUDDART KENNEDY M.C in the CIRQUE TOURCOING.	MB
	14th		Normal Routine.	MB
	15th		Church parade and Sacred Concert at TOURCOING	MB
	16		Normal routine.	
	17		Lecture on "Alsace Lorraine" by Mr Masterman Smith at Army Cinema	[illegible]

Instructions regarding War Diaries and Intelligence Summaries are contained in F. S. Regs., Part II. and the Staff Manual respectively. Title pages will be prepared in manuscript.

WAR DIARY
or
INTELLIGENCE SUMMARY.
(Erase heading not required.)

Army Form C. 2118.

Place	Date	Hour	Summary of Events and Information	Remarks and references to Appendices
	Dec			
TOURCOING	17		TOURCOING at 1030 hrs. Lecture much appreciated by men.	[illegible] Capt
	18		Normal routine	
	19		"	
	20		"	
	21		"	
	22		"	
	23		"	
	24	}		
	25	}	Christmas festivities	
	26	}		
	27		Lecture on 'Agriculture' by Capt G.S. Taylor at the CIRQUE Cinema Hall at 1030 hours. Lecture was under Corps arrangements.	
	28		Normal routine	
	29		"	
	30		"	
	31		"	

1/1/19

[illegible] Capt
for General Staff
4th Division

14th Division.
G.S. 1570.

G.O.C. | G.S.O.1 | G.S.O.2 | G.S.O.3

XV Corps.

The following programme is submitted in accordance with instructions in XV Corps No. A.C. 75/3, dated 12/11/18:-

Inspection of 41st Infantry Brigade Group on Friday November 22nd near BONDUES.

Inspection of 42nd Infantry Brigade Group on Saturday November 23rd at HERSEAUX.

Inspection of 43rd Infantry Brigade Group on Monday November 25th at TOURCOING.

Inspection of 15th Bn. Loyal North Lancashire Regt. (Pioneers) and 14th Machine Gun Battalion on Tuesday November 26th near TOURCOING.

Inspection of 14th Divisional Artillery on November 30th near TOURCOING.

Inspections to commence, in all cases, at 10.00 hours.

As the 14th Divisional Artillery are calibrating at TILQUES and do not return until November 26th, atdate late in November has been suggested.

As the troops have not been exercised lately in Ceremonial it is suggested that the March Past in para. 3 of the above quoted Corps order should be by Platoons instead of by Companies.

The actual localities selected will be notified later.

T.H. Hill Whitson
Lt Col GS for Brigadier General
Commanding 14th Division.

18/11/18.

Ev

14th Division No. G.S.1568

G.O.C.
G.S.O.1
G.S.O.2
G.S.O.3

41st Inf. Bde.
42nd Inf. Bde.
43rd Inf. Bde.
C.R.A.
C.R.E.
14th M. G. Bn.
15th L. N. Lancs. Regt. Pioneers.
Q.
14th Div. Train.

For information

The Corps Commander would like to inspect the troops of the 14th Division at an early date.

Infantry Brigade Groups will parade separately.

The R.F.A. and M. G. Bn. will parade combined.

1. The Troops, formed up in line of Quarter Column at close order will present arms when the Corps Commander reaches the Saluting Point, The Union Jack being "broken" at the same time.

2. During the Inspection the massed Marching Bands (Divisional Band) in case of R.A.) will play a TROOP.

3. The Troops will march past by Companies (or Batteries) reforming on the Parade Field. The Massed Bands will follow the last unit playing until it reaches its position.

4. The Troops will advance in Review Order and give a General Salute.

5. The Troops will march to quarters in column of route, Bands at the head of each Battalion.
As each Battalion reaches the Corps Commander the Band will wheel off the route and play its Battalion past following in rear of the last unit and playing it away.
Battalion Commanders will fall out bedides the Corps Commander and each Platoon will salute when passing.

6. Please forward to this Office as soon as possible the dates suggested for this inspection and the actual locality selected.

[signature]
Lieut-Colonel.
General Staff.
14th Division.

17/11/1918.

G.O.C.	
G.S.O.1	
G.S.O.2	
G.S.O.3	

14th Division
G.S.1578

XV Corps.

Parade grounds for the Corps Commander's inspections will be as follows:-

Friday 22nd.	41st Infy.Bde.	36/E 18 b 6.3.
Saty. 23rd.	42nd Infy.Bde.	AERODROME HERSEAUX A 6.c.
Monday 25th.	43rd Infy.Bde.	N of TOURCOING S 13 d
Tuesday 26th.	M.G.Battn.) Pioneers.)	36/F 1 b 8.8 Road entrance in X 26 b.

Parade ground for the Divisional Artillery inspection on 30th inst. will be notified later.

Eric Smithers Lieut
for Major-General.
Commanding.
14th Division.

20/11/18.

GENERAL STAFF,
14TH
DIVISION.
No.........................
Date.........................
File.........................

14th Division No.G.S.1575

41st Inf. Bde.
42nd Inf. Bde.
43rd Inf. Bde.
15th L.N.Lancs. Regt. Pioneers.
14th M. G. Bn.
C.R.E.

G.O.C.	
G.S.O.1	
G.S.O.2	
G.S.O.3	

GENERAL STAFF, 14TH DIVISION.
No.
Date.
File.

Reference G.S.1565 dated 18th inst.

At the Corps Commander's inspections of Brigade Groups

First Line Transport
Lewis Guns
and Trench Mortars

Will be on Parade.

An interval of 30 yards will be maintained between Units and First Line transport.

for Lieut-Colonel. Capt
General Staff.
14th Division.

19/11/1918.

Copies to - C.R.A.
AQ.
14th Div. Train.

14th Division
G.S.1898

41st Infy. Bde.
42nd Infy. Bde.
43rd Infy. Bde.
C.R.A.
15th L.N.Lancs. R.
14th M.Gun Battn.
Q.

G.O.C.	
G.S.O.1	
G.S.O.2	
G.S.O.3	

Reference 14th Division G.S. 1878 of 20th inst.

1. Formations and units will be inspected on date and place therein laid down with the exception of 41st Infy. Brigade who will be inspected on Wednesday 27th inst., and not on Friday 22nd inst.

2. The hour for the inspections in each case will be 10-30.

3. Dress will be drill order.

4. On Tuesday 26th inst., the troops to be inspected will be under command of Lt-Col. B.[illegible] DSO.

5. Q will notify Pioneers and Machine Gun Battalion of band arrangements for the inspection on Tuesday 26th inst.

for Lieut-Colonel.
General Staff.
14th Division.

21/11/18.

14th Division G.S. 1578.

XV Corps.

Parade Grounds for the Corps Commander's inspections will be as follows :-

Friday 22nd.	41st Infy.Bde.	36/E 18 b 8.3.
Saty. 23rd	42nd Infy.Bde.	AERODROME, HERSEAUX. A 6.c.
Monday 25th	43rd Infy.Bde.	N. of TOURCOING S 13.d.
Tuesday 28th	M.G.Battn.) Pioneers.)	36/E 1.b.8.8. Road entrance in X 26 b.

Parade ground for the Divisional Artillery inspection on 30th instant will be notified later.

(sd) Eric Smithers, Lieut.
for Major-General,
Commanding 14th Division.

20/11/18.

---- ---- ----

14th Division, G.S.1588.

41st Infantry Brigade.
42nd Infantry Brigade.
43rd Infantry Brigade.
C.R.A.
18th Bn. L.N. Lancs. Regt.
14th Machine Gun Battalion.
"Q".

G.O.C.	
G.S.O.1	
G.S.O.2	
G.S.O.3	

For information with reference to my G.S. 1585 of 21/11/18.

[illegible] Capt
for Lieut-Colonel,
General Staff,
14th Division.

22/11/18.

14th Division No. G.S.1595

G.O.C.	
G.S.O.1	
G.S.O.2	
G.S.O.3	

XV Corps.

Reference my G.S.1578 of 20th inst.

The location of the Parade Ground for the inspection of the Pioneer and M.G. Battalions on Tuesday the 26th inst. will be 28/X.24.a.4.2 and not as therein stated.

Brigadier General.
Commanding 14th Division.

23/11/1918.

Copies to - 15th L.N.Lancs. Regt.
14th M. G. Bn.

"A" Form

Army Form C. 2121
(In pads of 100.)

MESSAGES AND SIGNALS.

No. of Message..............

Prefix.............. Code..............m | Words. | Charge.

Office of Origin and Service Instructions

Sent
At..............m.
To..............
By..............

This message is on a/c of: G.S.O. 1 / G.S.O. 2 / G.S.O. 3 Service.

(Signature of "Franking Officer.")

Recd. at..............m.
Date..............
From..............
By..............

TO 15 L N LAN REGT
14 M G BATTN
Q

Sender's Number.	Day of Month.	In reply to Number.	AAA
G356	25		

Corps Commanders inspection arranged for tomorrow 26th is cancelled AAA Your troops will be inspected when Division is reviewed AAA Date for latter not yet fixed AAA Addsd Pioneers + MG Battn repeated Q

P.15

From 14 DIV
Place
Time

The above may be forwarded as now corrected. (Z)

Censor.

Signature of Addressor or person authorised to telegraph in his name.

W P Whitfield Capt

This line should be erased if not required.

App. A

14th Division - General Staff

War Diary - December 1918

VOL. XLVI.

Army Commander's Inspection
10 Dec. 1918

XV Corps No. A.C. 75/8.

H.Q. 14th DIVISION No. A250 28 NOV 1918 "A" & "Q" BRANCH

Headquarters,
14th Division.
38th Division.
40th Division.

---

1. The Army Commander proposes to inspect all Divisions of the XV Corps early in December.

2. Copies of Ceremonial Training have been applied for and on receipt will be issued to Divisions.

3. To ensure uniformity, the following will be the general outline of parades :-

- R.A. and Divisional Troops will be formed on the right of the line under the command of the C.R.A. Divisional Band in rear of the centre.
- Infantry Brigades in line of Quarter Columns, at close intervals, with massed Brigade Bands in rear of each Brigade; to be formed up on the left of Divisional Troops.

All arms including Machine Guns, Trench Mortars and Lewis Guns to be carried.

Should space not admit of the whole Division being on parade the inspection of the 3 Infantry Brigades will be held separately from Divisional Troops.

4. The Inspecting Officer will be received by 'General Salute'. On the Divisional Commander's 'caution', repeated by Brigade Commanders, Battalion Commanders will give the first part of the executive command, each Brigadier holding up his right arm to its full extent. The executive word will be given simultaneously by all Battalion Commanders when the Brigadiers drop their right hands at the signal of the Divisional Commander, (either by bugle call, or by lowering a lance to the ground) ; all Bands will at the same time play the 'General Salute'. During the inspection, the Divisional Band will play a 'Troop' for Divisional Troops, and Brigade Bands for their own Brigades. As the inspection of each formation is concluded, Bands will place themselves on the right of their formations, in position to lead them on to the Saluting Base.

5. Formations will march off in succession at 100 yards distance. When marching past, each Band will play the various units of its formation past the Saluting Point. When its last unit reaches the Saluting Point, each Band will advance and follow the rear Company, continuing to play until it reaches its position in rear of the centre of the formation, where it will be in position for the advance in Review Order.

As soon as the last Company of each Battalion reaches 'B' Flag (50 yards from the Saluting Point), the Battalion will be closed to Quarter Column, and then move to the left in fours. On reaching the parade line, it will again wheel and move into its original position changing ranks on the march.

6. The Troops will advance in Review Order. This depends on all Bands starting together and the Halt being sounded at the end of a Bar.

7. Should the Army Commander inspect the troops in Column of Route when marching to their quarters, Battalion Bands will lead their Battalions and form up opposite the Inspecting Officer until the last platoon has passed; each Band will then follow the Battalion, continuing to play until the Battalion has marched away. In column of Route, the distance between Battalions will be 50 yards.

The following notes on the characteristic faults in all Ceremonial Parades compiled by the Corps Commander are added for your information :-

(1) General Salute.

P.11

0264

(i) General Salute. Units do not present arms simultaneously, and the motions of the rifle are too hurried.
Rear companies of Battalions not being in same alignment.
Ranks in the Band not covered off from the front.

(ii) Inspection of Troops. The band ceases playing too soon, the Band of the last formation should continue to play until the Inspecting Officer reaches the Saluting Point.

(iii) March Past. Unnecessary delay in moving into position on the Saluting Base; the Brigade Major failing to supervise the dressing of the right markers of the companies of the leading Battalion, and delaying to report to the Brigadier when the leading Battalion is ready to start. There is no necessity to wait for the rear Battalions to get dressed.
The Battalion Adjutant having satisfied himself that the markers are dressed on the line of flags and that Companies are at right angles to the Saluting Base, should place himself at 'A' Flag (50 yards from the Saluting Point) from where he can correct distances etc.
Bands not forming up opposite the Saluting Point correctly, files not covered from the front, and the Bandmaster not knowing how to regain his position in rear of the original alignment (Bands should follow rear companies of formations).
Right Guides (C.S.M's) not marching on the Flags.

(iv) Advance in Review Order.
The centre of the Troops not being opposite the Saluting Point; the Band not commencing to play at the word 'Quick March'; Band not playing the right number of bars.

(v) Marching off in Column of Fours.
Platoon officers turning round to give commands; sections of fours not properly dressed; men 'squinting' instead of looking the Inspecting Officer boldly in the face; Band ceasing to play instead of following the last company and playing them off the ground. (The temporary clash of music of two bands playing at the same time is preferable to the cessation of music and the rear troops breaking step in consequence).

G. Frith

27/11/18.
JWD.

Brigadier-General,
D.A. & Q.M.G., XV Corps.

14th Division
S.G.1807

---

1. The Army Commander proposes to inspect all Divisions of the XV Corps early in December.

2. Copies of Ceremonial Training have been applied for, and on receipt will be issued to units.

3. To ensure uniformity, the following will be the general outline of parades :-

R.A. and Divisional Troops will be formed on the right of the line under the Command of the C.R.A.
Infantry Brigades in line of Quarter Columns, at close intervals, with massed brigade bands in rear of each Brigade to be formed up in order on the left of Divisional Troops.
All arms, including Machine guns, Lewis guns, and Stokes guns to be on parade.

Should space not admit of the whole Division being on parade, the inspection of the 3 Infantry Brigades will be held separately from Divisional Troops.

4. The Inspecting Officer will be received by 'General Salute'. On the Divisional Commander's 'caution' repeated by Brigade Commanders, Battalion Commanders will give the first part of the Executive command, each Brigadier holding up his right arm to its fullest extent.
The executive word will be given simultaneously by all battalion commanders when the Brigadiers drop their right hands, on the signal of the Divisional Commander (either by bugle call, or by lowering a lance to the ground); all bands at the same time playing the 'General Salute'.
During the inspection, the Divisional band will play a 'Troop' for Divisional troops, and Brigade Bands for their own Brigades. As the inspection of each formation is concluded, Bands will place themselves on the right of their formations in position to lead them on to the saluting base.

5. Formations will march off in succession at 100 yards distance. When marching past, each band will play the various units of its respective formations past the Saluting point. When its last unit reaches the Saluting Point, each band will advance and follow the rear company continuing to play until it reaches its position in rear of the centre of the formation, when it will be in position for the advance in Review Order.

6. Should the Army Commander inspect the troops in Column of Route when marching to their quarters, Battalion Bands will lead their battalions and form up opposite the Inspecting Officer until the last platoon has passed; each Band will then follow the Battalion, continuing to play until the Battalion has marched away. In column of route the distance between Battalions will be 50 yards.

/7.

7. The following are the characteristic faults in all Ceremonial parades :-

(i). General Salute. Units do not present arms simultaneously, and the motions of the rifle are too hurried.
Rear companies of Battalions not being in same alignment. Ranks in the Band not dressed, and file not covered.

(ii). Inspection of Troops. The Band ceases playing too soon. The Band of the last formation should continue to play until the Inspecting Officer reaches the saluting point.

(iii). March Past. Unnecessary delay in moving into position on the Saluting Base; the Brigade Major failing to supervise the dressing of the right markers of the companies of the leading battalion, and delaying to report to the Brigadier when the leading Battalion is ready to start. There is no necessity to wait for the rear Battalions to get dressed.
The Battalion Adjutant having satisfied himself that the markers are dressed on the line of flags and that Companies are at right angles to the Saluting Base should place himself at 'A' flag, (50 yards from the Saluting point) from where he can correct distances, etc.
Bands not forming up opposite the Saluting Point correctly, files not covered from the front and the Bandmaster not knowing how to regain his position in rear of the original alignment; (Bands should follow rear companies of formations)
Right Guides (C.S.Ms.) not marching on the flags.

(iv). Advance in Review order. The centre of the troops not being opposite the Saluting Point; the Band not commencing to play at the word "Quick march"; Band not playing the right number of bars.

(v). Marching off in column of fours. Platoon Officers turning round to give commands; sections of fours not properly dressed; men "squinting" instead of looking the Inspecting Officer boldly in the face; band ceasing to play instead of following the last Company and playing them off the ground. (The temporary clash of music of two bands playing at the same time is preferable to the cessation of music and the rear troops breaking step in consequence.)

* * * * * * *

The above instructions are forwarded for information and guidance.

T.E.L. Hutchinson (signature)

14th Division
26/11/1918

Lieut.Colonel
General Staff

14th Division
G.S.1684

H H H
41/42/43rd Infy. Bdes.
6 C.R.A.
1 C.R.E.
1 15th L.N.Lancs.Regt.
1 14th M.G.Battn.
1 D.A.P.M.
1 A.D.M.S.
----

1. The Division will parade for inspection by the Army Commander on Tuesday 10th December at 11.00 hours.

Formations:-

Artillery	on right in line at half interval.
R. E.	in line.
Infantry	Brigades in line of battalions in close column; in numerical order from the right.
Pioneers) M.G.Battn.)	In the order given - each in close column.

2. Lewis Gun Limbers

Four lewis gun G.S.limbered wagons will accompany each Infy. and Pioneer Battn. and will form up in a line five yards in rear of the rear Company in close column. The lewis gun G.S.wagons will not march past.

3. Machine guns

Eight Machine gun limbered G.S.wagons will accompany the M.G.Bn. and will be formed up and march past in rear of the rear Company similarly to the Infy. lewis gun limbered wagons.

4. Stokes Mortars on pack animals will form up as a battery in rear of the centre of each Bde. They will march past in line in rear of the last company in each Brigade.

5. Lewis guns

On arrival at the Parade ground, Lewis guns will be removed from the limbers and carried by one of the Gun team. The men carrying the guns will be in the supernumery ranks of their companies, 8 per Coy.

During the march past and during movement, these guns will be carried at the 'slope'; at all other times they will be held at the 'order'.

6. Companies of Infy, Machine gun, and Pioneer Battns. will all be sized and equalised.

7. During the march past, a distance of 100x will be maintained between Brigades, inclusive of normal distance. The leading Infy. Brigade will march past 200x behind the Artillery.

The distance between battalions will be 60x inclusive of normal interval.

8. Brigades and Battalions assembling on the Saluting base prior to the march past will be closed up so much as possible.

9. The Infantry, Pioneer and M.G.Battns. will not follow the route taken by the R.F.A. in the march past but will wheel on to the 'A' marker (Blue flag)

10. After passing the saluting point, battalions will form close column on the move on reaching the 'D' Marker (Blue flag) Thence, to the position for the advance in review order, three square wheels will be made.

/11. Dress.

11. Dress.
Drill order, without water-bottles, Box respirators, haversacks and entrenching equipment - waterproof sheets will be carried.

12. Markers
Markers to report to a Divisional Staff Officer at the Saluting point at 10-30 hrs.

13. Troops will move in accordance with March Table attached.

14. The D.A.P.M. will report at the Saluting point, with 6 M.M.P., at 10-30 hrs.

15. The A.D.M.S. will detail an ambulance to be at BREVECQUE Farm (F 26. a. 8. 8.) at 11-00 hrs.

J. E. H. Whitaker
Lieut-Colonel.
General Staff.
14th Division.

8/12/18.

Copies to :-

/ 14th Div. 'Q'
/ XV Corps 'G'
/ XV Corps 'A'

MARCH TABLE to accompany G.S.1684.
Reference Sheet No 9799

Serial No.	Unit	Starting Point	Route	Remarks.
1	R.F.A.	F. 9 b 1. 5.	MOUVEAUX	Not to pass the Cross Roads in F. 9 b 3.1 before 09-15.
2	R.E.	F. 9 b 1. 5.	MOUVEAUX	Will march unders orders of B.G.R.A.
3	41st I.B.	E. 18 c 3. 1.	Farm de BOCARNE	
4	43rd I.B.	F. 10 d 5. 1.	Main LILLE Road F 26 d 3. 1.	Head of column not to pass MOUVEAUX- MARCQ Rd. before 10-00.
5.	42nd I.B.	WATRELOS SQUARE	ROUBAIX Track F 26 d 1.1.	Not to pass Cross Roads in F 21 c 5. 9. before 10-00.
6	14th M.G.Bn.	F 9 b 3. 1.	Fm. de PRES.	To be clear of Cross Roads in F 8 d by 09-15.
7	15th L.N. Lancs.R.			To march under orders of B.G. Commdg. 43rd Infy. Bde.

Troops will march back to billets in the order in which they leave the Parade Ground, using the same roads by which they marched to it.

App. B

14th Division - General Staff

War Diary - December 1918

Volume XLVI

Torchlight Tattoo -
Cross-country Race
Boxing

| G.O.C. |
| G.S.O.1 |
| G.S.O.2 |
| G.S.O.3 |

A. 321/1.

1. It is proposed to hold a Torch Light Tattoo in the 1st week of December, in the Grand Place, ROUBAIX.

2. A practice field marked out to represent the Grand Place at ROUBAIX is being prepared in the neighbourhood of CROIX (36/L.10).

3. Formations and Units will detail personnel as follows to report to Captain J.A. Campbell, High land L.I., attd Div. H.Q., at the Square, CROIX (36/L.9.d.6.8) by 4 p.m. to-morrow, 14th instant, for training as torch-bearers etc. :-

C. R.A.	1 Captain, 1 Subaltern, 100 O.R.,
C. R.A.	All trumpeters (in addition to above).
C. R.E.	1 Subaltern, 15 O.R.
41st Infantry Bde.	1 Captain, 2 Subalterns, 120 O.R.
42nd Infantry Bde.	1 Captain, 2 Subalterns, 120 O.R.
43rd Infantry Bde.	1 Captain, 2 Subalterns, 120 O.R.
14th Bn., M.G. Corps	1 Subaltern, 30 O.R.
15th L.N. Lancs.R.	1 Subaltern, 30 O.R.
A.D.M.S. ...	1 Subaltern, 20 O.R.
Div. Train	5 O.R.
Div. Train ...	All trumpeters (in addition to above).

4. The personnel mentioned in para. 3 will consist of picked men who are not likely to reach the top of the Leave Roster before 5th December as it is most important that the men are not changed, thorough training being essential if the Tattoo is to be a success.

5. The 41st Infantry Brigade will detail a Field Officer to Command the composite Unit : name of the Officer selected to be notified to this Office by wire as soon as possible. The Unit will be billeted in CROIX and will not be available for any other purpose than the Tattoo, without reference to this Office.

The 42nd Infantry Brigade will detail an Adjutant and 43rd Infantry Brigade a Quartermaster.

Cooks, Orderlies etc. will be found from the personnel of the Unit.

Rations will be demanded from S.S.O. for whole Unit for consumption 16th instant and onwards.

6. All personnel will reach CROIX on 14th instant with rations for consumption on 15th instant.

7. Each Infantry Brigade will detail 1 Cooker and 1 Limbered G.S. Wagon, and the A.D.M.S. 1 Water Cart ; complete turnsout to report to Captain Campbell at the same place, date and hour as the personnel.

8. Instructions as regards training will be notified to the C.O. of the Unit by the A.A. & Q.M.G.

9. Any Officers or N.C.Os who have any knowledge of Torch Light Tattoos will be included in the numbers mentioned in para. 3.

10. All Pipe, Brass and Drum & Fife Bands in the Division will report at 10 A.M. at the Square, CROIX, on alternate days commencing 15th inst. : haversack rations will be taken. Lorries will be provided as far as possible to convey bands to and from their Units, on application to 'Q' Office ; 24 hours' notice must be given.

J. A. Carfield Lt Col

A.A. & Q.M.G.,

14th DIVISION.

13th November, 1918.
H.M.

COPIES TO :
"Q"
C. R.A.
C. R.E.
41st Infantry Bde.
42nd Infantry Bde.
43rd Infantry Bde.
14th Bn., M.G. Corps.
15th L.N. Lancs. Rgt.
14th Div. Train.
S.S.O.
A.D.M.S.
Capt. Campbell.
Sergeant Heller.

G.O.C.
G.S.O 1 ✓
G.S.O.2
G.S.O 3

14th DIVISIONAL BOXING COMPETITION.

1. The Divisional Boxing Competition will take place on Decr. 3rd and 4th 1918 at TOURCOING.

2. The Competition will be open to the following classes -

Featherweight	...	9 st. and under.
Lightweight	...	9.9 st. and under.
Welterweight	...	10.7 st. and under.
Middleweight	...	11.6 st. and under.
Catch Weights	...	over 11.6 st.

8 oz. Gloves 3 - two minute Rounds.
20 ' Ring.

3. Officers' Competitions will be arranged if four entries are received for any of the above Weights.

4. Entries will be limited to 2 Competitors for each Weight from the following Units,-

(1) Div. H.Q. (consisting of No. 1 Sec. Div. Signal Coy. 215th Employment Coy.)
(2) 46th Brigade, RFA, including X/14 T.M. Battery.
(3) 47th Brigade, RFA, including Y/14 T.M. Battery.
(4) 14th D.A.C.
(5) 14th Divisional R.E.
(6) to (15) Each Infantry Battalion and Pioneer Battalion.
(16) 14th Battn., M.G. Corps.
(17) 14th Divisional R.A.M.C.
(18) 14th Div. Train.
(19) 14th Div. M.T. Coy.

5. Any man on the strength of a Unit on the 16th November is eligible to compete for his Unit even though he may have been transferred to another Unit since that date.

T51

6. A Silver Medal will be given to the Winner at each Weight and a Bronze Medal to Runners up. A prize will also be awarded to the best loser in the whole Competition.

7. The Winner and Runner up at each Weight will represent the 14th Division at the XV Corps Boxing Competition which will take place about December 10th.

8. Entries stating Number, Rank and Name, Unit and Class must be sent to reach Brigade Major 41st Infantry Brigade by 18.00 November 27th.

9. Competitors will weigh in at 11.00 on Decr. 3rd at a place to be notified later and arrangements will be made for Competitors to be billetted in TOURCOING during the Competition.

10. Further details of the Competition will be issued later.

14th Division G.S.1568.

14th Divisional Cross Country Race.

1. A Divisional Cross Country Race will be held (weather and other circumstances permitting) on Friday December 6th.

2. The Course will be 3½ miles. Hour of assembly and starting point will be notified later.

3. The event is limited to a team of 18 runners from each of the following Units :-

Divisional H.Q. (including No.1 Section Div.Sig Coy. & D.E.C.
Brigades R.F.A.
D.A.C.
Divisional R.E.
Battalions.
Divisional Train.
Divisional M.T. Coy.
Divisional R.A.M.C.

4. Prizes will be given to the first three teams which complete the course.

5. Teams will be placed in order of merit according to the smallest number of totalled marks gained by each team.

6. The winning team will be entered for the XV Corps Cross Country Race, open for one team of 18 runners from Divisions, Corps H.A., Labour and Corps Troops, to be held about December 18th.

7. The following conditions are to be observed :-
(a) S.D. Boots must be worn, otherwise no restrictions as to kit.
(b) Team numbers, which will be provided by the Committee, must be worn on the chest.
(c) Each of the 18 runners in each team must complete the course.

N.B. Further local conditions and directions will be issued when the actual course has been selected.

8. Any man on the strength of a unit on Novr. 18th can compete for that Unit.

9. Entries for the Competition to be sent to 14th Division G. by 12.00 hours December 4th.

No entry will be received after the date and hour named.

[signature]

Miscellaneous Sports Committee.

18th November, 1918.

Copies to :-

41/42/43 Infantry Brigade.	C.R.E.
C.R.A.	15th L.N. Lancs. Regt.
14th M.G. BN.	14th Div. Train.
14th Div. Sig.Co.	A.D.M.S.
14th Div. M.T.Co.	D.A.D.O.S.
D.A.D.V.S.	D.A.P.M.
Q.	D.G.O.
Camp Commdt.	Senior Chaplain, C. of E.
D.M.C.	

14th Division.
Q.S.1678.

41/42/43 Bdes. C.R.A. C.R.E. 14th Div.Sigs. E.O.
14th M.G.Bn. 15th L.N.Lancs. D.A.P.M. D.G.O.
A.D.M.S. 14th Div.Train. Camp Commdt. S.C., C.of E.
14th M.T. Coy. "Q". D.E.C. D.A.DV.S. D.A.D.O.S.

The Divisional Cross Country Run will take place at 1430 hours Monday December 9th. The Starting Place will be 36/F.26.a.4.4.

The Course will be marked with flags, all of which must be left on the left-hand side.

There will be 3 Tally Posts at each of which each runner will be given a tally. Any runner who is unable to produce his 3 tallies at the winning post will disqualify his team.

All teams must finish complete - within ¾ of an hour after the first man *in the race* has passed the winning post - otherwise the team will be disqualified.

The team scoring the lowest number of marks will win. Should 2 or more teams score the same number of marks, the team which finishes complete first will win.

Teams have been given the following numbers :-

No. 1	Div. RAMC.	No. 9	Div. R.E.
2	15th L.N.Lancs.	10	18th Y. & L. Regt.
3	47th Bde. RFA.	11	14th M.G. Battn.
4	12th Suffolk Regt.	12	6th Wilts.Regt.
5	20th Middlesex Regt.	13	33rd London Regt. (RF)
6	Div. Train.	14	16th Manchester Regt.
7	14th A. & S. Highlanders	15	10th H.L.I.
8	29th Durham Light Infy.	16	D.A.C.

Numbers are forwarded herewith. These must be sewn on the front of the competitor's jersey. At the Starting point teams will form up in order of the numbers, from the RIGHT.

W. Beaumont.
Captain,
Misc. Sports Committee.

Copy to:-
XV Corps.

G.O.C.	
G.S.O.1	
G.S.O.2	✓
G.S.O.3	

14th Division No. G.S.1703

41/42/43 Bdes.	C.R.A.	C.R.E.	14th Sig. Coy.	E.O.
14th M.G.Bn.	15th L.N.Lancs.	D.A.P.M.		D.G.O.
A.D.M.S.	14th Div. Train.	Camp Cmdt.		S.C., C of E.
14th M.T.Coy.	Q. D.E.C.	D.A.D.V.S.		D.A.D.O.S.

The Result of the Divisional Cross Country Run which took place on Monday 9/12/1918 was as follows :-

Place.	Unit.	Marks.
First	14th M. G. Battalion.	492
2nd.	47th Bde. R.F.A.	520
3rd	12th Suffolk Regt.	576
4th	15th L.N.Lancs.	601
5th	33rd London Regt. R.B.	611
6th	29th Durham L.I.	640
7th	Divl. R.A.M.C.	971
8th	Divl R.E.	1032
9th	20th Middlesex Regt.	1315

2. First in :-

Lieut. MORCOM 33rd London Regt. R.B.
Time 21 mins. 48 secs.

Second in

No. 3066 Pte FAIRY 15th L.N.Lancs. Regt. Pioneers.

J.Beaumont Capt
Captain.
Misc. Sports Committee.

11/12/1918.

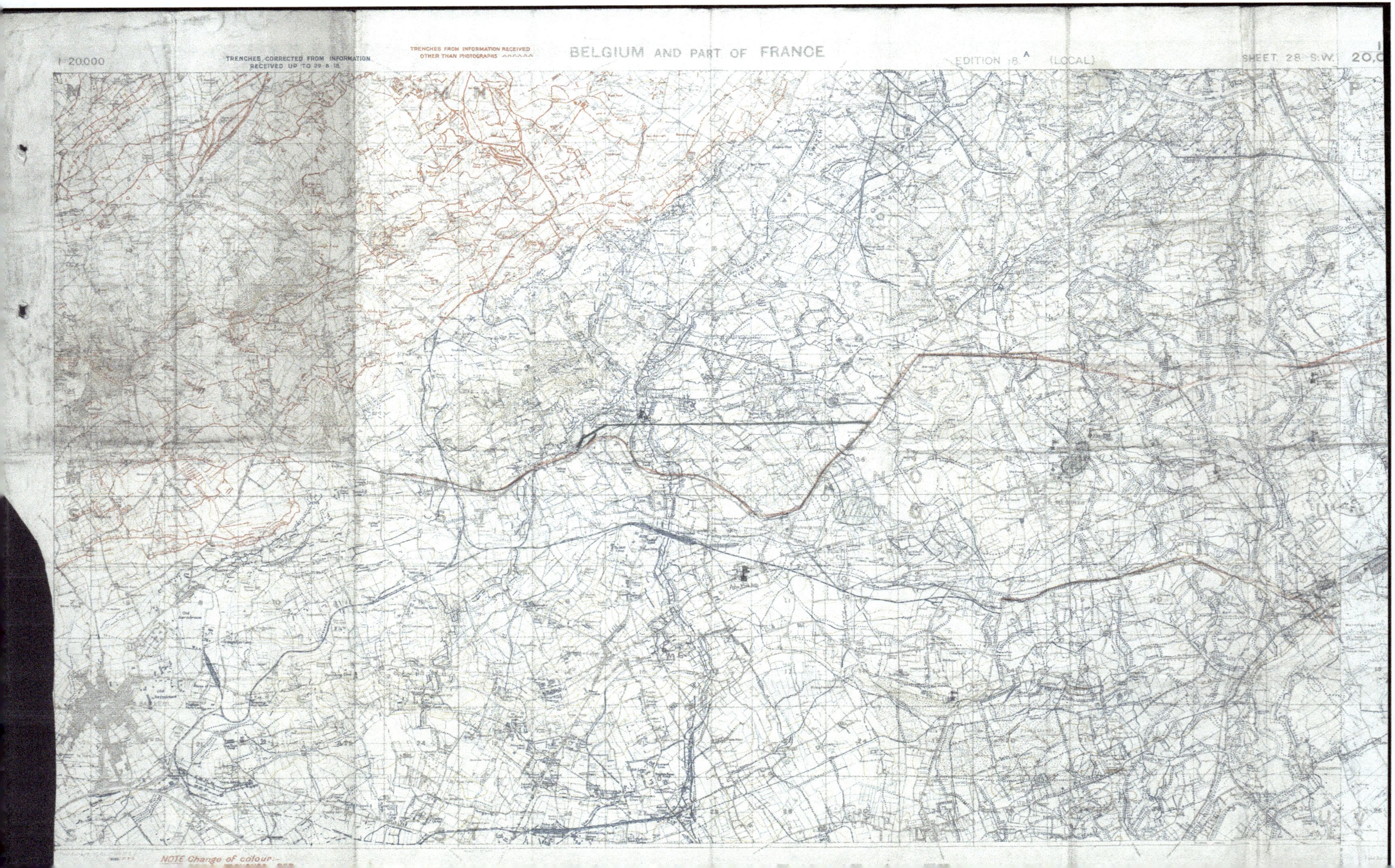
1:20,000
TRENCHES CORRECTED FROM INFORMATION RECEIVED UP TO 29-8-18.
TRENCHES FROM INFORMATION RECEIVED OTHER THAN PHOTOGRAPHS
BELGIUM AND PART OF FRANCE
EDITION 18A (LOCAL)
SHEET 28 S.W.
NOTE Change of colour

BELGIUM AND PART OF FRANCE

28 S.W. | 1/20,000 | TRENCHES CORRECTED FROM INFORMATION RECEIVED UP TO 6-9-18. | EDITION 8.A (LOCAL) | SHEET 28 S.E.

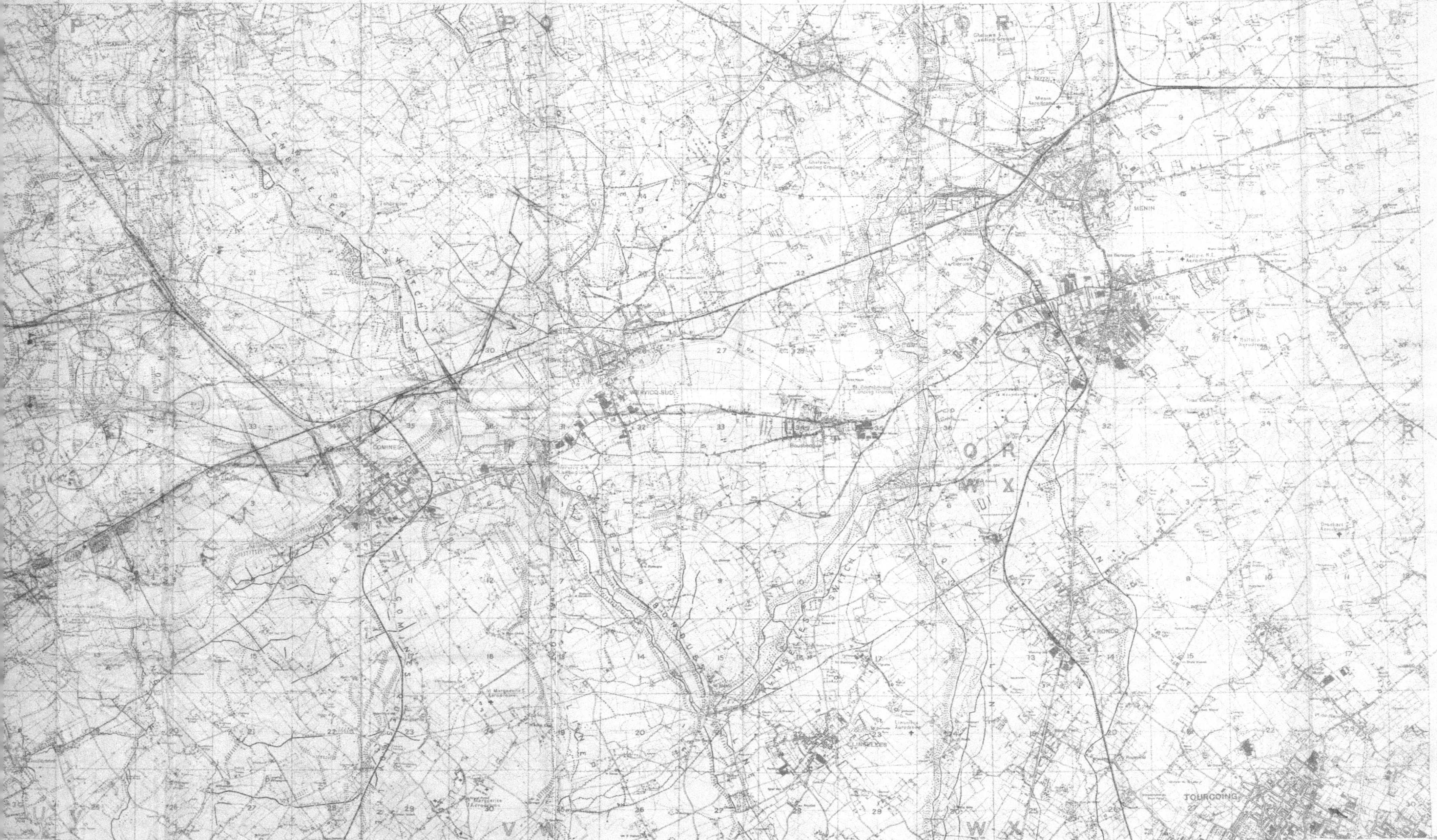

NOTE. Change of colour :- GERMAN TRENCHES -- BLUE.

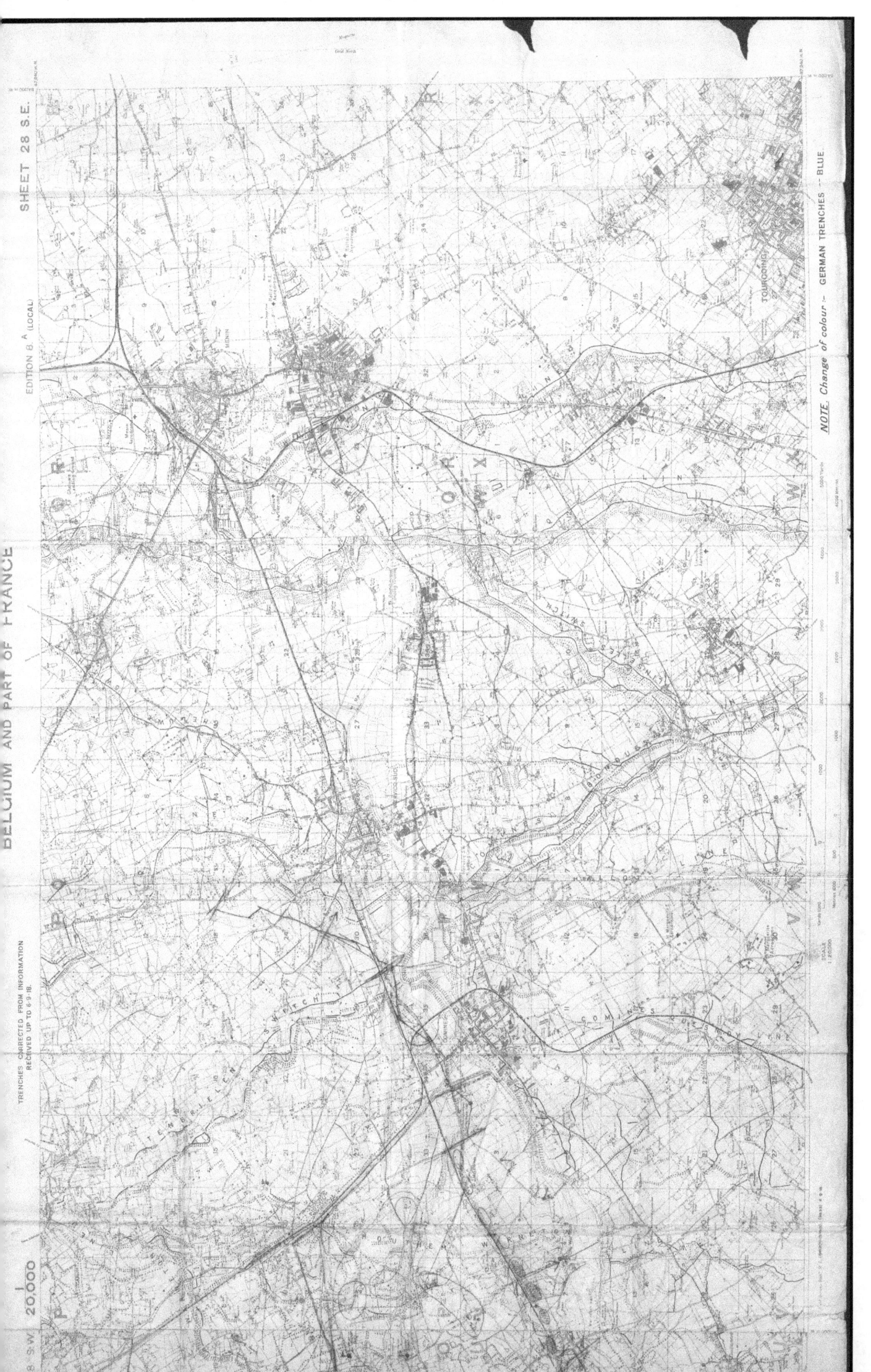

28 SE
1/20000

Confidential

14th Division - General Staff

War Diary

VOLUME XLVII - 1st - 31st January 1919.

Instructions regarding War Diaries and Intelligence Summaries are contained in F. S. Regs., Part II. and the Staff Manual respectively. Title pages will be prepared in manuscript.

WAR DIARY
or
INTELLIGENCE SUMMARY.
(Erase heading not required.)

Army Form C. 2118.

Place	Date	Hour	Summary of Events and Information	Remarks and references to Appendices
	Jan 1919			
TOURCOING	1		Normal routine	[illegible] Capt
	2		G.O.C. inspected 15th Bn L.N. Lan. Regt (P.) One Company Marching order, One Company Billets & Accounts, & One Company Interior Economy.	
	3		Normal routine	
	4		"	
	5		"	
	6		G.O.C. inspected Machine Gun Battalion at 1000 hours.	
	7		Prof Seccombe lectured to Div H.Q. Div Troops & 121 Inf Bde group at 1030 hours on "War Causes & War Issues", and to 43 Inf Bde group at MARCQ at 14.30 on "League of Nations". Both lectures good. G.O.C left for Conference at War Office at 0300 hours.	
	8		Normal routine	
	9		Corps Commander interviewed Brigade Commanders & Brigade Majors at No. 1. Mess at 1030 hours.	
	10		Normal routine	
	11		Lecture by Mr Muddock to 42 Inf Bde on "Old Russia" at 1030 hours	

1577 Wt. W10791/1773 500,000 1/15 D. D. & L. A.D.S.S./Forms/C. 2118.

Instructions regarding War Diaries and Intelligence Summaries are contained in F. S. Regs., Part II. and the Staff Manual respectively. Title pages will be prepared in manuscript.

WAR DIARY
or
INTELLIGENCE SUMMARY.
(Erase heading not required.)

Army Form C. 2118.

Place	Date	Hour	Summary of Events and Information	Remarks and references to Appendices
	Jan.			
TOURCOING	11 (Cont)		at HERSEAUX. Lecture not appreciated by the troops.	[illegible] Capt
	12		Church parade at ROUBAIX. Troops marched past the Army Commander. A detachment of 400 men representative of all units of the Division attended.	
	13		Normal routine.	
	14		"	
	15		"	
	16		Lecture by Rev T. P. Williams to 43rd Inf Bde at 1030 hours at BONDUES. Lecture well delivered & appreciated.	
	17		Normal routine	
	18		"	
	19		"	
	20		Lecture by Mr J Baker on "Czeco Slovaks & Jugo Slavs" at 1030 hours at Cinema, Rue des Anges Tourcoing.	
	21		Lecture by Mr. E. L. Hatzfeld on "Round the World in War time" to 42 Inf Bde at HERSEAUX at 1030 hours. Lecture much	

1577 Wt. W10791/1773 500,000 1/15 D. D. & L. A.D.S.S./Forms/C. 2118.

Instructions regarding War Diaries and Intelligence Summaries are contained in F. S. Regs., Part II. and the Staff Manual respectively. Title pages will be prepared in manuscript.

WAR DIARY
or
INTELLIGENCE SUMMARY.
(Erase heading not required.)

Army Form C. 2118.

Place	Date	Hour	Summary of Events and Information	Remarks and references to Appendices
	Jan			
TOURCOING	21 (Cont)		appreciated by all who attended. A party of 3 Officers + 14 O.R. of the American Army under Capt Rasmussen gave a demonstration of the Basket ball game to representatives of the Division at 14.30 hours at the LYCÉE, TOURCOING. Corps Commander + G.O.C. were present.	
	22		Normal routine. Presentation of Colours practice parade.	
	23		Units practicing for the Presentation of Colours parade	
	24		" " "	
	25		Presentation of colours to units of the Division by the Corps Commander in the Grande Place ROUBAIX at 11.00 hours.	App H
	26		Normal routine. Snow.	
	27		Lecture by Mr F.W. Gill to 43 Inf Bde at BONDUES at 10.30 hours on "A cycling tour through England". Lecture well received by troops.	
	28		Normal routine.	
	29		Normal routine	
	30		Normal routine	
	31		Normal routine	

1 February 1919

[signature]
Major
General Staff
14 Division

GENERAL STAFF, 14TH DIVISION. No. ... Date ... File ...

1577 Wt. W10791/1773 500,000 1/15 D. D. & L. A.D.S.S./Forms/C. 2118.

APPENDIX A

G.O.C.	
G.S.O.1	
G.S.O.2	✓
G.S.O.3	

14th Division.
G.S. 2087.

PRESENTATION OF COLOURS TO UNITS OF 14th DIVISION.
by Lieut. General Sir Beauvoir de Lisle, K.C.B., D.S.O.,
Commanding XV Corps
on 25th January 1919 at Roubaix

1. The presentation to take place in the GRANDE PLACE, ROUBAIX, at 1100 hours, 25th January, 1919.

2. Each unit receiving Colours, which will be presented by the Corps Commander, Lieut.-General Sir Beauvoir de Lisle, K.C.B., D.S.O., to be represented by a Guard consisting of 1 Captain, 1 Subaltern, 2 W.Os. 6 Sergeants and 32 Rank & File.
Dress - Drill Order, without haversacks, S.B.Rs. or water-bottles.

3. If very cold, greatcoats will be worn.

4. The Colour party to consist of 1 Second Lieutenant, 2 Coy. Sergt-Majors and 2 Corporals as coverers, found out of the numbers enumerated in para. 2.

5. The Parade will be Commanded by Brigadier-General Sweny, D.S.O. Commanding 41st Infantry Brigade.

6. The Captain in command of each Guard will be placed 3 paces in front of the second file from the right.

7. The troops will be formed up as per sketch attached.

8. The Parade ground will be picketed and lined by 150 men of the 41st Infantry Brigade, as per attached sketch.

9. All Divisional Bands to be on parade and to be placed as indicated on sketch attached; the Senior Bandmaster to conduct. The Pipers of the Highland Light Infantry and Argyll and Sutherland Highlanders to be on the platform above the steps of the MAIRIE.

10. The Drums and Colours, uncased, to be placed on the pavement just in front of the Centre Door of the MAIRIE.

11. Before the arrival of the Corps Commander, bayonets will be fixed.

12. The Corps Commander will be received by a General Salute.

13. The proceedings will then be as follows :- Troops will slope, then order arms.

14. The Brigadier-General Commanding will then give the Command "Colour Parties will take post - quick march" on which Colour parties will place themselves in line 5 yards from the Drums.

15. The Service of the Dedication of Colours will then be conducted by the various Chaplains to the Forces.

16. At the termination of the Service, the Corps Commander will present the Colours to the Officer of each Unit.

The Officers to whom the Colours will be presented will advance up to the Drums, the Colour parties remaining 5 yards distant.

/17

17. As each Officer receives his Colour, he will join his/Colour party and remain at attention at "the Order".

18. As soon as all the Colour parties have received the Colours and rejoined the Colour parties, the Colour parties will be ordered by the Brigadier-General Commanding,'Colour parties - Slope arms - . Colours will be at the "Carry" - about turn" - when all Colour parties will wheel right about (and the Colours will be "carried").

(The Massed Bands will then play "Scipio" (Handel) 8 bars).

19. On the Bands ceasing, the Brigadier-General Commanding will give the Command -"Colour parties will take post - slow march" on which each Colour party will march to the Centre of its Unit, halting 6 paces from the Centre - Colours carried.

(The Pipers will play " Scotland the Brave").

20. When the Colour parties are thus posted, the Brigadier-General Commanding will give the order -"Colour Guards - present Arms".

(The Bands will play "GOD SAVE THE KING").

21. The Brigadier-General Commanding will then give the order - "Slope Arms" and on this order Colour parties will wheel right about and resume the position described in para. 7.

22. The Brigadier-General Commanding will then give the order - "The Colour Guards will march past".

23. The 41st Infantry Brigade will then form up in Column of Guards, at close intervals. The Colour party 3 paces in front of each Guard.

The 42nd Infantry Brigade will move to the right in fours and form up behind the 41st Infantry Brigade.

The 43rd Infantry Brigade will follow the 42nd Infantry Brigade.

24. The March Past will be carried out in Column of Guards at 40 yards interval and will be played past by the Massed Bands.

The Pipers of the Argyll and Sutherland Highlanders and the Highland Light Infantry will play the Argyll & Sutherland Highlanders, Suffolks, Middlesex and Highland Light Infantry past.

The Salute will be taken by the Corps Commander.

Units will then march back to Quarters, where arrangements will be made by Brigadier-Generals Commanding for the proper reception and custody of the Colours.

25. The Corps Commander will present the Colours to the following units :-

18th York & Lancs.Regt.
29th Durham L.I.
15th Loyal North Lancs.Rgt.
16th Manchester Regt.
14th Argyll & Sutherland Highlanders.
12th Suffolk Regt.
20th Middlesex Regt.
10th Highland Light Infantry.

/26

23. N.C.Os. and men to form the colour guards will be specially selected, and should not be those who will be demobilised before 25th instant

Colour parties must be drilled and practised in the Slow March.

27. A party from 41st Infantry Brigade will be detailed to erect the pile of drums in front of ROUBAIX Church, and for their removal.

28. A practice parade will be held on Wednesday 22nd inst. at 1100 hours, at 29/S 19 b 5.5. All personnel who are to parade on 25th will attend this practice.

27. Following thispractice parade, the massed bands and pipes will practise their marches etc. under the senior band-master and pipe-major respectively.

28. Q.branch will arrange lorries to bring detachment of 43rd Infantry Brigade from their billets to the parade ground on Wednesday 22nd instant.

Q. will also arrange lorries to bring 42nd Brigade detachment from HERSEAUX to ROUBAIX on 25th instant.

29. B.G.C. 41st Infantry Brigade will detail one field officer and eight others to command the men lining the Square on 25th.

These officers and men will not be required on 22nd instant.

[signature]

14th Division
20/1/1919

Lieut.Colonel
General Staff

Copies to :-

4 — 41 Infantry Bde.
4 — 42 Infantry Bde.
4 — 43rd Infantry Bde.
1 — 15th L.N.Lancs.Regt.
1 — Q. Branch.
1 — Senior Chaplain C.of E.
1 — C.R.A.
1 — C.R.E.
1 — 14th M.G.Battn.
1 — 14th Train.
1 — 14th Signal Coy.
1 — A.D.M.S.
D.A.P.M.
D.A.D.V.S.
1 — D.A.D.O.S.
1 — A. D. C.
1 — XV Corps.
1 — A.P.M. ROUBAIX.

(C.R.A. to XV Corps: For information)

SKETCH MAP TO ACCOMPANY 14TH DIVISION G.S. 2067.

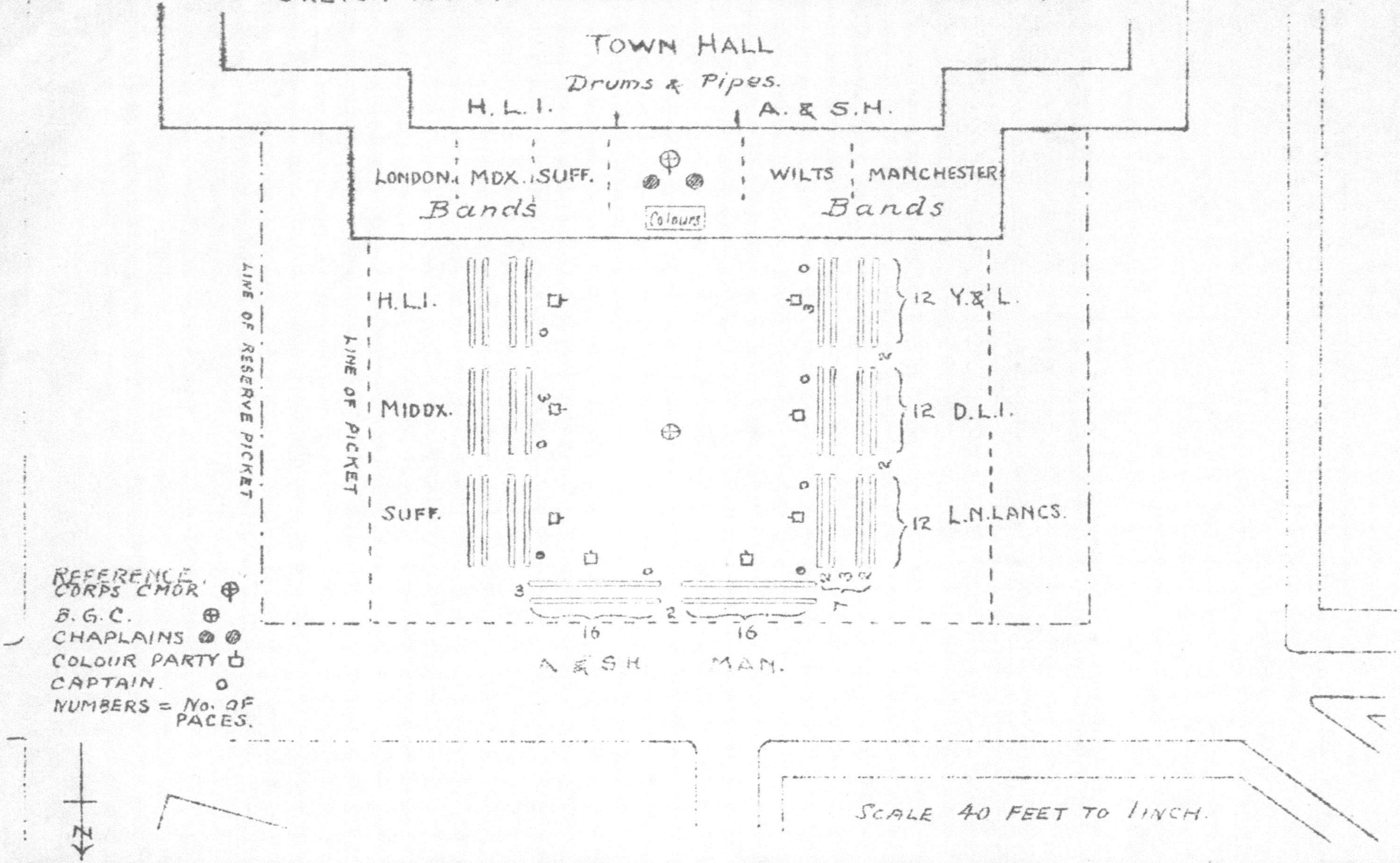

Green line shows position of troops lining street.

SKETCH MAP TO ACCOMPANY ~~14th DIVISION G.S. 2067.~~

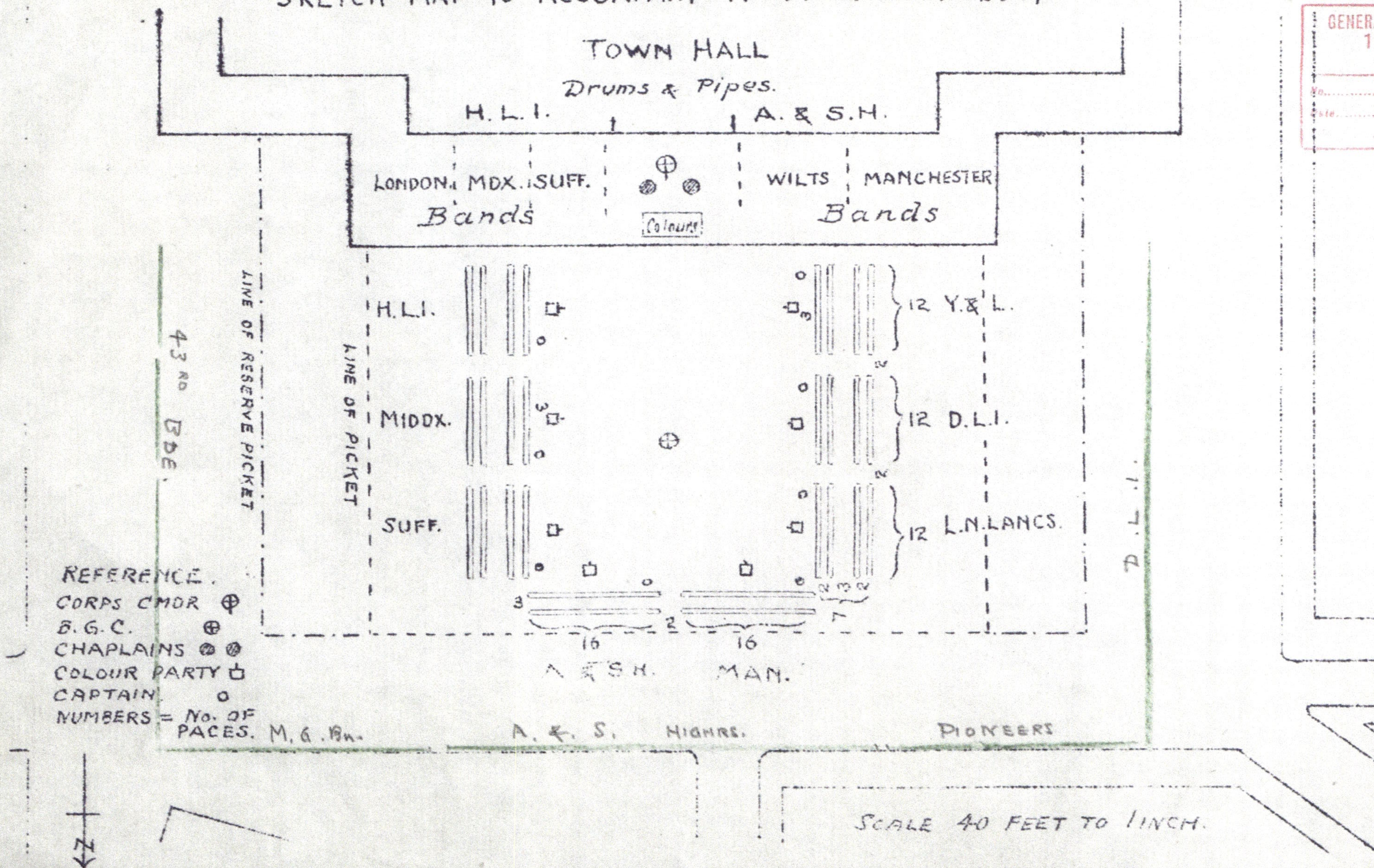

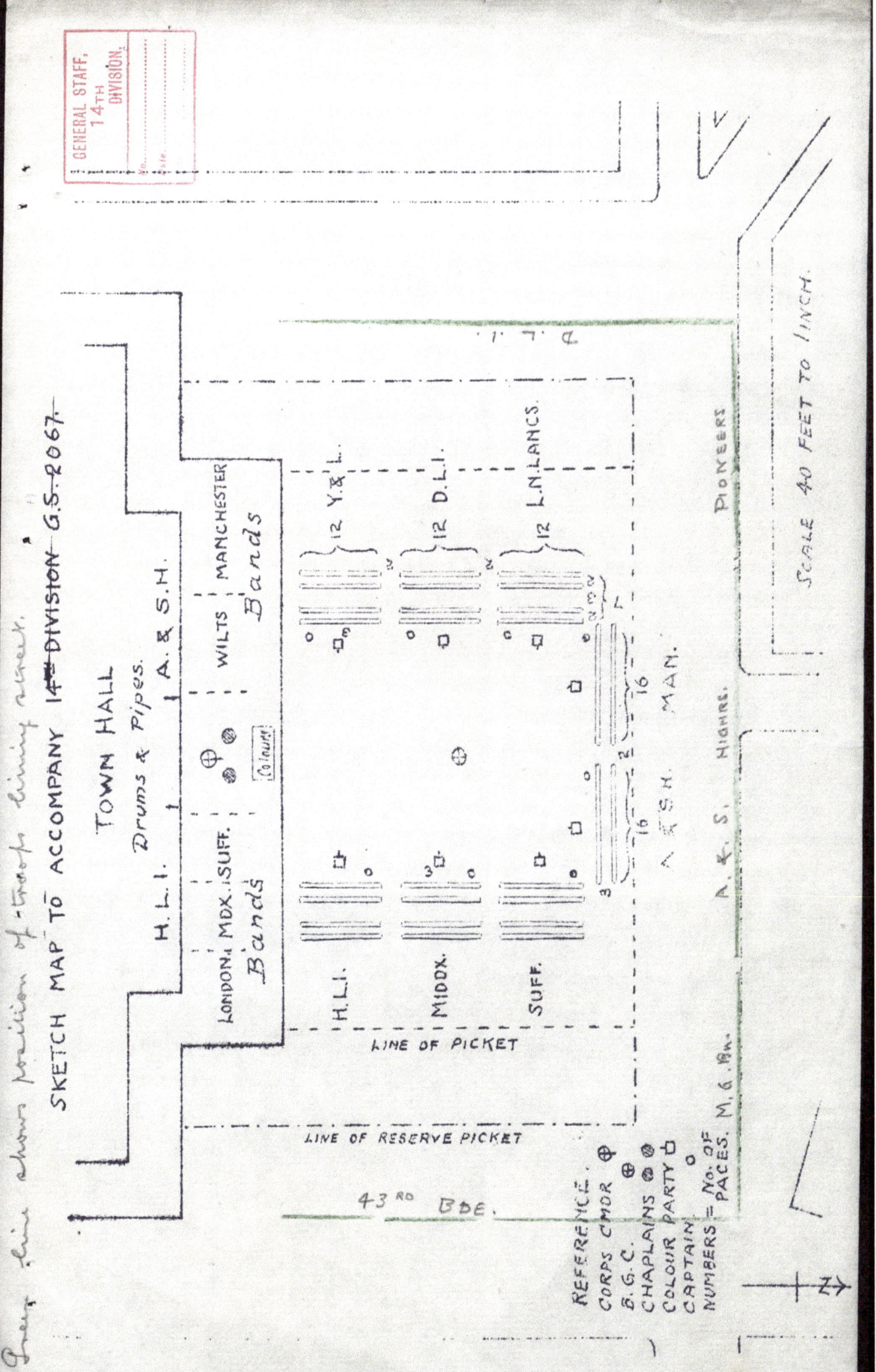

PRESENTATION OF COLOURS.

Address to the Troops by Lieutenant-General
Sir BEAUVOIR de LISLE, K.C.B., D.S.O.,
Commanding XV Corps.

In recognition of the services rendered to the Empire by your Battalion His Majesty The King has been pleased to present you with colours, thereby placing you on the same footing as the distinguished permanent Battalions of your Regiment.

In this campaign colours have not been carried into action as was formerly the custom but I hope that in future campaigns the old custom will be resumed. In consequence there are many who do not realise all that the colours stand for. A Battalion, being composed of individuals, can cease to exist; its spirit can never die. The soul of the Battalion is represented by its colours, and to defend the honour of a Regiment men have willingly given their lives in the past and will again in the future.

On demobilization your colours will be deposited in some place of honour probably in the cathedral and in the future you will perhaps conduct with pride your children and your childrens children to see the emblem of the Battalion in which you fought in the great war.

Should this occur, never fail to remind them of the fighting spirit of our great nation and how all right minded men rallied at the call of duty to defend our shores from invasion and humanity from oppression.

Should this call be heard in the lives of future generations may one and all again rally to the colours of the Regiments wherever it may be necessary to unfurl them.

* ** * ** *

Vol 46

Confidential

14th Division - General Staff

War Diary

1st - 28th February 1919 - VOLUME XLVIII

Army Form C. 2118.

Instructions regarding War Diaries and Intelligence Summaries are contained in F. S. Regs., Part II. and the Staff Manual respectively. Title pages will be prepared in manuscript.

WAR DIARY
or
INTELLIGENCE SUMMARY.
(Erase heading not required.)

Place	Date	Hour	Summary of Events and Information	Remarks and references to Appendices
	Feb			
TURCOING	1		Normal Routine.	W. J. Frolish Capt
	2		Normal Routine	
	3		Normal Routine	
	4		Normal Routine	
	5		Normal Routine	
	6		" " Lecture by Mr. Hilaire Belloc.	[illegible] Major G.S.
	7.		G.O.C + G.S.O.2 visited Battalions of 42 Inf. Bde. Lecture by Lord Denbigh	
	8.		Normal routine.	
	9.		Normal routine.	
	10.		Normal routine.	
	11		G.O.C. visited 42 Inf. Bde.	
	12.		Normal routine.	
	13.		Normal routine.	
	14.		Normal routine	
	15		Normal routine	
	16		Normal routine.	

1577 Wt. W10791/1773 500,000 1/15 D. D. & L. A.D.S.S./Forms/C. 2118.

Instructions regarding War Diaries and Intelligence Summaries are contained in F. S. Regs., Part II. and the Staff Manual respectively. Title pages will be prepared in manuscript.

WAR DIARY
or
INTELLIGENCE SUMMARY.
(Erase heading not required.)

Army Form C. 2118.

Place	Date	Hour	Summary of Events and Information	Remarks and references to Appendices
Tourcoing France.	February 17		G.O.C. C.R.A. & Infantry Brigade Commanders attend Army Commanders Conference at MOUVEAUX.	
	18		Orders received for draft of 12th Suffolk Regt. to proceed on Feb. 20th to join Army of Occupation. ([struck through]).	
	19th		Royal Artillery Band visited Tourcoing.	
	20th		" " " " "	
	21		Farewell dinner to G.O.C. at the Officers Club. Tourcoing.	
	22		Normal routine.	
	23		" "	
	24		" "	
	25		" "	
	26		G.O.C. proceeded on leave to England. B.G.C. 43 Inf. Bde. assumes command of the Division	
	27		Normal routine.	
	28		" "	[signature] Major G.S.

Instructions regarding War Diaries and Intelligence Summaries are contained in F. S. Regs., Part II. and the Staff Manual respectively. Title pages will be prepared in manuscript.

WAR DIARY

~~or~~

~~INTELLIGENCE SUMMARY.~~

(Erase heading not required.)

Army Form C. 2118.

HQ G S 14 D

V8 47

Ceased

Place	Date	Hour	Summary of Events and Information	Remarks and references to Appendices
TOURCOING	March 1st 1919	—	Routine work as usual	
	2		Major E.W.H. Wade, M.C. G.S.O.2 proceeded on leave to UK	
	3		Nothing to report	
	4		Ordinary work as usual.	
	5		Nothing to report.	
	6		Work as usual	
	7		Routine work as usual	
	8		Nothing to report	
	9		Ordinary work as usual	
	10		Orders received to close down Education Office and forward stores to H.Q. Second Army	
	11		Camp Library Books to be forwarded to H.Q. Second Army.	
	12		Nothing to report	
	13		Captain A.T. Eggington M.C. R.E., Divisional Education Officer proceeded, independently to UK. for demobilization.	
	14-15		Nothing to report.	

Instructions regarding War Diaries and Intelligence Summaries are contained in F. S. Regs., Part II. and the Staff Manual respectively. Title pages will be prepared in manuscript.

WAR DIARY

~~or~~

~~INTELLIGENCE SUMMARY.~~

(*Erase heading not required.*)

Army Form C. 2118.

Place	Date	Hour	Summary of Events and Information	Remarks and references to Appendices
	March 16th			
TOURCOING	1919		Division inspected by Commander-in-Chief British Armies in France.	
	17-20		Nothing to report.	
	21		Major-General P.C.B. Skinner CMG DSO returned from leave.	
	22		Major E.W.H. Wade M.C. returned from leave	
	23		Brigadier-General P.C.B. Skinner CMG DSO proceeded to take command of an Infantry Brigade, Midland Division, RHINE Army.	
	24	1200hrs	14th Division ceased to exist.	

March 24th 1919.

E.W.H. Wade.
Major G.S.

1577 Wt. W10791/1773 500,000 1/15 D. D. & L. A.D.S.S./Forms/C. 2118.

WAR DIARY.

A.D. 316.

1. The following Cadre on transfer to England will entrain at CROIX on March 21st, 1919, detrain at DUNKIRK.

14th Bn. M.G. Corps, Cadre "A" Serial No. F.8.

2. In addition, 80 Other Ranks, 12th North Staffs. (40th Div.) are proceeding by the same train.

3. 40th Division are issuing all orders for the move of personnel mentioned in para 2.

4. Train arrangements and times Units will report at CROIX will be issued when received.

5. The 14th M.G. Battalion will arrange direct with the 14th Divisional Train for rations to be placed in the Train in accordance with G.R.O. 6046.

6. Attention is directed to Q.M.G. instructions 721 Q.A. issued under this office number A.D. 296 dated 16-3-19.

7. Captain C.F. [illegible], 14th Division Headquarters, will remain at railhead during the whole of the entrainment and will be responsible for the reports called for in para 19 of Q.M.G's 721 Q.A.

8. On completion of entrainment on 21st March, O.C. Detachment 14th M.G. Battalion will send all remaining animals to the LINSELLES Horse Camp.

9. Instructions for the attachment of 14th M.G. Battalion details to 15th Bn. L.N. Lancs. have been issued seperately.

10. ACKNOWLEDGE.

[illegible signature]
Major,
D.A.Q.M.G.,
14th Division.

19-3-19.
J.F.B.

Distribution to:-
14th M.G. Bn.
15th Bn. L.N. Lancs.
14th Div. Train.
LINSELLES Horse Camp.
Signals.
A.D.M.S.
D.A.D.O.S.
File.
War Diary.
XV Corps "Q"

www.ingramcontent.com/pod-product-compliance
Lightning Source LLC
Chambersburg PA
CBHW080917230426
43668CB00014B/2146